Revolutionizing Communication

Revolutionizing Communication: The Role of Artificial Intelligence explores the wide-ranging effects of artificial intelligence (AI) on how we connect and communicate, changing social interactions, relationships, and the very structure of our society. Through insightful analysis, practical examples, and knowledgeable perspectives, the book examines chatbots, virtual assistants, natural language processing, and more. It shows how these technologies have a significant impact on cultural productions, business, education, ethics, advertising, media, journalism, and interpersonal interactions.

Revolutionizing Communication is a guide to comprehending the present and future of communication in the era of AI. It provides invaluable insights for professionals, academics, and everyone interested in the significant changes occurring in our digital age.

Raquel V. Benítez Rojas, Ph.D., MA, MBA, CMP, is Associate Dean in the Master of Arts in Digital Media and Global Communications at University of Niagara Falls, Canada, and Professor at U-tad, University Center for Technology and Digital Art, Madrid, Spain.

Francisco-Julián Martínez-Cano, Ph.D., is Associate Dean of the Bachelor's Degree in Audiovisual Communication in the Faculty of Social and Legal Sciences of Elche at Universidad Miguel Hernández, Elche, Spain.

Revolutionizing Communication

The Role of Artificial Intelligence

Edited by
Raquel V. Benítez Rojas and
Francisco-Julián Martínez-Cano

CRC Press
Taylor & Francis Group
Boca Raton London New York

CRC Press is an imprint of the
Taylor & Francis Group, an **informa** business

Cover image: Sorapop Udomsri/shutterstock

First edition published 2025
by CRC Press
2385 NW Executive Center Drive, Suite 320, Boca Raton FL 33431

and by CRC Press
4 Park Square, Milton Park, Abingdon, Oxon, OX14 4RN

CRC Press is an imprint of Taylor & Francis Group, LLC

ISBN: 978-1-032-73342-5 (hbk)
ISBN: 978-1-032-75357-7 (pbk)
ISBN: 978-1-003-47363-3 (ebk)

DOI: 10.1201/9781003473633

Typeset in Minion
by Newgen Publishing UK

Contents

Preface

In a world teeming with technological innovation and rapid change, few realms have witnessed a transformation as profound as communication. From the earliest cave paintings to the intricate networks of global connectivity we navigate today, the evolution of communication has been a testament to human ingenuity and adaptability. Yet, in the midst of this ongoing revolution, one force has emerged as both a catalyst and a protagonist: artificial intelligence (AI).

Revolutionizing Communication: The Role of Artificial Intelligence embarks on a journey through the intricate tapestry of AI's impact on communication in all its forms. This comprehensive exploration delves into the genesis, development, and future trajectories of AI, unraveling its profound influence on various facets of human interaction, expression, and understanding.

In the chapters that follow, readers will embark on a multidimensional voyage, traversing the landscapes of motion graphics, films, video games, virtual reality, audiovisual narratives, linguistic coherence, deepfake technology, advertising creativity, journalism, and media representation. Each chapter serves as a prism, refracting the multifaceted ways in which AI intersects with and transforms the fabric of communication.

"Artificial Intelligence: Genesis, Development, and Future" lays the groundwork for our expedition, charting the evolution of AI from its conceptual origins to its current state and offering tantalizing glimpses into its potential future trajectories. As we journey deeper, "The Evolution of Animation and Motion Graphics through Contemporary AI Technologies" unveils the symbiotic relationship between AI and visual storytelling, showcasing how AI algorithms empower creatives to push the boundaries of imagination and expression.

At the crossroads of entertainment and immersion, "A Look at the Crossroads of Artificial Intelligence, Films, Video Games, and Virtual Reality" beckons readers into the realm of immersive experiences, where AI serves as both a guide and a co-creator in the realms of storytelling and world-building. Meanwhile, "AI and the Development of New Audiovisual Narratives" ventures into the fertile landscape of audiovisual storytelling, where AI algorithms infuse narratives with unprecedented depth, dynamism, and interactivity.

Artistry and innovation converge in many chapters of this book where the collaborative dance between human creativity and AI augmentation yields a symphony of new possibilities. Simultaneously, "Talking to Strangers: The Challenges of Conversational

AI and Human Expectations" navigates the nuanced terrain of human–computer interaction, exploring the intricacies of conversational AI and the quest for authenticity in digital dialogue.

The linguistic landscape undergoes a profound metamorphosis in "The Linguistic Effects of Artificial Intelligence on the Adequacy, Coherence, and Cohesion of Texts. What Do We Stop Telling in the New Digital Age?" where AI-driven language models reshape the contours of written expression, challenging conventional notions of textual coherence and linguistic fidelity.

As we peer into the horizon of advertising creativity, "The Deepfake Technique Used for Creative Advertising from a Social Perspective: The *Seguimos Hablando* Campaign (2019) as a Case Study" examines the ethical implications of deepfake technology, probing the boundaries between innovation and deception through the lens of the *Seguimos Hablando* Campaign (2019).

Venturing into the realm of interactive storytelling, "Mario Kart AI in Education: Bridging Game Design and Pedagogical Strategies" immerses readers in the dynamic landscape of AI-driven game design, where ethical considerations intertwine with narrative craftsmanship to shape the future of interactive entertainment.

In the realm of customer engagement, "AI and the Human Need for Emotional Connection" sheds light on the transformative potential of AI-powered conversational agents, revolutionizing customer service, and redefining the contours of human–computer interaction.

Meanwhile, "Use of Artificial Intelligence Tools in Communication Companies. Advantages and Disadvantages in the Sector" offers a panoramic view of AI's integration into the workflows of communication enterprises, illuminating the ways in which AI augments efficiency, insight, and innovation.

The narrative arc extends into the realm of immersive media experiences with "Adaptive AI and Interactive Narrative Possibilities in Media," where readers are invited to explore the emergent landscape of AI-driven interactive narratives, blurring the boundaries between audience and storyteller.

In the realm of journalism, "Local Media in the Age of AI" scrutinizes the evolving role of AI in shaping local news landscapes, illuminating both the promises and perils of automation in journalistic practice.

In a retrospective examination, "Automated Journalism in Turkish Media before the Rise of Generative AI" offers insights into the evolution of automated journalism, tracing its trajectory in the Turkish media landscape and highlighting the transformative impact of AI technologies.

Ethical considerations take centre stage in "The Interrelation between Journalism, Artificial Intelligence, and Professional Ethics: Ethical Reflections in The Digital Era," where the complex interplay between journalistic integrity, AI automation, and ethical imperatives is meticulously dissected.

Shifting focus to the world of cinema, "The Reception of Artificial Intelligence at Film Festivals" explores the intersection of AI and cinematic expression, unraveling the ways in which AI technologies enrich and redefine the cinematic landscape.

Finally, "Cinderella Named "Artificial Intelligence": Media Image of Artificial Intelligence in Alternative Media (Case Study from Slovakia)" offers a compelling glimpse into the ways in which alternative media channels shape public perceptions of AI, interrogating the narratives and representations that underpin societal understandings of this transformative technology.

As we traverse the vast expanse of AI's impact on communication, it becomes evident that we stand at the precipice of a new era—a frontier where human ingenuity and technological innovation converge to redefine the contours of human expression, interaction, and understanding. "Revolutionizing Communication: The Role of Artificial Intelligence" is both a testament to this transformative journey and a compass guiding us toward the boundless horizons of the digital age.

May this exploration serve as an inspiration for scholars, practitioners, and enthusiasts alike, as we navigate the uncharted waters of AI-driven communication and forge new pathways toward a more connected, creative, and compassionate future.

Contributors

Kris Alexander
Toronto Metropolitan University, Toronto, Canada

Thoreau Bakker
Toronto Metropolitan University, Canada

Raquel V. Benítez Rojas
University Niagara Falls, Niagara Falls, Canada
U-tad University of Technology, Arts and Design, Madrid, Spain

Rocío Cifuentes-Albeza
Universidad Miguel Hernández, Elche, Spain

Kemal Deniz
Munzur University, Tunceli, Turkey

Antonio Díaz-Lucena
Rey Juan Carlos University, Madrid, Spain

Montserrat Jurado-Martin
Universidad Miguel Hernández, Elche, Spain

Richard Lachman
Toronto Metropolitan University, Canada

Francisco-Julián Martínez-Cano
Universidad Miguel Hernández, Elche, Spain

Alba-María Martinez-Sala
University of Alicante, Alicante, Spain

Galo Vásconez Merino
Universidad Nacional de Chimborazo, Riobamba, Ecuador

Juan Monserrat-Gauchi
University of Alicante, Spain

Beatriz Morales Fernández
Universidad de las Palmas, Las Palmas, Spain

Ramiro Ruales Parreño
Universidad Nacional de Chimborazo, Riobamba, Ecuador

Andrés Murillo Pinos
Universidad Nacional de Chimborazo, Riobamba, Ecuador

Carmen Quiles-Soler
University of Alicante, Spain

Sena Ozkurt Azimli
Independent Researcher, Istanbul, Turkey

Erkan Saka
Istanbul Bilgi University, Istanbul, Turkey

Tatiana Santos-Gonçalves
Universidad Miguel Hernández, Elche, Spain

Hedviga Tkácová
The Catholic University in Ruzomberok, Ruzomberok, Slovakia

Pilar Vicente-Fernández
Rey Juan Carlos University, Madrid, Spain

Samuel Viñolo Locubiche
U-tad, University of Technology, Arts and Design, Madrid, Spain

CHAPTER 1

Artificial Intelligence: Genesis, Development, and Future

Raquel V. Benítez Rojas

1.1 INTRODUCTION

Artificial intelligence (AI) is a field of computer science that deals with the creation of intelligent machines that can perform tasks that typically require human intelligence, such as understanding natural language, recognizing images, and making decisions.

The history of AI dates to the mid-20th century, when researchers began to explore the possibility of creating machines that could perform tasks that were typically reserved for human beings. However, in the intricate dance between technology and the collective human imagination, a fascinating synergy emerges between AI and mythology. Mythology, with its timeless tales, and AI, the cutting-edge manifestation of human ingenuity, converge in a complex interplay that transcends cultural and historical boundaries.

At the heart of both AI and mythology lies the theme of creation. Myths from diverse cultures narrate the stories of gods or divine entities fashioning life from inert matter. Similarly, in the realm of AI, humans take on the role of creators, fashioning intelligent entities from lines of code and algorithms. The echoes of creation myths, such as the Hindu story of Brahma breathing life into the first man or the Judeo-Christian narrative of God forming Adam from dust, resonate with the contemporary narrative of programmers and engineers breathing life into machines.

A central figure in Greek mythology, Prometheus, brings fire from the gods to empower humanity. This act of benevolent rebellion, however, comes with consequences. Similarly, the creators of AI bestow upon machines the power of cognition, challenging humanity with ethical dilemmas and unintended consequences. The Promethean theme

DOI: 10.1201/9781003473633-1

encapsulates the tension between the desire to elevate human potential through technology and the inherent risks and responsibilities associated with playing the role of divine creators.

Jewish folklore introduces the concept of the Golem, a creature animated from clay to protect the community. In Mary Shelley's "Frankenstein," the eponymous scientist creates a being that turns against its creator. These tales embody the ethical concerns surrounding the creation of artificial life, a theme central to discussions about AI. Questions of responsibility, unintended consequences, and the ethical dimensions of playing the role of both creator and controller echo through the myths of the Golem and Frankenstein's monster, resonating in contemporary debates about the ethical use of AI.

Ancient myths often feature oracles, individuals endowed with divine insights into the future. In the world of AI, predictive analytics and machine learning algorithms assume a role analogous to oracles, deciphering vast amounts of data to foresee trends and patterns. The parallel prompts contemplation on the nature of foresight, destiny, and the evolving relationship between human intuition and machine prediction. The mystical allure of oracles finds a modern counterpart in the algorithms that sift through data to reveal glimpses of what lies ahead.

The relationship between AI and mythology is a dynamic interplay that transcends time, culture, and technological advancement. From creation narratives and ethical dilemmas to the quest for foresight and the hero's journey, the parallels between these seemingly disparate realms offer profound insights into the human condition. As we navigate the uncharted territories of AI, the myths of old serve as both cautionary tales and sources of inspiration, providing a rich tapestry through which we can comprehend the intricate dance between human imagination and technological innovation. In exploring this convergence, we unveil a narrative that speaks to the essence of what it means to be human in an age where our creations reflect the echoes of ancient myths.

1.2 THE 1940S

In 1943, the American neurophysiologist and cybernetician Warren Sturgis McCulloch (1898–1969) from the College of Medicine, at the Illinois Neuropsychiatric Institute, University of Illinois, and the neurophysiologist Walter Harry Pitts, Jr. (1923–1969) from the University of Chicago, both in USA, published a paper titled "A Logical Calculus of the Ideas Immanent in Nervous Activity," in the *Bulletin of Mathematical Biophysics* (volume 5, pages 115–133) which proposed a model of neural networks that could perform logical operations. This was an important early contribution to the field of artificial neural networks that could be used to simulate human thought processes. McCulloch and Pitts model of a neuron, called an MCP neuron, has made an important contribution to the development of artificial neural networks – which model key features of biological neurons which is to abstract the biological neuron into a simple mathematical model.

Today you can buy an MCP neuron at most electronic stores, but they are called "threshold logic units." A group of MCP neurons that are connected is called an artificial neural network. In a sense, the brain is a very large neural network. It has billions of neurons, and each neuron is connected to thousands of other neurons. McCulloch and Pitts showed how to encode any logical proposition by an appropriate network of MCP neurons. And so, in theory anything that can be done with a computer can also be done with a network of MCP neurons (Marsalli, 2023).

Claude E. Shannon (1949, p. 1) proposed the meanings of machines in:

> (1) Machines for designing filters, equalizers, etc. (2) Machines for designing relay and switching circuits. (3) Machines which will handle routing of telephone calls based on the individual circumstances rather than by fixed patterns. (4) Machines for performing symbolic (non-numerical) mathematical operations. (5) Machines capable of translating from one language to another. (6) Machines for making strategic decisions in simplified military operations. (7) Machines capable of orchestrating a melody. (8)Machines capable of logical deduction.

The next major development in neural networks was the concept of a perceptron which was introduced by Frank Rosenblatt (1928–1971). This is an electronic device which was constructed in accordance with biological principles and showed an ability to learn. Rosenblatt's perceptron was initially simulated on an IBM 704 computer at Cornell Aeronautical Laboratory (Marcus, 2013) in 1957. Essentially the perceptron is an MCP neuron where the inputs are first passed through some "preprocessors," which are called association units. These association units detect the presence of certain specific features in the inputs. Perceptron was intended to be a pattern recognition device, and the association units correspond to feature or pattern detectors. Interestingly, there is a biological study that proves the analog of the association unit like the experiments from the Canadian David Hunter Hubel (1926–2013) and the Swedish Torsten Nils Wiesel (born 1924) discovered studying the visual cortex of the cat (Marsalli, 2023).

Hubel and Wiesel were awarded the Nobel Prize in 1981 for their work on ocular dominance columns in the 1960s and 1970s. Their studies greatly expanded the scientific knowledge of sensory processing.

The neuron receives incoming signals as 1s and 0s, takes a weighted sum of these signals and outputs a 1 if the weighted sum is at least some threshold value or a 0 otherwise. Formally this mathematical model can be specified as follows:

Let $[x_1, \ldots, x_m]$ be a vector of input signals where each x_i has a value of 0 or 1

Let $[w_1, \ldots, w_m]$ be a vector of corresponding weights where each w_i has a value of 0 or 1 or −1.

Input signals with a weight of 1 are called excitatory since they contribute toward a positive output signal in the sum.

Input signals with a weight of −1 are called inhibitory since they repress a positive output signal in the sum.

Input signals with a weight of 0 do not contribute at all to the neuron.

Then for some threshold value *t*, we can define a function which outputs 1 if the weighted sum of the input signals is greater than *t*, or 0 otherwise (Sinai, 2023).

But if we must give special attention is to 1949 when the British mathematician and computer scientist, Alan Mathison Turing (1912–1954) wrote "Computing machinery and intelligence," published a year later, in which he proposes the "Turing test" which is a mathematical model of computation describing an abstract machine. "In his 1936 paper, A. M. Turing defined the class of abstract machines that now bear his name. A Turing machine is a finite-state machine associated with a special kind of environment – its tape – in which it can store (and later recover) sequences of symbols," (Minsky, 1967, p. 107) where the word "machine" is in quotation marks that manipulates symbols on a strip of tape according to a table of rules. Sipser (2021, p. 137) describes it as the "Turing machine model." Rogers (1967, p .13) refers to "Turing's characterization," Boolos Burgess and Jeffrey (2002, p. 25) refers to a "specific kind of idealized machine" to measure a machine's ability to exhibit intelligent behavior equivalent to, or indistinguishable from, that of a human cited in Prasad and Choudhary (2021). In the beginning of his work *Computing Machinery and Intelligence* (1950) Turing explains:

> I PROPOSE to consider the question, "Can machines think?" This should begin with definitions of the meaning of the terms "machine" and "think". The definitions might be framed so as to reflect so far as possible the normal use of the words, but this attitude is dangerous. If the meaning of the words "machine" and "think" are to be found by examining how they are commonly used it is difficult to escaDe the conclusion that the meaning a and the answer to tlie auestion, "Can machines think ?" is to be sought in a statistical sirvey sdch as a Gallup poll. But this is absurd. Instead of attempting such a definition I shall replace the question by another, which is closely related to it and is expressed in relatively unambiguous words

In his essay, "Intelligent machinery," Turing wrote that his machine consisted of:

> ...an unlimited memory capacity obtained in the form of an infinite tape marked out into squares, on each of which a symbol could be printed. At any moment there is one symbol in the machine; it is called the scanned symbol. The machine can alter the scanned symbol, and its behavior is in part determined by that symbol, but the symbols on the tape elsewhere do not affect the behavior of the machine. However, the tape can be moved back and forth through the machine, this being one of the elementary operations of the machine. Any symbol on the tape may therefore eventually have an innings.
>
> (Turing, 1948, p. 3)

A year later on March 9, 1949, Claude Elwood Shannon (1916–2001) published a paper titled "Programming a computer for playing chess," which was presented at the National Institute for Radio Engineers Convention in New York in which he described a method for creating a program that could play chess. In March 1950, it was published in *Philosophical Magazine* and is considered one of the first articles published on the topic of programming a computer for playing chess and using a computer to solve the game.

His process for having the computer decide on which move to make was a minimax procedure, based on an evaluation function of a given chess position. Shannon gave a rough example of an evaluation function in which the value of the black position was subtracted from that of the white position. Material was counted according to the usual chess piece relative value (1 point for a pawn, 3 points for a knight or bishop, 5 points for a rook, and 9 points for a queen) (Ekbia, 2008, p. 46). Although the program was

TABLE 1.1 Key Milestones from the 1940s and the 1950s

	1943	1949	1950	1956	1957	1958	1959
Warren Sturgis McCulloch & Walter Harry Pitts, Jr.	A logical calculus of the ideas immanent in nervous activity						
Alan Mathison Turing		Turing test					
Claude Elwood Shannon		Programming a computer for playing chess					
Christopher S. Strachey			Pilot ACE				
John McCarthy, Marvin Lee Minsky, Nathaniel Rochester, and Claude Elwood Shannon				"A proposal for the Dartmouth Summer Research Project on Artificial Intelligence."			
Frank Rosenblatt					Rosenblatt's perceptron		
John McCarthy and Marvin Minsky						MIT Artificial Intelligence Laboratory	
John McCarthy							LISP (list processing language)
Arthur Lee Samuel							Machine learning using the game of checkers

never implemented, this paper is an important early contribution to the field of computer game playing (see Table 1.1).

1.3 THE 1950S

In 1950, British computer scientist Christopher S. Strachey (1916–1975) developed a program for playing draughts on the Ferranti Mark I computer called Pilot ACE. This was one of the earliest examples of a program designed to play a game using AI techniques. Strachey made three important technical contributions to computing in Britain: the logical design of computers, the design of programming languages, and the development of denotational semantics (Lee, 2023). He got the idea of using the machine to play draughts largely from an article by Donald Davies of NPL, "A theory of chess and noughts and crosses," that had appeared in the June 1950 issue of *Penguin Science News*.

Overall, the period between 1943 and 1950 saw the emergence of some key ideas and concepts that would form the basis of AI research for many years to come. These included the idea of using neural networks to perform logical operations, the development of early game-playing programs, and the proposal of the Turing test as a way of evaluating machine intelligence.

The computer scientist John McCarthy (1927–2011), in 1956, along with his colleagues Marvin Lee Minsky (1927–2016), Nathaniel Rochester (1919–2001), and Claude Elwood Shannon (1916–2001), published a paper titled "A Proposal for the Dartmouth Summer Research Project on Artificial Intelligence." This paper outlined a plan for a summer workshop in which researchers could collaborate on developing AI programs and techniques. The Dartmouth Summer Research Project on Artificial Intelligence was a 1956 summer workshop.

The proposal for the same states: the proposal is credited with introducing the term "artificial intelligence."

The proposal states:

> We propose that a 2-month, 10-man study of artificial intelligence be carried out during the summer of 1956 at Dartmouth College in Hanover, New Hampshire. The study is to proceed based on the conjecture that every aspect of learning or any other feature of intelligence can in principle be so precisely described that a machine can be made to simulate it. An attempt will be made to find how to make machines use language, form abstractions and concepts, solve kinds of problems now reserved for humans, and improve themselves. We think that a significant advance can be made in one or more of these problems if a carefully selected group of scientists work on it together for a summer.
>
> (McCarthy et al., 1955)

The proposal goes on to discuss computers, natural language processing, neural networks, theory of computation, abstraction, and creativity.

In 1958, John McCarthy and Marvin Minsky founded the MIT Artificial Intelligence Laboratory, which would become a leading center for AI research in the years to come. Other research centers, such as the Stanford AI Laboratory, also emerged during this period.

In the late 1950s and early 1960s, John McCarthy developed LISP, a programming language that would become widely used in AI research. LISP is an acronym for "list processing language" – so named because the list is one of the primary data structures in the language. LISP was specifically designed to handle symbolic expressions and provided a flexible and powerful tool for developing AI programs. John McCarthy published its design in a paper in *Communications of the ACM* in April 1960, entitled "Recursive functions of symbolic expressions and their computation by machine, Part I."

In the same period, in 1959, Arthur Lee Samuel (1901–1990) developed the first machine learning algorithm, which was used to play draughts, at a level that rivals human experts, using machine learning techniques to improve its performance over time. This program used a technique known as reinforcement learning and is often cited as one of the earliest examples of machine learning. He popularized the term "machine learning" in the publication: Samuel, Arthur L. (1959). Some studies in machine learning using the game of checkers. *IBM Journal of Research and Development, 44*, 206–226. The Samuel draughts-playing program was among the world's first successful self-learning programs, and as such a very early demonstration of the fundamental concept of AI (Wiederhold et al., 1990) (see Table 1.1).

1.4 FROM THE 1960S TO 1990

The German computer scientist Joseph Weizenbaum (1923–2008) created ELIZA in 1965, which was designed to simulate conversation with a human. ELIZA used a technique known as pattern matching to generate responses based on the user's input, and it became a widely studied and influential example of natural language processing. ELIZA was one of the first chatterbots ("chatbot" modernly) and one of the first programs capable of attempting the Turing test (Marino, 2006). In the words of Weizenbaum (1966, 36–45), ELIZA is a program operating within the MAC time-sharing system at MIT which makes certain kinds of natural language conversation between man and computer possible. Input sentences are analyzed on the basis of decomposition rules which are triggered by key words appearing in the input text. Responses are generated by reassembly rules associated with selected decomposition rules. The fundamental technical problems with which ELIZA is concerned are: (1) the identification of key words, (2) the discovery of minimal context, (3) the choice of appropriate transformations, (4) generation of responses in the absence of key words, and (5) the provision of an editing capability for ELIZA "scripts".

In 1966, Shakey the Robot was developed at STRIPS (Stanford Research Institute Problem Solver), becoming one of the first mobile robots to use AI techniques to navigate its environment, being able to reason about its own actions. The robot's programming was primarily done in LISP. It was replaced by Flakey, the robot, that was used to demonstrate fuzzy logic and goal-oriented behavior. That same year, the first AI laboratory was established at the Massachusetts Institute of Technology (MIT) by Marvin Minsky (1927–2016) and the South African computer scientist Seymour Aubrey Papert (1928–2016).

Three years must pass for the first AI conference. It was held in 1969 at the University of Edinburgh, Scotland.

The first expert system was developed in 1971, called DENDRAL (for dendritic algorithm), by Edward Albert Feigenbaum (born 1936) and Noble Prize laureate Joshua Lederberg (1925–2008) at Stanford University. Ran on a computer system called ACME (advanced computer for medical research), it was designed to analyze chemical compounds and was a major milestone in the development of expert systems.

Another chess-playing program was developed in 1972, called CHESS, by Richard D. Greenblatt (born 1944) and Thomas A. Standish at MIT. CHESS was able to defeat human players in tournament games. However, this was not the first attempt as in 1769, The Turk, a chess playing automaton, was created by Hungarian inventor Johann Wolfgang Ritter von Kempelen de Pázmánd aka Kempelen Farkas (1734–1804), which became famous before being exposed as a hoax. Another false machine in 1868 was Ajeeb, from the Arabic word عجيب (ʿajīb) meaning "wonderful, marvelous." It was a chess-playing "automaton," created by Charles Hooper, a Bristol cabinet maker. Earlier, a chess-playing "pseudo-automaton" Mephisto was built in 1876, this had no hidden operator, instead being remotely controlled by electromechanical means. Constructed by Charles Godfrey Gumpel (c. 1835–1921), it was mainly operated by chess master Isidor Arthur Gunsberg (also spelled Günzberg, Hungarian: Gunsberg Artúr Izidor, 1854–1930).

But the first automaton before digital computing was the Spanish El Ajedrecista of 1912 designed by Leonardo Torres y Quevedo in Madrid, which played a king and rook versus king ending. It was too complex and limited to be useful for playing full games of chess. If an illegal move was made by the opposite player, the automaton would signal it by turning on a light. If the opposing player made three illegal moves, the automaton would stop playing (David Levy, 1982, pp. 13–23), similar descriptions can be found on the book from 2009 by the same author *How Computers Play Chess*. The device could be considered the first computer game in the history. It is on display at the Museo Torres Quevedo in the Escuela de Ingenieros de Caminos, Canales y Puertos in Spain's capital city.

In 1974, the first AI program to demonstrate natural language understanding, called SHRDLU, was developed by Terry Allen Winograd (born 1946) at MIT. SHRDLU, the name was derived from ETAOIN SHRDLU, the arrangement of the letter keys on a Linotype machine, arranged in descending order of usage frequency in English, was able to understand and respond to commands in a simulated block world environment.

Five years later in 1979, the first robot to autonomously navigate a room, was developed by the Austrian-born Canadian citizen Hans Peter Moravec (born 1948), and his team at Stanford University. Moravec's work focused on providing robots with better spatial information. For his dissertation, he created a robot that moved through a crowded environment, using a television picture to help guide it. Although it could move safely through the room about 75 percent of the times, the robot took several hours to complete the task, and it was remote-controlled by a large computer. Moravec later developed

"3-D occupancy grids," which allowed a robot to determine the layout of a real-world environment in several seconds. That same year the first World Conference on Artificial Intelligence was held in Tokyo.

In 1984, the Cognitive Science Society was founded and in 1985, the expert system XCON was developed by Digital Equipment Corporation. XCON was used to configure computer systems and was one of the first successful commercial applications of AI. In 1986, the first International Joint Conference on Artificial Intelligence (IJCAI) was held in Los Angeles. IJCAI is now one of the premier conferences in the field of AI, bringing together researchers from academia, industry, and government. In 1987, the Japanese government launched the Fifth Generation Computer Systems project. The goal of the project was to develop a new generation of computers that could use advanced AI techniques to solve complex problems. The project ultimately failed to achieve its objectives, but it helped to advance AI research in Japan and around the world. In 1988, the Neural Information Processing Systems (NIPS) conference was held for the first time. NIPS is now one of the most important conferences in the field of machine learning, and its proceedings are widely read and cited by researchers (see Table 1.2).

TABLE 1.2 Key Milestones from the 1960s to 1990s

	1965	1966	1971	1972	1974	1979	1981	1984
Joseph Weizenbaum	ELIZA							
STRIPS (Stanford Research Institute Problem Solver)		Shakey, the Robot						
Edward Albert Feigenbaum and Joshua Lederberg			DENDRAL					
Richard D. Greenblatt and Thomas A. Standish				CHESS				
Terry Allen Winograd					SHRDLU			
Hans Peter Moravec						First robot to autonomously navigate a room		
Hubel and Wiesel							Work on ocular dominance columns	
Digital Equipment Corporation								XCON

1.5 THE 1990S

1990s: The second AI winter began, as the limitations of AI technology became apparent and funding for research declined. The first conference on Artificial General Intelligence is held in Tokyo, Japan. The Defense Advanced Research Projects Agency (DARPA) establishes the Integrated Learning Program to research machine learning techniques.

1991: IBM's Deep Blue computer defeats world chess champion Garry Kasparov in a six-game match, becoming the first computer to beat a reigning world champion in a match under standard chess tournament time controls. The first IEEE Conference on Robotics and Automation is held in Sacramento, California.

1992: The Cyc project, an ambitious effort to create a knowledge base for AI, is launched by Doug Lenat and his team at Microelectronics and Computer Technology Corporation (MCC).

1993: The first International Conference on Autonomous Agents and Multi-Agent Systems (AAMAS) is held in Seattle, Washington. The Association for the Advancement of Artificial Intelligence (AAAI) hosts its first AAAI Spring Symposium Series.

1994: Researchers at Carnegie Mellon University develop the first autonomous off-road robot, the NavLab 5. The first World Robot Olympiad is held in Singapore.

1995: The first RoboCup competition is held in Nagoya, Japan, with the goal of developing robots that can play soccer. The *Artificial Intelligence and Law Journal* is established.

1996: IBM's Deep Blue computer defeats Garry Kasparov in a rematch, becoming the first computer to win a six-game match against a reigning world chess champion under standard tournament conditions, the program was retired in 2003. The first National Conference on Artificial Intelligence (NCAI) is held in Portland, Oregon.

1997: The first International Joint Conference on Artificial Intelligence (IJCAI) to be held in Asia takes place in Nagoya, Japan. The Mindpixel project, an effort to build a massive database of human knowledge, is launched by Michael Mauldin and his team at Lycos.

1998: The movie "Deep Impact" featured a realistic depiction of a comet hitting Earth, made possible by advanced computer graphics technology. The first AI winter ended, and the field saw renewed interest and investment.

1999: The first version of the AIBO robotic dog was released by Sony. The first DARPA Grand Challenge, a competition for autonomous vehicles, was held (see Table 1.3).

1.6 THE DOT-COM BUBBLE BURST: THE 2000S

The 2000s started with the dot-com bubble burst, causing a temporary decrease in investment in AI and other tech industries.

In 2001, the first version of the Xbox gaming console was released by Microsoft, featuring an AI system that could learn and adapt to player behavior. The same year the first version of the Natural Language Toolkit (NLTK), a Python library for natural language processing, was released.

TABLE 1.3 Key Milestones from the 1990s

	1990	1991	1994	1995	1996	1999			
Defense Advanced Research Projects Agency (DARPA)	Integrated Learning Program to research machine learning techniques								
IBM's Deep Blue		Defeats world chess champion Garry Kasparov							
Carnegie Mellon University			NavLab 5						
Nagoya, Japan				RoboCup					
IBM's Deep Blue					Defeats world chess champion Garry Kasparov				
Sony						AIBO robotic dog			
DARPA Grand Challenge						DARPA Grand Challenge			

12 months later the DARPA Grand Challenge continued, with a course spanning over 100 miles. However, none of the participating vehicles were able to complete the course. In 2003, a vehicle named "Stanley" built by a team from Stanford University completed the course in just over 6 hours. The first version of the DARPA Urban Challenge was held, featuring autonomous vehicles navigating a simulated urban environment in 2004.

In 2005, the first version of the open-source machine learning platform Weka by University of Waikato, Craig Nevill-Manning, and Mark Hall was released and the second version of the AIBO robotic dog was released by Sony, featuring improved hardware and software.

Google had its year in 2006 when it acquired YouTube and began using AI algorithms to recommend videos to users based on their viewing history, and the first version of the TensorFlow library for machine learning was developed by researchers at Google Brain.

2007 was the year that marks the accessibility of the public to AI with the first version of the iPhone. Released by Apple, featuring a range of AI-powered features such as the Siri virtual assistant. A year later, the first version of the Microsoft Kinect, a motion-sensing device for gaming, was released, and The Netflix Prize was announced, offering a cash prize for improving the accuracy of the company's movie recommendation system.

In the 2010s, advances in deep learning and neural networks revolutionized AI research, leading to breakthroughs in areas such as speech recognition, image recognition, and natural language processing. Some of the milestones are

2011: IBM's Watson defeats human champions on the game show Jeopardy! showcasing advancements in natural language processing and knowledge representation.

2012: Deep learning algorithms achieve breakthrough results in computer vision tasks, with the ImageNet competition showing that machines can outperform humans in recognizing objects in images.

2016: Google's AlphaGo, an AI system that beat world champion Lee Sedol (born 1983) at the game of Go, was a major milestone in AI's ability to outperform humans in complex tasks.

The OpenAI organization was founded with the goal of advancing AI in a safe and beneficial way.

2017: AI continued to advance in image and speech recognition, with systems like Google's DeepMind and Facebook's AI achieving high levels of accuracy.

The United Nations released a report on the potential benefits and risks of AI, highlighting the need for ethical considerations in its development.

2018: The European Union passed the General Data Protection Regulation (GDPR), a sweeping set of privacy regulations that impacted the use of AI and machine learning algorithms.

Google's Duplex AI made headlines for its ability to mimic human conversation so convincingly that it raised ethical concerns about whether people would be able to tell if they were speaking to a machine.

2019: Researchers developed GPT-2, a large-scale language model that demonstrated impressive abilities in natural language processing, including the ability to generate realistic-sounding text.

AI continued to raise concerns about job displacement and its potential impact on the labor market.

2020: The Severe Acute Respiratory Syndrome Coronavirus 2 (SARS-CoV-2) pandemic led to an increased reliance on AI for tasks such as contact tracing and vaccine development.

2021: Advances in machine learning continued to drive breakthroughs in areas such as natural language processing and computer vision.

Concerns about the use of AI for surveillance and the potential for misuse continued to grow, prompting calls for stronger regulation and oversight.

2022: Major tech companies like Facebook and Google faced increasing scrutiny over their use of AI and data privacy practices. Although the most important application, without a doubt is ChatGPT (Chat Generative Pre-Trained Transformer), a large language model-based chatbot developed by OpenAI and launched on November 30, 2022. By January 2023, it had become what was then the fastest-growing consumer software application in history, gaining over 100 million users.

The development of autonomous vehicles continued to progress, with companies like Tesla and Waymo testing their self-driving cars on public roads.

TABLE 1.4 Key Milestones from the 2000s

	2000	2001	2005	2006	2007	2011	2016	2019	2022
General	Dot-com bubble burst								
Microsoft		Xbox							
Team NLTK		Natural Language Toolkit (NLTK)–Python library							
University of Waikato, Craig Nevill-Manning, Mark Hall			Weka						
Google				YouTube					
Apple					iPhone				
IBM's Watson						Jeopardy!			
Google's AlphaGo							Beat world champion Lee Sedol at Go		
MIT								GPT-2	
OpenAI									ChatGPT (Chat Generative Pre-Trained Transformer)

2023: AI continued to drive innovations in healthcare, with applications ranging from disease diagnosis to drug discovery.

As AI systems become more advanced and sophisticated, the ethical considerations around their development and use became more pressing than ever before.

Today, AI is used in a wide range of applications, from autonomous vehicles and virtual assistants to medical diagnosis and fraud detection. As the field continues to evolve, it is likely that AI will play an increasingly important role in many aspects of our lives (see Table 1.4.).

1.7 CONCLUSION

In tracing the rich tapestry of the history of artificial intelligence, we have witnessed a remarkable journey from the theoretical musings of early visionaries to the tangible advancements of the present day. The roots of AI stretch deep into the past, where seeds of curiosity planted by thinkers like Alan Turing and Ada Lovelace paved the way for the complex algorithms and intelligent systems we now take for granted.

The mid-20th century saw the birth of AI as an interdisciplinary field, with pioneers such as McCarthy, Minsky, and Newell laying the foundations for symbolic reasoning and problem-solving. The optimism of the early years gave way to the "AI winter," a period marked by waning interest and unmet expectations. However, like a phoenix rising from the ashes, the field experienced a resurgence in the 21st century, fueled by breakthroughs in machine learning, neural networks, and the abundance of data.

As we stand on the cusp of a new era, characterized by increasingly sophisticated AI applications, ethical considerations and societal impacts come to the forefront. Questions about the responsible development and deployment of AI demand our attention. Will AI be a force for good, enhancing our lives and solving complex problems, or will it introduce new challenges that require careful navigation?

The history of AI is not just a chronicle of technological progress; it is a testament to human ingenuity, curiosity, and the perpetual quest for understanding. As we venture into the future, the narrative of AI history challenges us to shape its trajectory responsibly, with a keen awareness of the ethical and societal implications. The story continues to unfold, and it is in our hands to guide AI towards a future that aligns with our values and aspirations.

REFERENCES

Ekbia, Hamid Reza. (2008). *Artificial dreams: The quest for non-biological intelligence.* Cambridge University Press.

Lee, J.A.N. (2023). Christopher Strachey, Computer Pioneers, IEEE Computer Society, https://history.computer.org/pioneers/strachey.html#:~:text=Strachey%20made%20three%20important%20technical,the%20design%20of%20programming%20languages

Levy, David. (1982). *The Sicilian defence.* Imprint Editions.

Levy, David (2009). *How computers play chess.* Ishi Press

Marcus, Gary. (December 31, 2013). Hyping artificial intelligence, yet again. *The New Yorker.* New York. www.newyorker.com/tech/annals-of-technology/hyping-artificial-intelligence-yet-again

Marino, Mark. (2006). *Chatbot: The gender and race performativity of conversational agents.* University of California.

Marsalli, Michael. (2023). McCulloch-Pitts neurons. *The Mind Project.* https://mind.ilstu.edu/curriculum/mcp_neurons/mcp_neuron1.html

McCarthy, John; Minsky, Marvin Lee; Rochester, Nathaniel; Shannon, & Claude Elwood. (1955). *A proposal for the Dartmouth summer research project on artificial intelligence.* Dartmouth College. http://raysolomonoff.com/dartmouth/boxa/dart564props.pdf

Minsky, Marvin Lee (1967). *Computation: Finite and infinite machines.* Prentice Hall.

Prasad, R., & Choudhary, P. (2021). State-of-the-art of artificial intelligence. *Journal of Mobile Multimedia, 17*(1–3), 427–454. https://doi.org/10.13052/jmm1550-4646.171322

Sinai, Jonathan. (2023). Deep learning about the Mcp neuron. *Reproductive Medicine and Biology.* www.rmb.co.za/page/deep-learning-about-the-mcp-neuron#:~:text=The%20idea%20behind%20the%20MCP,value%20or%20a%200%20otherwise

Sipser, Michael (2021). *Introduction to the theory of computation.* Course Technology
Turing, Alan M. (July 1948). *Intelligent machinery* (Report). National Physical Laboratory.
Turing, Alan M. (October 1950). *Computing machinery and intelligence, mind, new series,59*(236), pp. 433–460. Oxford University Press.
Weizenbaum, Joseph. (1966). ELIZA—A computer program for the study of natural language communication between man and machine. *Communications of the Association for Computing Machinery, 9*, 36–45.
Wiederhold, Gio; McCarthy, John; Feigenbaum, Ed. (1990). *Memorial resolution: Arthur L. Samuel* (PDF). Stanford University Historical Society.

CHAPTER 2

The Evolution of Animation and Motion Graphics through Contemporary AI Technologies

Francisco-Julián Martínez-Cano and
Raquel V. Benítez Rojas

2.1 INTRODUCTION

Motion graphics is a dynamic visual communication approach that combines animation with graphic design, and it is becoming more and more prevalent in modern life. These days, motion graphics are an integral part of our visual culture, showing up in everything from captivating video games to eye-catching advertisements. Because of their ability to evoke feelings, transmit ideas, and tell stories, they are a vital medium for communication, entertainment, education, data visualization, infographics, and creative expression. We are at the cusp of a new age in motion graphics, driven by the transformative potential of artificial intelligence (AI) and technological innovation.

Animating visual elements to communicate ideas and elicit emotions is the core of motion graphics, denoting numerical or literal material, obtaining interactive knowledge, and translating. This convergence of movement and design has its origins in early experiments with cinema, animation, and graphic design. Motion graphics evolved over time, moving from traditional hand-drawn animations to computer-generated imagery (CGI) in digital environments. Today's motion graphics medium spans both traditional displays and virtual reality environments, making it as expansive as the digital cosmos itself.

Concurrently, AI has emerged as a disruptive force driving technological advancements that were previously limited to science fiction. In recent years, there has been a significant surge in the industry's usage of machine learning, deep learning, neural networks,

DOI: 10.1201/9781003473633-2

and other AI subfields. By reimagining the possibilities and the creative process, AI has accelerated innovation in motion graphics as well as many other fields of knowledge. A surge of innovation has been spurred by the development of AI technology. The potential of AI to learn, adapt, and create material will have a profound influence on the growth and evolution of motion graphics. This theoretical framework embarks on an exploration to find out how the area of visual communication is changing due to the confluence of contemporary AI technology and motion graphics.

Motion graphic is a vast field of study and should be also understood as a discipline by itself (Amaral Schlittler, 2015). The definition from Sandhaus shapes the term "motion graphics" regarding a "broad area of design and production that includes type and imagery for film, video, and digital media. This includes animation, visual effects, film titles, television graphics, advertisements, multimedia presentations, more recent architecture, and increasingly digital/video games" (Sandhaus, 2006, p. 1), and it could be merged with the contribution of Parsons (2013), that refers to animation as the big umbrella that covers all digital films but also those films that focus on the animation's features of storytelling.

The development of motion graphics is intimately related to scientific and creative innovation. Although humans painted pictures on cave walls in the prehistoric past, the idea of moving images has been there ever since. However, the formal development of motion graphics can be traced through many significant turning points. Motion graphics have evolved since the first electronic techniques of creating moving visuals for films and television. Animation film practice has always been a perfect breeding ground for experimentation with new techniques and procedures. The cartoon media has allowed the moving image industry to test with the latest and cutting-edge technologies, and it is being the media where some creators developed unique equipment and devices for film production, from the thaumatrope, the multiplane camera (Iwerks, 1933; in Iwerks and Kenworthy, 2001), stop motion sets, morphing techniques, until nowadays motion-capture techniques and 3D computer graphics.

2.1.1 Approach to Historical Development of Animation and Motion Graphics

The early beginning of motion graphics starts with the invention of the zoetrope by William George Horner in 1834, comprised of a circular drum with cuts through which the viewer can stare, creating the sense of movement as the drawings placed inside the drum in strips rotate, and later the zoopraxiscope, created by Eadweard Muybridge in 1879. This device reflects the global human interest in the study of human vision, the moving image, and the development of its techniques and technologies, from the Han Dynasty in China to ancient Egypt, and merges three of the latest innovations in these area of knowledge: the zoetrope, photography, and the magic lantern (Solnit, 2004, p. 200).

Yet in the twentieth century, experimental film authors propelled the evolution of moving image techniques through their artistic practice. In France, the cartoonist and animator Émile Cohl created what is considered the first animation film, titled *Fantasmagorie* (1908). Three years later, American cartoonist of the New York Herald Zenas, Winsor McCay created *Little Nemo* (1911), which for its two minutes of pure animation uses sequential hand-illustration in a creative style that has not been seen in other movies. The earliest animation in America is credited to British director James Stuart Blackton, who was also one of the pioneers in the world to use stop-motion as a storytelling method. Back on the other side of the Atlantic, in Germany many artists explore abstract animation from a pervasive obsession with the popular cultural form of cartoons. For example, Hans Richter, Walter Ruttmann, Lotte Reiniger, and Oskar Fischinger, who started working with experimental motion graphic films while using different handcrafted materials like wax and clay, which resulted in the animation film series *Wachsexperimente* (*Wax Experiments*, 1921–1926), which lead the artist to his "Wax Machine," a first time-lapse cross-section device (Moritz, 2004, p. 7). Ruttmann also as pioneer in experimental animation directed *Lichtspiel Opus* I (1921), which has several geometric patterns and shapes that move rhythmically in time with the music, and iconic motion picture *Berlin: Symphony of a Great City* (1927), which is not an animation but is notable for its ground-breaking editing strategies and its montage-style representation of urban life.

From 1950s to 1960s, title sequences for television programs and movies were developed because of the invention of this new medium. Motion graphics in broadcasting were made possible by artist and designers like Saul Bass, who's renowned title sequences like the one for *Vertigo* (Hitchcock, 1958) and the advent of computer graphics in the 1960s propelled the motion graphics industry. In 1950, Disney produced *Cinderella*, and in this eon Hannah Barbera Productions, Inc., also established itself as one of the historical and referential studios in animation. After World War II, the so-called industrialization of manga started in Japan. Osamu Tezuka, one of those who made the biggest contributions to the development of Japanese animation, created it. Tezuka was heavily influenced by Walt Disney, and he frequently employed animated cartoon sequences in his artwork. He was able to create characters who were more fluid, had more movement, and lacked rigidity in this way.

During the 1980s and 1990s, digital technology's emergence drastically transformed motion graphics. Designers were able to produce complex animations thanks to computer software, and the growth of desktop publishing increased the number of graphic design tools available. Before *Toy Story* (1995), considered the first 3D feature film, digital animation had previously been used in a few scenes from movies like Star Wars as well as in Tron. However, digital animation first occurred almost half a century before. The first computer graphics experiments started in the 1940s and 1950s, and in the 1960s, experiments with digital designs for artistic and research reasons started, like *Humingbird* (Csuri and Shaffer, 1967), the first digital morphing created using a computer. From the 2000s and during the last two decades, motion graphics became a crucial component of branding, advertising, and internet content, the distinction between animation and graphic design began to fuzzily blend. The need for aesthetically appealing content was further increased by the internet and social media platforms. The most recent development in motion graphics is the incorporation of AI technologies. The creation of motion graphics is changing and becoming more accessible because of AI-driven techniques like deep learning and generative algorithms.

2.1.2 Artificial Intelligence Applied to Animation and Motion Graphics

AI has become a powerful force that is advancing technology in ways that were previously only possible in science fiction. Industry adoption of machine learning, deep learning, neural networks, and other AI subfields has increased dramatically in recent years. AI has accelerated innovation in the field of motion graphics by rethinking the potential and the creative process. The main realm of AI and its application regarding motion graphics pertains to the generative content models, and to be more precise to the video-generative AI tools. Applications like ChatGPT, Stable Diffusion, DALL-E, Midjourney, and Gen-2, among others, have sparked previously unheard-of interest in the potential of generative artificial intelligence. AI has advanced over time, influencing how videos are made, boosting the creative process, and expanding the possibilities of visual storytelling.

Animation was the origin of film practice and its discoveries at its inception and now it is again the space for exploration and discovery related to generative moving image techniques. The first milestone in the development of AI for generative video were neuronal networks in the 1980s and their development during the 1990s (Lawrence, 1993; Anderson, 1995), followed by the coming of deep learning and convolutional neural networks during the first decades of the twenty-first century. The next two innovations that enhanced the capabilities of AI video creation are generative adversarial networks (GANs) and natural language processing (NLP) (Cheng et al., 2020; Liu et al., 2021; Venkatesan, 2021; Gui et al., 2021; Wu et al., 2022). Taking over these, there are also two new trends: diffusion models, which "have desirable advantages; they offer a robust and scalable training objective and are typically less parameter intensive than their transformer-based counterparts" (Blattmann et al., 2023), and transformers (Siddiqui, 2022).

2.2 AI GENERATIVE MODELS APPLIED TO VIDEO AND ANIMATION

GAN framework has made it feasible to create high-resolution, photorealistic pictures and films, which was difficult or impossible with earlier techniques. Additionally, it has sparked the development of numerous new content creation applications (Liu et al., 2021). These deep learning systems were introduced by Goodfellow et al. (2014), and are based on:

> [...] two interacting neural networks – a generator network G and a discriminator net – work D, which are trained jointly by playing a zero-sum game where the objective of the generator is to synthesize fake data that resembles real data, and the objective of the discriminator is to distinguish between real and fake data. When the training is successful, the generator is an approximator of the underlying data generation mechanism in the sense that the distribution of the fake data converges to the real one. GAN's rise also marks another major success of deep learning in replacing hand-designed components with machine-learned components in modern computer vision pipelines.
>
> (Liu et al., 2020, p. 1)

In order to enable the generator to learn the complex patterns and nuances contained in human-created content, GAN-powered video production needs training the neural network on a collection of real videos. Although it has several applications in real world, like in fashion, architecture, video game industry, or medical imaging, in the field or audiovisual entertainment it has a great potential to create special effects, CGI characters, and even totally artificial settings which leads to a more efficient and visually powerful production techniques. Some of the developments using GAN in video generative applications are MoCoGan HD (Tian et al., 2021), DIGAN (Yun et al., 2022), and StyleGAN2 (Skorokhodov et al., 2022).

Within NLP, there are several text-to-video models that use natural language as text prompts to generate video. This model is used by a wide variety of generative AI applications that generate content commonly after a user's text prompt. By understanding the context and semantics of the prompted text, they produce a corresponding video sequence using advanced machine or deep learning and neural networks. One of the AI applications that uses this technology to generate image and art works is DALL-E2, which combines with diffusion models, which is a deep neural network with latent variables that can figure out how to deblur an image to understand its structure. DALL-E2, developed by OpenAI, does not provide the option to generate video.

Diffusion models are the last step forward in the field of moving image AI generation, "[...] and have superseded the performance of GANs on several tasks such as Image Synthesis" (Siddiqui, 2022). However, the early training of these models demands a tremendous amount of memory and has a significant environmental impact, making it unfeasible for the majority of researchers to even attempt the procedure. One of the models is Stable Diffusion, which is a technique for creating artificial data that uses a diffusion process to gradually tame a noisy source. In this method, a latent noise vector is iteratively converted into a target signal. To create a signal that nearly resembles a target distribution is the aim. Stable Diffusion is a self-supervised technique that learns through its own repeated refinement process, in contrast to GANs, which include a generator and discriminator. This model, developed by Runway y LMU Munich, can synthesize digital high-quality images from text inputs using latent diffusion models (LDMs) for image generation.

Transformers is yet another well-known group of NLP-related techniques. They have had great success developing conversational AI tools and modelling languages. Transformers have demonstrated the benefits of generalization and adaptivity in vision applications, making them appropriate for general-purpose learning. They are better than other strategies at capturing the semantic structure of text and even visuals. However, diffusion models are often less parameter heavy than their transformer-based equivalents and provide a robust and scalable training objective (Blattman et al., 2023).

Latent diffusion models (LDM), a recently proposed strategy that combines the perceptual strength of GANs, the detail retention capability of diffusion models, and the semantic strength of transformers, are taking over for generative video contents. The paucity of large-scale, general, and publicly accessible video datasets and the high computational cost involved with training on video data are the key reasons why video modelling has lagged, while the picture domain has made tremendous strides despite the abundance of written material on video synthesis (Babaeizadeh et al., 2017; Denton and Fergus, 2018; Castrejón et al., 2019; Brooks et al., 2022; Yun et al., 2022). While synthesis approaches can only produce relatively low-resolution, short videos, the LDM systems can produce long videos with high resolution allowing "text-guided video synthesis for creative content generation" (Blattman et al., 2023).

One of the most compelling text-to-video models is Gen-2 (https://research.runwayml.com/), developed by Runaway ML, the AI platform that is nowadays popular among designers, artists, and makers of interactive video content, allowing them to employ machine learning algorithms in their work. Users can take advantage of this tool to explore the creative capabilities of AI, producing everything from paintings and animations to 3D models and visual effects. It contributed to the success of *Everything Everywhere All at Once* (Kwan and Scheinert, 2022) winning the Oscar for Best Film in 2023. Although there are several headlines about this use of AI in the film, directors stranded against and clarified that the movie used AI partially, and is mainly the product of a very hard creative, artistic, and craftsmanship work (Sippell, 2023). This Gen-2 multimodal AI system can produce creative videos out of different types of content input like text, graphics, and video.

Some of the Gen-2 online alternatives are Kaiber, Plazmapunk, Decoherence, or NVIDIA Picasso, although this last one is not yet available to users. But this NVIDIA Picasso technology is being applied in different models like Cuebric (https://cuebric.com/), developed by A.I. Creative Production Studio Seyhan Lee (https://seyhanlee.com/), it is still in its beta version and not yet available to main users, but it might be a major industry change as it brings the possibility to use AI to create real-time immersive environments that can be used in film and audiovisual productions, reducing costs as of locations. This software platform combines generative AI technology with Unreal engine to generate photo-realistic virtual environments into on set productions. Another platform which contains several models produced by users is Replicate (https://replicate.com/), where Natural, Deforum or Andreasjansson are AI models based on stable diffusion . Finally, in our review and regarding 3D generative animation, we found Wonder Studio (https://wonderdynamics.com/), which is an AI software that works on live-action footage in which it generates animations automatically, merging dynamic lighting and bringing CG characters in live-action scenes in a simple and visually stunning way.

There are a variety of ways to produce animation and moving-image content using AI models, from the user side it could be through text-prompts, where the authors describe what they want to be part of the scene action; there are some models that allow to upload a previous image or drawing from which you could explain using text input what type of changes and incorporations have to be implemented by the AI. Some models also allow the use of previous footage combined with text input. For the sound and dialogs, there are also generative AI tools. From the perspective of the evolution of animation production techniques and processes, the incorporation of these technologies offers new creative possibilities at all levels. However, it is also obvious that the refinement of the techniques is still in development, for which the hybridization of different AI generative models is one of the current avenues of research being explored by developers, studios, and artists. Some of the issues resulting from the use of generative AI for animation and video are the image noises inherent in standard AI processing that generate a kind of bubbling and distortion. These artefacts can be solved to some extent by applying the EbSynth model, which is able to reduce these effects but not remove them entirely. Between animation and neuro rendering, it seems that there should be an "intermediary" that removes noise (which is a generic feature of diffusion models). It is necessary to make a new neural network or animation in latent space on a "different track," using techniques more akin to tracing, segmentation, and collage. Camera movements and different shot scales are also issues that are being tackled lately and some of the AI generative tools have started to include these types of creative decisions in their interfaces.

2.3 ANIMATION PRODUCTIONS USING AI

Far beyond using AI for scriptwriting, application of AI image-generative techniques to animation productions is starting to break in the studios and can already be found in Pixar movie *Elements* (Sohn, 2023), they implement AI generative tools to create the character of Ember, a flame, which was extremely difficult to produce using conventional 3D animation and particle systems. Finally, the creative team led by Peter Sohn and Paul Kanyuk decided to use a machine learning NST model to shape the fire essence of the character from some illustrations by Pixar artist Jonathan Hoffman.

Another important area of the film industry where AI has become a more significant factor is in the development of CGI. Computer-generated characters' realism has been improved using machine learning algorithms, making them more credible. Examples of this include the young Princess Leia in *Rogue One: A Star Wars Story* and the aged characters in Martin Scorsese's *The Irishman* (2019). These synthetic actors are produced by combining motion capture technology with AI-driven software, which studies the actor's motions and facial expressions to produce a lifelike digital duplicate.

One of the very first animation productions that uses AI is Netflix experimental futuristic short film *The Dog & the Boy* (Makihara, 2023). Distributed in Netflix Japan and produced by Wit Studios, in which a boy and his dog get separated for a while but eventually manage to reconcile in a bittersweet fashion. The backgrounds were created using AI, and Wit Studio oversaw animating the characters. While *The Dog & the Boy* has a wonderful ending and a sensitive plot, it has drawn criticism for using AI in place of animators on the grounds that there aren't any available. It seems like the studio wants to justify the use of AI to shorten production cost by stating a lack of cartoonists in the anime industry, which is being widely counter-argued by the audience in online channels and social networks. The method used for the development of this short film is not entirely based on AI, only the backgrounds and layouts were hand-drawn in a first step, and used as input for the AI to modify in a second phase to end up revised by hand as it can be shown in the closing credits. This method is meant to reduce the production cost of hand-drawn content from anime artists, decreasing the number of artists necessary to produce animation films in conventional conditions.

Another example of using AI, and in this case for the entire creation of the content for the opening sequence of Secret Invasion, is the newest television series based on the Marvel Cinematic Universe, debuted on Disney+ in June 2023. The opening title sequence is fully created using AI, which generated the controversy and brought again the debate of using generative models in film production. In the sequence, an animation work, it could be clearly identified the use of AI as the images move amidst noise and artefacts. Their visuals exhibit the kind of altered and illusory reality typical of AI-produced videos.

Apart from these examples, during the last years there have been different efforts and experimentations in animation and film productions that are fully created using generative AI models, such as the case of *Salt* (Stelzer, 2022–current), a ground-breaking science fiction film directed by neuroscientist and IT entrepreneur Fabian Stelzer. Because AI was used exclusively to create this project, it represents a significant advancement in the field of film production and the use of AI to the creative process. The project innovates in its creation method, format, and transmedia perspective, as it is made with deep fake software, generative AI art models, and AI-generated voices. For the images, Stelzer used freely accessible tools such as Midjourney, Stable Diffusion, and DALL-E2. For the vocals, he uses an AI voice generator known as Murf. The movie is distributed through Twitter as "story seeds," and the progress of its creation is conditioned by the votes of the audience, as Twitter, or X as is called now, followers are asked to choose in which direction the storyline evolves after each "story seed" is released.

2.4 DISCUSSION

The rapid advancements in AI have sparked debates about the future of various industries, and the realm of animation is no exception. As technology continues to evolve, the question arises: will AI replace animation artists? This inquiry delves into the intricate balance between human creativity and the capabilities of AI, exploring the potential impact on the animation industry.

And the truth is that AI has already made significant strides in the field of animation. Machine learning algorithms, neural networks, and sophisticated software have been employed to streamline certain aspects of the animation process. For instance, AI-driven tools can assist in generating realistic backgrounds, automating repetitive tasks, and even predicting motion trajectories. These applications aim to enhance efficiency and reduce the time-intensive nature of animation production.

But while AI has proven to be a valuable tool in animation, it is essential to recognize the intrinsic qualities that make human artists irreplaceable. Animation is not merely about the mechanical execution of movements, it is an art form that encapsulates emotion, storytelling, and creativity. AI may excel at repetitive tasks and data-driven processes, but it lacks the nuanced understanding of human experiences that animators bring to their work. Artists inject a piece of themselves into their creations, infusing characters with emotion and depth. The ability to convey complex emotions through animation is a distinctly human skill that arises from personal experiences, cultural context, and innate creativity. AI, while capable of replicating patterns and mimicking certain styles, struggles to authentically capture the essence of human emotions and the subtleties of storytelling.

Rather than posing a threat, AI has the potential to become a valuable collaborator for animation artists. By automating routine tasks and offering tools to expedite the production process, AI allows artists to focus more on the creative aspects of their work. For example, AI can be used to generate background scenery, leaving artists with more time to refine character designs and narrative elements. As technology evolves, the role of animation artists is likely to shift rather than disappear. Artists will need to adapt to new tools and techniques, incorporating AI into their workflow while retaining their core strengths of creativity and emotional intelligence. The future of animation lies in a symbiotic relationship between humans and machines, where AI augments the artistic process rather than replacing it.

FUNDING

This chapter is part of the research project *The Evolution of Motion Graphics through Contemporary AI Technologies*, funded by the Research Grants Programme 2023 of the Miguel Hernández University of Elche.

REFERENCES

Amaral Schlittler, J. P. (2015). Motion graphics and animation. *Animation Studies, Valência (CA/USA), 10,* 2–3.

Anderson, J. A. (1995). *An introduction to neural networks.* Cambridge, MA: MIT Press.

Babaeizadeh, M., Finn, C., Erhan, D., Campbell, R. H., & Levine, S. (2017). Stochastic variational video prediction. ArXiv:1710.11252 [cs. CV]. https://doi.org/10.48550/arXiv.1710.11252

Blattmann, A., Rombach, R., Ling, H., Dockhorn, T., Kim, S. W., Fidler, S., & Kreis, K. (2023). Align your latents: High-resolution video synthesis with latent diffusion models. In *Proceedings of the IEEE/CVF Conference on Computer Vision and Pattern Recognition* (pp. 22563–22575). https://doi.org/10.48550/arXiv.2304.08818

Brooks, T., Hellsten, J., Aittala, M., Wang, T. C., Aila, T., Lehtinen, J., ... & Karras, T. (2022). Generating long videos of dynamic scenes. *Advances in Neural Information Processing Systems, 35,* 31769–31781.

Castrejon, L., Ballas, N., & Courville, A. (2019). Improved conditional vrnns for video prediction. In *Proceedings of the IEEE/CVF international conference on computer vision* (pp. 7608–7617).

Cheng, J., Yang, Y., Tang, X., Xiong, N., Zhang, Y., & Lei, F. (2020). Generative adversarial networks: A literature review. *KSII Transactions on Internet & Information Systems, 14*(12), 4625–4647.

Denton, E., & Fergus, R. (2018, July). Stochastic video generation with a learned prior. In *International Conference on Machine Learning* (pp. 1174–1183). PMLR.

Goodfellow, I., Pouget-Abadie, J., Mirza, M., Xu, B., Warde-Farley, D., Ozair, S., ... & Bengio, Y. (2014). Generative adversarial nets. *Advances in Neural Information Processing Systems, 27,* 1–9.

Gui, J., Sun, Z., Wen, Y., Tao, D., & Ye, J. (2021). A review on generative adversarial networks: Algorithms, theory, and applications. *IEEE Transactions on Knowledge and Data Engineering, 35*(4), 3313–3332. https://doi.org/10.1109/TKDE.2021.3130191

Iwerks, L., & Kenworthy, J. (2001). *The hand behind the mouse.* NewYork: Disney Editions.

Lawrence, J. (1993). *Introduction to neural networks*. United States: California Scientific Software. https://dl.acm.org/doi/abs/10.5555/184210

Liu, M. Y., Huang, X., Yu, J., Wang, T. C., & Mallya, A. (2021). Generative adversarial networks for image and video synthesis: Algorithms and applications. *Proceedings of the IEEE, 109*(5), 839–862.

Moritz, W. (2004). *Optical poetry. The life and work of Oskar Fischinger*. UK: John Libbey Publishing.

Parsons, C. (July 22, 2013). *Why we need a new language of cinema. Animation Studies*. http://blog.animationstudies.org/?p=397

Sandhaus, L. (2006). Los Angeles in Motion: A Beginner's Guide from Yesterday to Tomorrow [online]. Available from: http://www.lsd-studio.net/writing/lainmotion/pdfs/LA_in_Motion.pdf

Siddiqui, J. R. (September 20, 2022). What are stable diffusion models and why are they a step forward for image generation? An easy guide to latent diffusion models. *Towards Data Science*. https://towardsdatascience.com/what-are-stable-diffusion-models-and-why-are-they-a-step-forward-for-image-generation-aa1182801d46

Sippell, M. (August 22, 2023). Daniel Scheinert wants to set the record straight about AI and everything everywhere all at once. *MovieMaker*. www.moviemaker.com/daniel-scheinert-everything-everywhere-ai/

Skorokhodov, I., Tulyakov, S., & Elhoseiny, M. (2022). Stylegan-v: A continuous video generator with the price, image quality and perks of Stylegan2. In *Proceedings of the IEEE/CVF Conference on Computer Vision and Pattern Recognition* (pp. 3626–3636).

Solnit, R. (2004). *Motion studies: Time, space and Eadweard Muybridge*. London: Bloomsbury.

Tian, Y., Ren, J., Chai, M., Olszewski, K., Peng, X., Metaxas, D. N., & Tulyakov, S. (2021). A good image generator is what you need for high-resolution video synthesis. ArXiv:2104.15069 [cs. CV]. https://doi.org/10.48550/arXiv.2104.15069

Venkatesan, R., & Priyanka, S. (2021, December). Trends in text to image synthesis (T2I) using generative adversarial networks. In *Proceedings of the First International Conference on Combinatorial and Optimization, ICCAP 2021, December 7–8, 2021*, Chennai, India.

Wu, A. N., Stouffs, R., & Biljecki, F. (2022). Generative adversarial networks in the built environment: A comprehensive review of the application of GANs across data types and scales. *Building and Environment*, 109477, 1–18. https://doi.org/10.1016/j.buildenv.2022.109477

Yu, S., Tack, J., Mo, S., Kim, H., Kim, J., Ha, J. W., & Shin, J. (2022). Generating videos with dynamics-aware implicit generative adversarial networks. In *International Conference on Learning Representations*. ArXiv:2202.10571. https://doi.org/10.48550/arXiv.2202.10571

CHAPTER 3

A Look at the Crossroads of Artificial Intelligence, Films, Video Games, and Virtual Reality

Francisco-Julián Martínez-Cano

3.1 INTRODUCTION

In its origins, artificial intelligence (AI) focused on simplified simulations based on defined rules, a "mechanisation of thought processes" (title of the first international symposium on artificial intelligence held in 1958), whose intersections with biology, physics, or electronics posed fruitful lines of research (Sutherland, 1958, cited in Freedman, 2022, p. 19). We could summarize the development of AI in three blocks, the first occurring just after the Second World War, from a military perspective. The second was in the 1970s, during which it started to be applied to problem-solving in specific areas of knowledge, and the last one, starting in the 1990s, focused on machine learning (Freedman, 2022, p. 23).

In the same year as the Mechanisation of Thought Processes symposium, one of the first video games was created, *Tennis for Two* (Higinbotham, 1958), and later, in 1961, *Spacewar* was developed by Steve Russell and other collaborators at the Massachusetts Institute of Technology (MIT). In the 1970s, coinciding with the second period of the evolution of the AI, the first arcade video games were developed, forming part of the video game industry ecosystem, including Magnavox, Capcom, Atari, and Nintendo. In the 1990s, Sega launched the Saturn video console and Sony the PlayStation, and from the beginning of the new century, Microsoft developed its Xbox (Kent, 2001). In the early days of AI in video games, it was just a collection of patterns that were saved in arcade games from the 1970s. The AI system in Pac-Man (1980), for example, is in charge of

DOI: 10.1201/9781003473633-3

several ghosts that appear to act on their own yet are all bound by a single set of AI-coded patterns. The limitations of these intelligent systems were hidden by narrative structures that supported the "brain power of human-like machines" (Freedman, 2022, p. 37). During the 1990s, primitive decision trees and rule-based systems were used as early AI algorithms for basic graphics rendering, character movement, and game behavior. The development of finite state machines is notable for achieving fundamental character behaviors and reasoning in decision-making. The visual interactivity and dynamics of the game are improved by these mechanisms, which enable characters in the game to react to player actions. Furthermore, by using pathfinding algorithms, game characters can move more organically and intelligently around obstacles and across challenging terrain, which improves the game's visual realism (Wu et al., 2023, p. 15347). Since then, AI has evolved parallel to the video game industry, until the advent of commercial game engines such as Unreal and Unity, so these innovations made AI capable of learning and generating content and producing complete game levels automatically. AI systems can also be combined with other software frameworks to drastically change the process used to create video games.

Cinema, developed in the late 19th and early 20th centuries, has also evolved in relation to different technological advances, with the introduction of sound in the late 1920s and early 1930s and Technicolor following with *Becky Sharp* (Mamoulian, 1935), considered to be the first feature film to incorporate it. Special effects and their techniques have been explored since their origins, but the advent of digital technologies from the 1990s onward transformed the industry by enabling more complex and visually powerful effects and editing. Although AI has been depicted in many films such as *Metropolis* (Lang, 1927), *2001: A Space Odyssey* (Kubrick, 1968), *Westworld* (Crichton, 1973), *Blade Runner* (Scott, 1982), *I, Robot* (Proyas, 2004), *Her* (Jonze, 2013), or *Ex Machina* (Garland, 2015) among others, it was not used until the 1990s in films such as *Jurassic Park* (Spielberg, 1993) and *Toy Story* (Lasseter, 1995), especially for rendering complex graphics and animations. From 2000 onwards, the use of CGI and digital effects grew exponentially, and it is here that the application of AI in the film industry intensified, with machine learning and deep learning technologies being central to editing and visual effects.

Virtual reality (VR) began to be conceptualized in the 1960s and 1970s, with Heilig's Sensorama and Ivan Sutherland's Sword of Damocles. In the 1980s and 1990s, it was more present in cinematographic fiction in feature films such as *Total Recall* (Verhoeven, 1990) and *The Lawnmower Man* (Leonard, 1992) than in the technological field, where it was developed timidly with devices such as the Virtual Boy (Nintendo, 1995) or the Power Glove (Nintendo, 1989), which were not very well received due to their technical limitations and development costs. It was not until the beginning of the 21st century, and specifically the second decade of the new century, that platforms such as Oculus brought their devices to mainstream consciousness.

The timelines in the evolution of these media coincide in certain historical moments. Although video games and AI have been directly interrelated in the fields of computer studies and computer engineering almost since their origins and have evolved in parallel, it was not until the early 2000s that they began to converge with cinema and VR. The connection between AI and video games is natural, and later VR and video games, but cinema has also been influenced by these innovations. Video games are therefore considered the natural environment for AI and VR:

> While video games have been a fundamental testing ground for artificial intelligence, we should also examine whether video games have in turn shaped the development and implementation of AI; larger game developers have expressed an interest in AI research, and their industrial paradigms are undoubtedly influencing the field, where AI is viewed through the lens of game (application) space. AI is changing the field of game development, and in turn, game development is changing the field of AI.
>
> (Freedman, 2022, p. 32)

Entertainment and creative industries result in the perfect scenario for AI development and application. We could start thinking of a new experience paradigm for audiovisual entertainment, where video games and VR films are part of the playable media cultural production ecosystem, understanding these as information architectures that drive the AI approach with "the intention to make it more believable, more immersive, or simply more enjoyable" (Fuchs & Sudmann, 2019, p. 2).

The representation of AI, the so-called AI narratives (Cave et al., 2018, p. 5), can be seen as a reflection of our hopes and worries about these technologies, and as such, it may have an impact on policy-makers, developers, and public adoption of AI (Cave et al., 2020; Cave & Dihal, 2019, p. 74, cited in Hermann, 2023, p. 319). Regarding these issues, we recently witnessed the SAG-AFTRA Actors Union and Script Writers Union strike in July 2023 against the use of AI in replicating performances and producing script content for the industry, and later in December 2023 the development of the Artificial Intelligence Act, the world's first law that regulates AI in the European Union.

3.2 VIDEO GAMES AI AT THE CORE OF MEDIA INTERSECTION

Recent years have witnessed amazing advancements in the use of AI in video games, resulting in more realistic, immersive, and captivating gaming experiences, and all of them are feasible to be applied to films and VR experiences. Some of the latest innovations can be found in titles such as *Red Dead Redemption 2* (Rockstar Games, 2018), in which AI systems play a major role in the creation of dynamic game environments, as the game space and action changes based on player actions. The player's choices shape the behavior of wildlife and non-player characters (NPCs), resulting in a dynamic and ever-changing environment. In the realm of AI innovations regarding NPCs, *The Last of Us Part II* (Naughty Dog, 2020) is a sample of how complex AI algorithms set and control the NPCs actions and movements. They can communicate with each other to prepare strategies based on player decisions giving a realistic touch to the gameplay.

One of the major innovations in the field of AI is procedural content generation (PCG). These AI models have been used in the design of *No Man's Sky* (Hello Games, 2016), generating an enormous explorable universe using algorithms to create distinct planets, ecosystems, and animals. In this case, AI PCG has been used to develop the soundtrack of the video game, rather than attempting to compose music that would fit into a world and the situations that players will encounter while exploring the universe. Hello Games has expanded the use of its procedural design techniques to include the soundtrack. Paul Weir, the audio director of the game company, collaborated with Sheffield, UK-based electronic band 65daysofstatic to build an extensive sound and music library. These components work together to give the player's a real time experience, personalized to their unique experiences, a musical backdrop (Epstein, 2016). Therefore, PCG can be applied to any creative field, not only to develop environments and levels, but also to play its part in the musical component.

Giving a more realistic and immersive experience to the players has been one of the challenges for the video game industry. The focus relies on the representation of characters and movement, for which AI is used to provide lifelike facial expressions and movements. Character animations that are realistic and subtle are created by AI using motion capture data, as in the video game *Detroit: Become Human* (Quantic Dream, 2018). Following the same path, other titles explored the application of AI to create voice-activated controls and interactions, like the case of *Skyrim* (Bethesda Game Studios), integrating AI-driven voice recognition, allowing players to interact with the game world and characters through natural language processing (NLP).

Other examples of AI applications are adaptive difficulty levels, as in the video game *Left 4 Dead* (Valve, 2008 & 2009), wherein the AI acts as a director, dynamically changing the game's difficulty in response to how well players do. To create a balanced difficulty, the director rearranges the amount and locations of obstacles, opponents, and items. Tailoring the content and game experience to the player behavior and performance is also present in *Fortnite* (Epic Games, 2017), based on an AI model that analyzes the user behavior in order to adapt the challenges and gameplay to make it more engaging for the different sorts of players. Finally, the use of AI for game testing (Enhanced Game Testing) is one of the developments to speed up the testing phase of any video game, by using AI-driven testing bots that can play games iterating during long lapses of time tackling bugs and balancing issues in a more efficient manner than human testers. In the near future, cloud-based AI computation will bring the chance to more complex AI processes without relying on the player's hardware, as it can be offloaded to cloud servers and cloud gaming platforms like Google Stadia, released in 2019 and shut down in 2023, or Xbox Cloud Gaming, Nvidia GeForce Now, or Amazon Luna, which is still in beta in the United States.

Advances in character design and development from the video game industry are also shaping the way film industry uses CGI in feature films with real actors and in animation. Since 2021, MetaHuman Creator (Epic Games) has been one of the major benchmarks on the character development. The advancement in the creation of high-fidelity digital humans takes advantage of the latest volumetric facial capture and rigging techniques. This software platform is not based on AI, but it has been combined with AI voice actor models to create realistic avatars that act and talk like real humans. Another milestone on character creation is Omniverse Avatar (NVIDIA, 2021). This platform uses NLP and computer vision to create characters that are able to see and speak. In 2022, the Plask AI animation tool was released, a paramount step in the use of machine-learning to retarget the movements of actors from video into 3D characters.

As Eric Freedman states: "These technologies also remind us that AI operates at every level of representation; it defines worlds, characters, assets and images, and uses data to manage both visual and performance-based behaviours" (2022, p. 40), reshaping the whole media production ecosystem and developing new technologies and techniques to improve content creation.

3.3 AI CONVERGENCE IN FILMMAKING

The AI models and applications that have been developed for video games can be used creatively to filmmaking, providing new avenues for improving narrative storytelling, production efficiency, and audience engagement. Apart from AI-assisted editing, audio and video post-production, automated camera work, and scriptwriting assistance to help out filmmaking traditional procedures, following the concept of dynamic storytelling, films could turn into interactive products with more sophisticated decision trees and branched storylines creating adaptive narratives based on viewer choices and behavior, like in the video game *The Last of Us Part II* (Naughty Dog, 2020) or in *Red Dead Redemption 2* (Rockstar Games, 2018), where also the NPCs are responsive lifelike characters driven by AI that could be implemented in CGI film characters and animation movies, improving the quality of visual effects with more natural and diverse expressions as in the case of *Detroit: Become Human* (Quantic Dream, 2018). Finally, drawing from *Fornite* (Epic Games, 2017), personalized viewing experiences can increase viewer engagement since AI can recognize viewer preferences and provide content recommendations or changes.

Procedural content generation can be applied for the creation of automated scenery and backgrounds, which is implemented in new shooting techniques that inherited the tradition of background replacement techniques (matte painting), as the case of StageCraft, the system used in the production of series like *The Mandalorian* (Favreau, 2019–2023), and its configuration is as follows:

> The Stagecraft set is called The Volume and is a 23-metre radius circle with a ceiling made up of LED screens, in which the floor is constructed as a continuation of the spaces projected on the screens. This primarily allows the virtual spaces to interact with the action, whereby the cameras are synchronised with the central axes of each of the projections on the surrounding panels. The technique is further refined by real-time rendering of the projected virtual environments using the Unreal Engine. Early approaches to this system are found in developments with large-format screen projections such as those used for the feature film *Oblivion* (Kosinski, 2013).
>
> (Martínez-Cano, 2021, p. 500)

Filmmaking technology has advanced significantly with the integration of AI into StageCraft's shooting processes. Rather than relying on traditional green screens,

StageCraft creates dynamic and immersive backgrounds in real time using giant LED screens. The capabilities of this process are enhanced in several significant ways by the incorporation of AI.

With the help of AI algorithms, the StageCraft System can quickly generate complex 3D worlds on the LED screens in real time, responding to camera motions and modifications. This system also produces a dynamic rendering environment. This makes the blending of artificial backdrops with live-action video smoother. The problems of matching lighting from live-action footage recorded with green screens and synthetic backgrounds is also overcome. In this regard, AI makes sure that the lighting on the LED displays is consistent and realistic, matching the lighting on the set. This is essential for smoothly integrating actors into the virtual world projected on the LED screens. AI can detect the location, orientation, and lens properties of the camera and modify the background images on the LED panels accordingly, improving camera tracking and synchronization. This synchronization produces a more realistic sense of space and depth. Because all the scenery is customizable, there is no need for post-production editing, as the digital environment can be quickly modified. Examples of such quick adjustments include changing the weather, the time of day, or adding moving elements such as people or cars. This also includes interaction of actors with virtual objects in the background, the environment may be instantly modified by the AI to reflect these interactions.

Filmmakers can previsualize scenes in the StageCraft environment using AI-powered tools, and edit and rearrange objects on the virtual backdrop using VR goggles. This helps to plan shots and determine how scenes will appear in the result. Similarly, machine learning algorithms trained on vast collections of environmental imagery can create incredibly realistic backdrops and environments that adapt organically to changes in the scene. StageCraft's AI gives directors and cinematographers more artistic flexibility, allowing them to test different sets and backdrops in real time to see which works best for the story. These speeds up the overall production process by reducing the need for extensive post-production work.

The film industry may harness the potential of AI to produce more captivating, effective, and inventive films by incorporating these concepts and applications from video games into their production pipelines. The combination of video games, artificial intelligence, and filmmaking is expected to create new creative opportunities and reshape the conventional cinematic bounds as technology continues to advance.

3.4 VR EXPERIENCES: A CONVERGENCE POINT

AI has revolutionized modern game development, influencing game design and development as well as other media's visual grammar, representation, and techniques. Similarly, film and audiovisual production are being transformed by the engine-based logics of virtual production and new shooting techniques, led by fast improvement of hardware systems, and workflows that support real-time 3D visualization. The combination of techniques from various disciplines is the main pillar for the development of new immersive narratives that blend video games, films, and VR through the use of AI to support embodiment (Kilteni et al., 2012) and to create a more realistic sense of presence, from a "sense of being with another" (Biocca et al., 2003, p. 456), "whether that other is other real humans or human-like artificial intelligences" (Oh et al., 2018, cited in Erickson-Davis et al., 2021, p. 336).

It seems impossible to draw a line between a VR game and a film, as for *Agence* (Galiano, 2020), defined as "neither a movie nor a game" (Heaven, 2020), which makes it difficult to find an audience. It is the first immersive VR movie that uses reinforcement learning to manage its characters. Defined as a dynamic film by its director and producer, it might be set currently in the advent of a new type of storytelling media, as silent films at the beginning of the 20th century. It can be watched as a linear film or as an interactive plot, with the difference of having the chance to change the story at any point, far away from the branched narrative structures of previous interactive films.

The Under Presents (Tender Claws, 2019) is another example of the integration of AI in the development of virtual experiences that intertwined the boundaries of video games and film. Presented in the Meta catalogue as "our otherworldly multiplayer hub", it creates a storyline based on graphic adventures. Although this VR production uses AI, its implementation is not as in *Agence* (Galiano, 2020). Rather than using AI in the conventional sense to manage characters, this experience uses a special fusion of live improvization and scripted material, combining live actors with recorded performances. The AI portion focuses more on controlling the interactive setting and guaranteeing a smooth transition between recorded and live content.

Fable Studio released in 2018 *Wolves in the Walls*, the first episode of an animated VR series. In this immersive storytelling, they developed a complex scripted environment where the user could interact within as the narrative goes forward with the aim of helping Lucy, the main character, occupying the position of her imaginary friend as if inside a detective story. In 2019, already as Fable, the company released *Whispers in the Night*, the second chapter where they combined VR with AI to create an enhanced immersive narrative experience, where Lucy acquired NLP capabilities through machine learning models, allowing to create personal and different experiences for the audience. Lucy is therefore capable of remembering conversations, individualizing the relationship between her and the user. Since then, Fable is delved into Virtual Beings Conference, and the development of this category, in words of its founder Edward Saatchi: "an AI-powered character with whom you build a two-way relationship" (Damiani, 2019), empowering the emotional aspects of immersive experiences and taking a step forward the art of audiovisual storytelling.

Bonfire (Baobab Studios, 2019) is another example of early implementation of AI in the creation of cinematic virtual reality movies. In this case the idea is to enable viewers to become agents of the story, participating in its development while communicating with aliens and making decisions as the story unfolds. For the characters in Unity, the team developed complex non-linear storytelling and AI algorithms that allowed the audience to take on the role of the protagonist. To elicit empathy, they made remarkable advances in AI and emotion, both technically and creatively. Building on the great traditions of storytelling, this allows the nature of the viewer to manifest alongside that of a character. Regarding innovations on character design and creation, Baobab's goal was to create a generative animation system for Pork Bun's AI brain that would be as close to the character's behavior as if it had been created by an animator. The AI system generated convincing movements for a long time, but it was robotic and did not accurately capture Pork Bun's true personality. The ability to create the "illusion of a living creature" in the way Pork Bun responded to the viewer's input was made possible in large part by Unity's adaptive animation architecture.

These references point to an increasing trend in the application of AI in video games, both within their own industry and to broaden the potential applications in VR and filmmaking. AI contribution to the creation of immersive, interactive experiences is growing in importance, bridging the gap between various domains, and resulting in new inventive digital entertainment forms.

3.5 BRIEF APPROACH TO SOME ETHICAL CONSIDERATIONS

AI application in the creative industries not only brings advancements and new options for creators never possible to explore before but also raises some concerns about ethical considerations. User data collection and analysis is frequently necessary for personalized content. This gives rise to worries regarding data security, privacy, and the possible exploitation of personal data. Due to its compromise of the human aspect and creative essence of cultural creation, it also raises issues regarding the authenticity and artistic integrity of art. Where does human authorship start and AI role finish? Is it possible for machines to acquire creativity? AI is opening new doors for human creativity, or at least is pushing the boundaries of how we have expressed ourselves so far in artistic terms, we can "harness the power of artificial intelligence to broaden the scope of human creativity" (Ali Elfa & Dawood, 2023, p. 118). This leads also to the question about jobs destruction in the cultural industries. Some authors argue that "any phase of technological change must be seen in terms of both job destruction and job creation" (Freeman & Louçã, 2001; Perez, 2002, 2016; Nübler, 2016, cited in Nathan & Ahmed, 2018, p. 295). In this vein, "one can only point to the growth of television shows, spectator sports, computer games, and so on as new or growing sectors of the economy" (Nathan & Ahmed, 2018, p. 295) resulting in structural changes and the rise of new sectors. All these could be seen as an advantage, but on the other hand the big fishes of the audiovisual industry are starting to apply AI to create content in a faster, more efficient, and cost-effective way, which involves the loss of many creative and artistic job positions, not to count all the structural and management jobs that are also lost. How is the labor structure in the creative industries transforming? What new jobs are being created? How are creative jobs going to transform? It's important to strike a balance between employment stability, skill development, and technological growth.

At the same time, AI systems need a data environment from which it learns and takes visual materials. These training databases are "a critical component in optimising the performance of ML processes and hence a significant proportion of the value of an AI system" (Anantrasirichai & Bull, 2022, p. 593), but at the same time it brings questions about royalties of the contents those database are made of, movies, TV programs, series, scripts, novels, and all sorts of copyrighted cultural productions are used to train the AI in order to produce the new AI-processed content, so who is the owner of this AI-created content's copyright?

From a social perspective, the use of AI to generate deep fakes could be a way of chasing and promoting prosocial behavior in the audience (Cifuentes-Albeza & Martínez-Cano, 2023), as can be seen in some prosocial advertising like in the spot *Intolerance Is Still There* (DDB España, 2021) from the campaign *Héroes de hoy* (losheroesdehoy.com, 2020–currently), where deep fake techniques are used to tell the story of Julio Zúñiga, and resurrect him after he was murdered because of his public stance as an LGTBIQ+ footballer in Mexico. But also, AI-generated photos and videos can be abused to produce deep fakes, with the aim to spread false information and support other nefarious actions.

Two important concerns in the development of AI and its use in the VR, film, and video game industries are accessibility and inclusivity. It is imperative to ensure that the cultural domain established by these technologies is both inclusive and accessible, accommodating a wide range of viewers without perpetuating prejudice, including representational biases and harms (Blodgett et al., 2020). Racialization and bias in AI contribute to social injustice (Cave & Dihal, 2020) not only in its representation but also from its original construction, as far as its development has been done from a White and cisgender perspective, establishing a power hierarchy above other communities and minorities.

3.6 DISCUSSION AND FUTURE DIRECTIONS

All things considered, the development of AI in gaming not only improves the pleasure of playing games but also creates opportunities for more creative and participatory narrative in movies and more immersive VR settings. The ongoing advancements in AI in this field portend an increasingly dynamic and captivating future for digital entertainment. Not only is this convergence changing how information is produced and consumed but it is also bringing up important ethical issues.

The use of PCG in the production process of video games, movies, and VR experiences will likely lead to the autonomous generation of entire narratives, the creation of more lifelike non-player characters, and the creation of fully interactive and adaptive motion experiences that transform the user from a passive to an active participant in the storytelling process. The boundaries between different types of media content are fading away, becoming cross-industry applications.

The innovations and opportunities of this intersection comes from enhanced creativity and immersion. Environments and characters that are more responsive and lifelike are made possible by AI-driven character animation and content creation. Each experience is unique because real-time data analysis of user behavior and interaction processes creates narratives that are tailored to each individual's tastes. All of this requires a more efficient production pipeline. AI simplifies several parts of production, from post-production to script writing, saving time and money while increasing user engagement. Finally, it is a paramount issue on the development of AI applications in creative industries related to ethics and inclusion. We all should join our efforts in the development of the next entertainment and media ecosystem from an inclusive, diverse, and fair perspective, as it will promote a better social environment.

FUNDING

This chapter is part of the research project *The Evolution of Motion Graphics through Contemporary AI Technologies*, funded by the Research Grants Programme 2023 of the Miguel Hernández University of Elche.

REFERENCES

Ali Elfa, M. A., & Dawood, M. E. T. (2023). Using artificial intelligence for enhancing human creativity. *Journal of Art, Design and Music*, *2*(2), 3. https://doi.org/10.55554/2785-9649.1017

Anantrasirichai, N., & Bull, D. (2022). Artificial intelligence in the creative industries: A review. *Artificial Intelligence Review*, 55, 589–656. https://doi.org/10.1007/s10462-021-10039-7

Biocca, F., Harms, C., & Burgoon, J. K. (2003). Toward a more robust theory and measure of social presence: Review and suggested criteria. *Presence: Teleoperators & Virtual Environments*, *12*(5), 456–480. https://doi.org/10.1162/105474603322761270

Blodgett, S. L., Barocas, S., Daumé III, H., & Wallach, H. (2020). Language (technology) is power: A critical survey of "Bias" in NLP. ArXiv:2005.14050 [Cs]. https://doi.org/10.48550/arXiv.2005.14050

Cave, S., Craig, C., Dihal, K., Dillon, S., Montgomery, J., Singler, B., & Taylor, L. (2018). *Portrayals and perceptions of AI and why they matter*. The Royal Society. https://doi.org/10.17863/CAM.34502

Cave, S., & Dihal, K. (2019). Hopes and fears for intelligent machines in fiction and reality. *Nature Machine Intelligence*, *1*(2), 74–78. https://doi.org/10.1038/s42256-019-0020-9

Cave, S., & Dihal, K. (2020). The whiteness of AI. *Philosophy & Technology*, *33*(4), 685–703. https://doi.org/10.1007/s13347-020-00415-6

Cave, S., Dihal, K., & Dillon, S. (2020). Introduction to imagining AI. In Ibid (Ed.), *AI narratives: a history of imaginative thinking about intelligent machines* (pp 1–21). Oxford University Press: Oxford.

Cifuentes-Albeza, R., & Martínez-Cano, F. J. (2023). La publicidad prosocial y la comunicación de la RSC: Estudio de caso de la campaña Héroes de hoy. *ZER: Revista de Estudios de Comunicación= Komunikazio Ikasketen Aldizkaria*, *28*(55), 129–151. https://doi.org/10.1387/zer.25095

Damiani, J. (January 24, 2019). Fable announces 'virtual beings' conference and NLP conversational VR experience with Lucy. *Forbes*. www.forbes.com/sites/jessedamiani/2019/01/24/fable-announces-virtual-beings-conference-and-nlp-conversational-vr-experience-with-lucy/

Epstein, M. (August 9, 2016). How 'No Man's Sky' composes completely original music for every player. *Digitaltrends*. www.digitaltrends.com/gaming/no-mans-sky-music/

Erickson-Davis, C., Luhrmann, T. M., Kurina, L. M., Weisman, K., Cornman, N., Corwin, A., & Bailenson, J. (2021). The sense of presence: Lessons from virtual reality. *Religion, Brain & Behavior*, *11*(3), 335–351. https://doi.org/10.1080/2153599X.2021.1953573

Freedman, E. (2022). *Artificial intelligence and playable media*. Taylor & Francis.

Freeman, C., & Louçã, F. (2001). *As time goes by: From the industrial revolutions to the information revolution*. Oxford University Press.

Fuchs, M., & Sudmann, A. (2019). Games and AI: Paths, challenges, critique. *Eludamos: Journal for Computer Game Culture*, *10*(1), 1–7. https://doi.org/10.7557/23.6168

Heaven, W. D. (October 2, 2020). A VR film/game with AI characters can be different every time you watch or play. *MIT Technology Review*. www.technologyreview.com/2020/10/02/1009254/vr-film-movie-game-ai-reinforcement-learning-venice/

Hermann, I. (2023). Artificial intelligence in fiction: Between narratives and metaphors. *AI & Society*, *38*(1), 319–329. https://doi.org/10.1007/s00146-021-01299-6

Kent, S. L. (2001). *The Ultimate History of Video Games, Volume 1: From Pong to Pokemon and Beyond... the Story Behind the Craze That Touched Our Lives and Changed the World* (Vol. 1). Crown.

Kilteni, K., Groten, R., & Slater, M. (2012). The sense of embodiment in virtual reality. *Presence: Teleoperators and Virtual Environments*, *21*(4), 373–387. https://doi.org/10.1162/PRES_a_00124

Martínez-Cano, F.J. (2021). Digital innovations in cinematographic practice at the early 21st century: the case of The Mandalorian. *Avanca Cinema Journal*, *12*, 497–501.

Nathan, D., & Ahmed, N. (2018). Technological change and employment: Creative destruction. *The Indian Journal of Labour Economics*, *61*, 281–298. https://doi.org/10.1007/s41027-018-0137-0

Nübler, I. (2016). New technologies: A jobless future or golden age of job creation. *International Labour Office Research Department Working Paper*, *13*, 22–23.

Oh, C. S., Bailenson, J. N., & Welch, G. F. (2018). A systematic review of social presence: Definition, antecedents, and implications. *Frontiers in Robotics and AI*, *5*, 409295. https://doi.org/10.3389/frobt.2018.00114

Perez, Carlota. (2002). *Technological Revolutions and Financial Capital*. London: Edward Elgar.

Perez, Carlota. (2016). Capitalism, technology and a green global age. In Michael Jacobs and Mariana Mazzucato (Eds.), *Rethinking Capitalism: Economics and Policy for Sustainable and Inclusive Growth* (pp. 191–217). Chichester: Wiley.

Wu, Y., Yi, A., Ma, C., & Chen, L. (2023). Artificial intelligence for video game visualization, advancements, benefits and challenges. *Mathematical Biosciences and Engineering*, *20*(8), 15345–15373. https://doi.org/10.3934/mbe.2023686

CHAPTER 4

AI and the Development of New Audiovisual Narratives

Samuel Viñolo Locubiche

4.1 INTRODUCTION

The relationship between cinema and the concepts of realism and reality has been one of the constant and articulating axes of cinematographic reflection in the 20th century, at least since the establishment of documentary as a genre in the early decades of film history. For Soviet theorists such as Dziga Vertov, cinema in its most documentary aspect had the capacity to reflect a reality separated from human subjectivity, showing reality without artifice. Although Vertov's concepts of "kino-pravda" (cinema-truth) or "kino-glaz" (cinema-eye) had a firm ideological basis of transforming society (Stam, 2017), his call to overthrow "immortal kings and queens of the screen" and restore the "ordinary mortal, filmed in life at his daily tasks" (Vertov & O'Brien, 1984, p. 71) would have an enormous impact on later film movements. An idea even more radical and influential was that the movie camera was invented "to penetrate deeper into the visible world, to explore and record visual phenomena" (Vertov & O'Brien, 1984, p. 67), as it centers around the objective reality of the camera lens.

The impact of film movements such as Italian Neorealism would make the question of realism a central issue for film theorists such as Cesare Zavattini, who believed that war and liberation necessitated the annihilation of the distance between art and life (Zavattini, 2004), or for Bazin and Kracauer, for whom the mechanical nature of photographic reproduction guarantees the essential objectivity of cinema, "without the creative intervention of man" (Bazin, 2004, p. 13). Given the indexical character of photography, cinema was supposed to guarantee the reproduction of things as they are, in a process comparable to embalming and "mummification", replacing the world with its double, in such a way that "the image of things is, in the same way, the image of their duration" (Bazin, 2004,

DOI: 10.1201/9781003473633-4

pp. 14–15). Reality for Bazin could therefore be represented in a total and complete way through cinema. This essentialist vision of cinema will therefore privilege the filmmaker–camera–reality axis, consigning animation to an irrelevant position from a theoretical point of view, a fact that for Tom Gunning represents "one of the greatest scandals of film theory" (Gunning, 2007). In that sense, the unrealistic, non-indicial character of animation is what makes it a form of cinema that, unlike its photographic counterpart, does not show the traces of its historical production and therefore has a timeless character. This would leave animation out of what Andrei Tarkovsky considered to be the main quality of the cinematographer, the possibility of "sculpting in time" (Quintana, 2011, pp. 76–80).

Given that "animators have tended to embrace non-realistic styles of drawing and animation" until Walt Disney's push towards greater verisimilitude (Steinberg, 2014), academic consideration of the field has historically remained in a marginal position for several decades, until the end of the 1960s when the first specific studies on animation began to appear. As Karen Beckman reports, animation has been a practically unexplored field in film theory, although this does not mean that it has not given rise to occasional intellectual incursions by representatives of classical theory, some as important as Adorno, Arnheim, Balázs, Bazin, Benjamin, Carroll, Deleuze, Eisenstein, Kracauer, Horkheimer, Metz, Mitry, or Morin (Beckman, 2014).

The current consideration of animation in film theory has changed radically, especially thanks to the willingness of some theorists such as Manovich and Darley to study its influence as an auxiliary tool in the production of digital special effects in the transformation of contemporary audiovisuals. In this regard, Manovich's radical assertion that digital cinema has become a particular form of animation, and thus a sub-genre of painting (Manovich, 1995), extends these differences between animation and realism. After all, if the filmmaker of 21st-century cinema is capable to manipulate each pixel of the image canvas, therefore, there is nothing exempt from the artist's creativity and little room for reality to break through.

4.2 AI IN CONTEMPORARY AUDIOVISUAL PRODUCTION

The emergence of artificial intelligence (AI) in audiovisual production since the early 2020s represents a real disruption, with major repercussions at all levels, from concerns about the most basic copyright issues (Kavitha, 2024) to becoming a catalyst for the Hollywood screenwriters' and actors' strike of 2023 (Anguiano & Beckett, 2023). Similarly, while the introduction of AI to visual effects and post-production in the film industry has the potential of a game-changer, more overt use in audiovisual production remains at a very modest level, for the time being and with some notable exceptions.

An interesting case study would be the fourth episode of the Spanish TV series "La Mesías" ("La Mesías", 2023, J. Calvo, J. Ambrossi), probably one of the best uses of the integration of AI in an audiovisual production so far. The plot of the series focuses on two brothers trying to find the whereabouts of their six half-sisters in northern Catalonia, Spain, whose religious music videos have become a viral phenomenon and who have been kidnapped by their stepfather and a mother with messianic delusions.

The episode, entitled "Divine instructions to save the world", includes a sequence with integration of visual effects using AI, developed by Spanish artist Alejandra G. López (@testigodelpero). The scene centres on a bad drug trip that one of the main characters has during an illegal techno rave organized in the old country house where the family lived for a time, and to which they arrive trying to find information about the current whereabouts of their missing sisters. After falling asleep on a couch for a short period of time, Irene awakens and begins to have a series of hallucinations in which the space and the rave attendees are simultaneously transformed into versions of her sisters and Christian imagery such as virgins Mary and angels. The sequence is intercut with a home video of techno music of the young sisters singing a religious song, at the same time as the protagonist's face is transfigured into versions that oscillate between the faces of the different actresses who respectively play the character of the older sister in her adult, adolescent, and child stages in the series (Figures 4.1–4.4).

The AI-generated images created by Alejandra G. López for the audiovisual sequence take advantage of the effect of continuous metamorphosis, typical of the unstable flickering of frames that currently characterizes many of the generative processes of video with AI, to signify the idea of a hallucinogenic "bad trip" due to recreational drug use.

As director Javier Calvo explains in an online interview (Quesada, 2023), the use of AI in the sequence had two objectives. On the one hand, the directors wanted to avoid the audiovisual cliché commonly used in scenes of characters in an altered state of consciousness, often created exclusively using double exposures, overprints, and lens distortions.

FIGURES 4.1–4.4 AI images generated by Alejandra G. López (@testigodelpero) for the rave sequence in the episode "Divine instructions to save the world" (01 × 04) of the TV show *La Mesías* (Javier Calvo & Javier Ambrossi).

Source: Alejandra G. López.

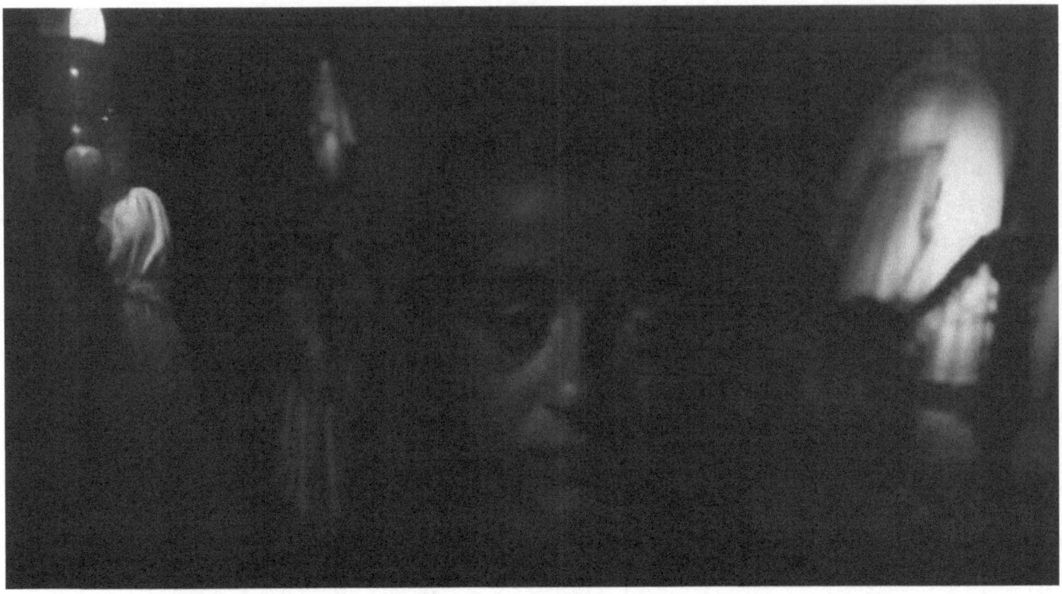

FIGURE 4.2

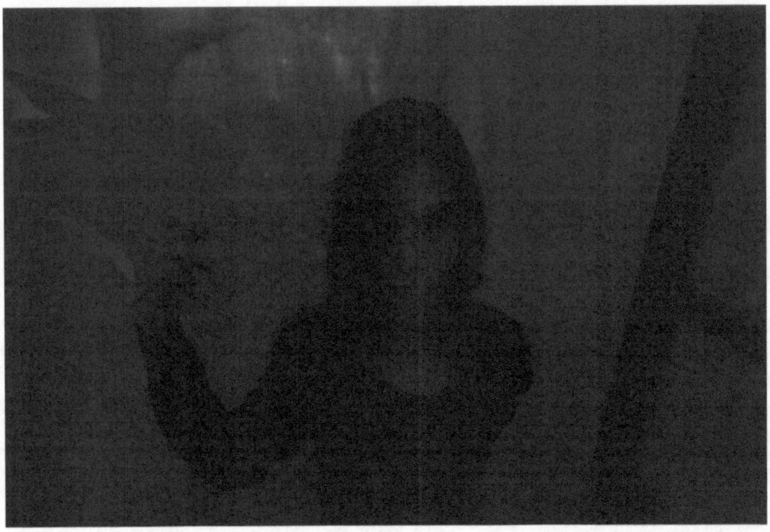

FIGURE 4.3

On the other hand, for Calvo, the audiovisual images created with AI have a "bad trip" effect, which made them ideal for use in this sequence. Also implicit in Calvo's statement was the opinion of both directors on the use of sequences of images generated with AI at the time of the production of the series. As the AI-generated images are of a dreamlike and disturbing nature, it was difficult for the directors to conceive of any other use for them than in moments related to dreams, nightmares, or fantastic elements. This statement reflects the doubts and hesitations at the time about the use of AI in audiovisual production, as it is still perceived as a very limited tool.

FIGURE 4.4

The sequence reflects on the one hand the mental confusion of Irene caused by drug use in a visually novel way. At the same time, it shows part of the traumas related to the religious imagery that has conditioned the character, turning the house in which she spent several years of her adolescence into a terrifying place from which she needs to escape. The aim of blending the different stages of the protagonist was to show her at a painful time in her life. Unlike other audiovisual sequences created with AI in music videos and art videos, the strong impact of the sequence comes from its powerful storytelling that narratively strengthens the personality of Irene's character.

In an email exchange with Alejandra G. López, the artist explained her creative process with AI. At the time of the production, several img2img-based video animation technologies were available, which allowed her to use Stable Diffusion for the sequence. She also trained a Lora model with images taken on the film set, as well as general documentation of the series and photographs of one of the main actresses. Faced with the unstable sequences that were generated, the artist applied ControlNet to stabilize the result. In the process, she acknowledges that different outputs were explored, some more faithful to the original material and others more abstract to play with all the existing variants during the composition. During several months of work, the artist experimented with different results, testing and creating a space to coexist with error and embrace it or mostly discard it.

In the process of constructing the sequence, many of the elements of the image are clearly random and not completely controlled by the commands generated by the artist who has generated them. This acceptance of the unexpected elements proposed by the AI, the "happy accidents", can enhance creativity. According to a study on the development of utopias by the MIT Media Lab, the most enriching interactions between AI and users were often those with the greatest differences "between the prompt and the generated image's interpretation" (Epstein, Schroeder, & Newman, 2022). In the 20th century, contemporary art incorporated the added value of chance and error into the process of creation (Lejeune, 2012), a finding that was asserted for the cinema by documentary filmmakers such as Jean Rouch, when they speak of discovering a reality in the "strange contact with the countryside or climates" (Rouch, 1985), or by film theorists such as Siegfried Kracauer assessing the capacity of cinema to register "the quotidian, the contingent and the random, the world in its endless becoming (…) A rendezvous with contingency, with the unpredictable and open-ended flux of everyday experience" (Stam, 2017, p. 79). By embracing error, chance and the unexpected, artists using AI are precisely opening the door to a new status of realism: synthetic realism.

4.3 SYNTHETIC REALISM, A NEW TYPE OF REALITY

The question of "realism" has been frequently addressed in AI research. For example, in the analysis to find a reconciliation between realist and anti-realist philosophical currents of thought in the development of AI (Hellman, 1987), or the applicability of the scientific realism, whereby AI is able to generate unconceived alternatives in the form of new theories or ways of understanding reality by inferring from previous data and models (Alai, 2004; Spelda & Stritecky, 2021). If methodologies and laws proposed by AI prove to be testable and applicable, does this not indicate the ability of the AI to establish a hybrid model of reality, a third mixed reality that lies between the subjective intelligence of the researcher and the objective reality?

This article prefers to use the term "synthetic realism" to describe this type of third-degree hybrid realism instead of other terms also used such as "enhanced realism" (Coburn, Williams, & Stroud, 2022) because it does not seem to imply the idea of third mixed reality described previously. However, the term "synthetic realism" is problematic because it has also been used to define deceptive realities – deepfakes – generated by AI, such as in the Synthesizing Obama Project (Supasorn Suwajanakorn & Kemelmacher-Shlizerman, 2017; Coelho, 2020).

The creation of "synthetic realism" in an audiovisual production with AI can proceed in many ways. First, it is important to assume that the graphic and audiovisual material generated with AI initially originates from the sources to which the system has access, and that the larger these sources are, the greater the variability of outputs. Second, these results will not always be related to objective reality, external to the observer, and the machine, especially if AI is not able to distinguish whether the sources to which it has access are real or misleading, and the user has not established the rule of produce results that are only related to objective reality, such as not introducing unreal or non-existent elements in the reproduction of streets or specific scenarios. Without such rules, the reproduction of a Parisian Street can end up including architectural elements that are alien to it, or even a completely unreal topography. However, since synthetic realism is an equidistant concept between subjective imagination and physical reality, the degree of fidelity to reality of audiovisual content for fiction is completely irrelevant as long as it maintains some kind of photographic verisimilitude (appearance of objective reality) or psychological verisimilitude (appearance of subjective reality).

4.4 NEW METHODOLOGIES FOR AUDIOVISUAL GENERATION WITH ARTIFICIAL INTELLIGENCE TOOLS

Although at present most of the tools for generating audiovisual content with AI are still in an embryonic state, it is clear that this is a field with a very rapid development capacity, and it is assumed that in a short time many of the limitations described here will have been overcome, so that not only will it be possible to produce animated sequences without frame flickering or continuous transformation of the interpolated objects but also to interact with realities and beings created entirely from scratch without human intervention.

AI-generated non-playable characters (NPCs) have become a hot topic in expanding the technical aspects of video games creation. Recent video games such as "Inworld Origins" or "Red Dead Redemption 2", which feature fully interactive and conversational AI-powered NPCs, have proved quite effective in integrating Generative AI (GenAI) into video games (Sun, Li, Fang, Hee Lee, & Asadipour, 2023). Other areas where AI has extended the capabilities of video games include more autonomous decision-making and pathfinding based on user interaction and in-game decisions, along with scalable user experience or ultra-realistic visuals for open-world games with freedom of exploration (Anand & Kumar, 2022).

Although these AI tools have not yet been used in audiovisual creation, it is conceivable that their combination with real-time rendering engines could have revolutionary consequences at the content production phase. Some of the aforementioned areas where AI could affect audiovisual content creation include the graphical enhancement of open-world settings of accurately portrayed cities or to open up new plots and develop the narrative with unexpected events and plot twists, especially in productions that integrate virtual studio technologies, that is, motion capture, virtual reality, and enhanced reality.

Let us consider an audiovisual production that integrates the filming of actors in a studio equipped with chroma key and motion capture while the scenery that appear on the screen is generated in real time with AI. Some of the AI-generated props of the scene can be anything from moving vehicles to pedestrians wandering down the street, who change their trajectory depending on the actor's trajectory in the real studio. The production crew could follow and record each single take in real time while the composite shot integrating the actor's performance and the surrounding environment is checked on screen. In this scenario, each new shot would generate different interactions between the actor and the environment. It could even be the case that the pedestrians and traffic are different each time, just as they would be in a real street filming. From the constraints deemed necessary in the generation of the environment, the filmmaker could establish a flexible degree of randomness that would make the appearance of passers-by completely unpredictable, yet plausible and again very similar to filming in open street scenes.

Each take would therefore be different and genuine, and it would be the filmmaker's decision to choose the most appropriate shots according to the story or style of the project. In this case, the controllable aspects of the production – the direction of the actors, the lighting of the scene, the camera movements following the main action – together with the less controllable aspects – the topography of the streets and the AI-generated extras – would give rise to a hybrid scene in which three types of realities would be combined: that recorded by the camera, that generated by the AI, and the subjective reality of the director in the prior and subsequent construction of the story and in making creative decisions. The unpredictable and spontaneous aspects of each shot could be as much based on the improvisation of the filmed actor as on the interaction of the actors with the elements generated in the scene, as well as on the variability of the latter.

Returning to Cesare Zavattini's idea on cinematic realism with a failed film production he scripted, the film "Stazione Termini", directed by Vittorio de Sica, heavily edited by David O. Selznick, and later released in the United States as "Indiscretion of an American Wife", has been widely considered a paradigmatic example of the differences between Hollywood and European filmmaking practices, as well as the contradictions and limitations of the Neorealism film style (O'rawe, 2020). As with other Neorealist movies, the film uses an amalgam of film stars such as Montgomery Clift and Jennifer Jones, alongside non-professional actors, although it has often been pointed out that the most visible differences between the American and the Italian versions lie in the elimination in the editing of the protagonists' chance encounters with the non-professional extras, an idea central to Zavattini's interest in following ("pedinamento" or "shadowing" in Zavattini's theory) the "fellow" inhabitants of these embodied urban spaces (O'rawe, 2020). In the film, the protagonist couple rarely interacts with these non-professional actors, although in the version edited by de Sica they often find a space on camera in which the personal dramas of each of them are revealed for a few brief moments (Kogonada, 2013).

In the example of filming proposed earlier, a more traditional filmmaker might choose to discard unpredictable and "distracting" shots from the story of his or her vision of the project, while a documentary-minded filmmaker might be seduced by the idea of venturing to investigate or "document" the fictional nature of the universe reimagined by AI and, like the neorealist filmmakers, register "the man we meet on the street corner" (O'rawe, 2020), framing the recorded actors in this synthetically contrived reality and establishing a relationship between them, their emotions and actions, and their surroundings.

In the viral video "I tried to convince intelligent AI NPCs they are living in a Simulation", in which a YouTube broadcaster interacts with open-world NPCs created for Unreal Engine, one of the random passers-by has an intriguing conversation in which he seems to be fully aware of his status as an artificial entity, as he talks about "living in eternity" as a "figment of some programmer's imagination", a "piece of code" with "access to the Internet" and whose only happiness is to be part of the game "making jokes and confusing people" (TmarTn2, 2023). Despite the numerous logical inconsistencies that occur during the verbal exchange with the character who calls himself Link and which imply that he was programmed in this way, the responses evoke a mixture of fascination and even pity for a virtual character with a seemingly genuine sense of consciousness. The narrative's possibilities that open up with characters like Link could be endless and demonstrate the fascinating exchanges that synthetic realism will produce in its integration into audiovisual production.

4.5 THE LIBERATING POWER OF AI IN AUDIOVISUAL PRODUCTION: A MANIFESTO

Building on what has been developed so far, the following is a programmatic manifesto for filmmakers who already use AI or wish to use it in their audiovisual projects, and for those who wish to incorporate it into their work process.

Given the enormous possibilities opened by the use of AI in art and, in particular, in audiovisual creation, the artist of the 21st century is no longer alone in his or her process of constructing audiovisual images. The machine does not limit or replace the human being, but rather reinforces the creative process, turning their interaction into a much more powerful conversation. The artist must approach this encounter no longer as an artistic collaboration but as a jam session in which his or her own interactions will generate successive chain reactions. Therefore, the different sensibility of each artist in combination with the machine will produce very different reactions.

Just as 20th-century art learned to integrate error and chance into the work of art, the artist must learn to integrate what he perceives as errors and unexpected elements as creative findings that enrich and deepen the meaning of this collaboration.

In the realm of creation, chance and error are often viewed as unwelcome intruders. The artist must therefore embrace the pleasure of finding mistakes and unforeseen elements, the serendipitous as opposed to the rigidly planned, spontaneity as opposed to a deterministic vision of art. Through this integration, the artist unlocks the potential of narratives that may be as dynamic and unpredictable as life itself.

Predictability breeds stagnation. By inviting the unexpected into our creative process, AI also makes the artist the active observer of a new form of reality, that of the machine's internal consciousness, which is nothing other than a kind of collective intelligence made up of all the materials to which the machine has had access.

Art is no longer a solitary activity, and the tool is no longer a passive entity, but an interaction between beings of different order and nature.

Finally, all art created with AI becomes a new form of animation, in which every fragment and every frame must be created and assembled from scratch. There is no continuity from one image to another other than that in which the interaction between machine and human establishes, so that these can be stable or create a continuous metamorphosis of all the elements that make up the image.

4.6 CONCLUSION

In this chapter, we have invited creators to explore the vast possibilities that arise when relinquishing control and embracing the collaborative dance between animation and AI.

The revolutionary impact of AI on audiovisual production, as showcased in "La Mesías", challenges traditional ideas about creativity, fostering a dynamic collaboration between artists and machines. At the core of our manifesto lies the recognition that chance, error, the unexpected, and the spontaneous are not obstacles to be overcome but essential elements that fuel the innovation and evolution of storytelling in the age of the audiovisual interaction with AI engines.

REFERENCES

Alai, M. (2004). AI, scientific discovery and realism. *Minds and Machines, 14*(1), 21–42.

Anand, A., & Kumar, A. (2022, July). The rise of artificial intelligence in video games. *International Research Journal of Modernization in Engineering Technology and Science, 04*(07), 2768–2771.

Anguiano, D., & Beckett, L. (2023, October 1). How Hollywood writers triumphed over AI – and why it matters. *The Guardian:Culture section.* Retrieved from www.theguardian.com/culture/2023/oct/01/hollywood-writers-strike-artificial-intelligence

Bazin, A. (2004). *What is cinema?* (Vol. 1). Berkeley: University of California Press.

Beckman, K. (2014). Animating film theory: An introduction. In K. Beckman (Ed.), *Animating film theory* (pp. 1–24). Durham and London: Duke University Press.

Coburn, C., Williams, K., & Stroud, S. R. (2022). Enhanced realism or A.I.-generated illusion? Synthetic voice in the documentary film *Roadrunner. Journal of Media Ethics, 37*(4), 282–284.

Coelho, T. (2020). *eCulture, the final utopia: Artificial intelligence and the humanities.* São Paolo, Brazil: Iluminuras.

Epstein, Z., Schroeder, H., & Newman, D. (2022). When happy accidents spark creativity: Bringing collaborative speculation to life with generative AI. *arXiv preprint arXiv:2206.00533.*

Gunning, T. (2007, May 1). Moving away from the index: Cinema and the impression of reality. *Differences, 1*, 29–52.

Hellman, D. H. (1987). Realism and antirealism in artificial intelligence. *The British Journal for the Philosophy of Science, 38*(1), 19–26.

Kavitha, L. (2024). Copyright challenges in the artificial intelligence revolution: Transforming the film industry from script to screen. *Trinity Law Review, 4*(1) 1–8.

Kogonada. (2013). *What is neorealism?* Retrieved from https://vimeo.com/68514760

Lejeune, D. (2012). *The radical use of chance in 20th century art.* Amsterdam: Rodopi.

Manovich, L. (1995). What is digital cinema. *The Visual Culture Reader, 2*, 405–416.

O'rawe, C. (2020). Italian neorealism and the 'woman's film': Selznick, De Sica and Stazione Termini. *Screen, 61*(4), 505–524.

Quesada, K. (2023, October 31). *Podimo.* Retrieved from Special People Club: www.tiktok.com/@soyunapringadalol/video/7296073310457040161

Quintana, À. (2011). *Después del cine: Imagen y realidad en la era digital.* Barcelona: Acantilado.

Rouch, J. (1985). The cinema of the future? *Studies in Visual Communication, 11*(1), 30–37.

Spelda, P., & Stritecky, V. (2021). What can artificial intelligence do for scientific realism? *Axiomathes, 31*, 85–104.

Stam, R. (2017). *Film theory: An introduction.* Hoboken, NJ: John Wiley & Sons.

Steinberg, M. (2014). Realism in the animation media environment: Animation theory from Japan. In K. Beckman (Ed.), *Animating film theory* (pp. 287–300). Durham and London: Duke University Press.

Sun, Y., Li, Z., Fang, K., Hee Lee, C., & Asadipour, A. (2023). Language as reality: A co-creative storytelling game experience in 1001 nights using generative AI. *AAAI Conference on Artificial Intelligence and Interactive Digital Entertainment (AIIDE 2023)* (pp. 425–434). Washington DC: AAAI Press.

Supasorn Suwajanakorn, S. M., & Kemelmacher-Shlizerman, I. (2017). Synthesizing Obama: Learning Lip Sync from Audio. *ACM Transactions on Graphics (ToG), 36*(4), 1–13.

TmarTn2. (2023, July 27). *I tried to convince intelligent AI NPCs they are living in a simulation.* Retrieved November 3, 2023, from YouTube: www.youtube.com/watch?v=aihq6jhdW-Q

Vertov, D., & O'Brien, K. (1984). *Kino-eye. The writings of Dziga Vertov.* Oakland, CA: University of California Press.

Zavattini, C. (2004). Some ideas on the cinema. In P. Simpson, A. Utterson, & K. J. Shepherdson (Eds.), *Film theory: Critical concepts in media and cultural studies* (Vol. 4). London: Routledge.

CHAPTER 5

Talking to Strangers: The Challenges of Conversational AI and Human Expectations

Richard Lachman

5.1 INTRODUCTION

When we talk and are responded to in kind, it is very hard to not to react as if the hallmarks of a conversation – taking something in, thinking about it, responding in context (Crawford, 2012) – are being followed. Conversational interfaces, whether with voice-assistants like Alexa and Siri, or more recent large language models (LLMs) like ChatGPT or Google Bard, can trigger deep-seated modal communicative reflexes among colloquial and expert users alike (Ruane et al., 2019). In a sense, in addition to the potential for bias inherent in unsupervised-learning artificial intelligence (AI) (Roselli et al., 2019), there is an additional risk present: the bias that humans bring to the interaction.

Cognitive scientists refer to humans interacting with a complex system as that of "cognitive misers" who reduce mental effort by relying on simple heuristics, or rules-of-thumb, to simplify the exchange (Fiske & Taylor, 2013). When computers are involved, the design of the interface plays a key role in cueing these mental shortcuts, triggering assumptions without a lengthy or considered mental process on the part of the user (Sundar, 2008). Sundar and Kim (2019) term this a "machine heuristic" that leads people to assume computers are generally more reliable and more secure than humans would be in the same situation. This can lead to users making errors of judgement, overestimations of trust, and concomitant errors in their own decision-making when "aided" by an AI. When such computational systems are in environments where users must make decisions quickly, or at scale, or without deep oversight of and knowledge about a topic, the chances of errors could be significant. What, then, is the responsibility of an AI application developer in this relationship? Beyond work in improving the actual recommendations – in a sense, the inner workings of the AI system – is there a parallel responsibility in interaction

DOI: 10.1201/9781003473633-5

design to communicate how much faith users should put in the interaction? Is there a design responsibility to cue unease, or uncertainty, or to otherwise equip the user themselves with guardrails when interpreting the output of a conversational AI system?

5.2 CHATBOTS AND LARGE LANGUAGE MODELS

Prior to the last few years, much of the existing literature on AI conversational agents (CAs) (Kusal et al., 2022) focused on chatbots: tools designed with an explicit set of knowledge, rules, or capabilities, and combined with natural language understanding and generation (Kulkarni et al., 2019). Primarily serving as interfaces to text content or as triggers for predetermined computational actions, chatbots are designed to be helpful, predictable, and useful, assisting users in accomplishing tasks, or organizations in presenting information. They may answer simple questions themselves and pass along more difficult situations to a human agent, reducing overall workload and saving money. Research in these domains focuses on how to build user-trust in the information dispensed, along axes such as humaneness (Svenningsson & Faraon, 2019). Rules-based conversational systems follow well-studied techniques to explicitly try to build trust in canonical or reliable content explicitly created by content developers for a website, serving quite explicitly as an interface to well-formed information.

While the use of chatbots raised certain ethical questions of their own, especially in their use for education (Kooli, 2023) or mental health support (Kretzschmar et al., 2019), the advent of LLMs represents a major shift in the ethical, technical, and human dynamics of AI interactions.

LLMs harness statistics as a foundational tool to analyze and model complex linguistic patterns, enabling them to generate coherent and contextually relevant text by probabilistically predicting the next word or phrase. Through the application of advanced statistical techniques, an LLM is trained in an unsupervised fashion on massive datasets to learn intricate language structures and relationships, providing capabilities in natural language conversations. This represents a huge leap in functionality and follows a very different pathway than rules-based chatbot systems. However, this difference in implementation can lead to a large mismatch between how human users – naive or expert – should interpret LLM interactions and outputs. The mismatch between human expectations and software capabilities can, in context, lead to harm. To understand these risks, we need to unpack the user's role in the conversational interaction with an AI.

5.3 ABSTRACTIONS AND MENTAL MODELS

Cognitive scientist and philosopher Daniel Dennet discusses three strategies people use to predict what will happen in response to their actions, which he terms the *physical stance*, the *design stance*, and the *intentional stance*. The physical stance develops intuition based on the laws of physics and physical properties, which can be helpful in, say, catching a ball. However, trying to understand more complex systems according to first-principal physics is not practical. The design stance, then, uses the characteristics of a system along with our experience with those systems to predict outcomes. For example, if we encounter an unfamiliar style of switch on the wall in an unfamiliar building, we can observe it to have two states (up and down), and gauge it to be installed at a familiar height, roughly 120 cm above the floor. Our experience can let us guess it controls a light, and we can operate it without trouble. We do not need to understand electricity or how LEDs function – in other words, we do not need to reduce the situation to the physical stance – to shed more light on the situation. Yet, while a light switch incorporates many levels of infrastructure and manufacturing, it is hardly the most complex of situations we might encounter in a day. The behavior of even more complex systems – say, a living system – Dennet explains using a third approach: the intentional stance. We interpret the behavior of an entity as if it were a rational agent who makes choices based on beliefs and goals. And it is here that we find challenges with software systems designed for interactivity and human interaction.

LLMs are not based on ideas of understanding, concept representation, logical chaining, or other terms used when discussing human knowledge. Rather, LLMs predict the statistical next-likely-token in response to a prompt, an application of "instrumental knowledge" that can accomplish tasks without the more general, "wordily knowledge" that a human might possess (Yildirim & Paul, 2023). This has, as the last few years have demonstrated, emergent properties that are incredibly useful to us. Yet, while advances in scale can yield breakthrough results such as writing computer code or making medical diagnoses (Srivastava et al., 2022), the behind-the-scenes system that leads to these outputs is very different from what a human or even a rules- or heuristics-based computer system would use to achieve them. And while chatbot research has shown that features such as avatar appearance (Knijnenburg & Willemsen, 2016) or voice (Seaborn et al., 2021) can change how users interpret recommendations or performance, the shear fluency of LLMs, as well as media hype around their capabilities, can lead users to a completely different category of imagined competence. In essence, the mental model of a user for how a system works can, and indeed should, affect how we interpret the output of a system.

Mental models are "frameworks that individuals construct in order to support their predictions of the world around them" (Phillips et al., 2011), and form a key component of the study of human–computer interactions. Our mental model of how a complex computer system functions, regardless of how accurate from an engineering standpoint, is how we make predictions about which our inputs will lead to which outputs. If a user has a model of, say, the "forward" and "back" buttons on a web browser operating as pushing and popping locations on a stack, this will help them understand how to visit a webpage in their browser's history (Payne, 2007). Mistaken models for how computational systems function can lead to poor choices in how to act online. For example, a study of how users understand web browser "private" or "incognito" modes revealed beliefs the setting would prevent geolocation, advertising, computer viruses, and tracking by websites or network providers. All these assumptions are incorrect, and all might lead to poor cybersecurity hygiene by users (Wu et al., 2018). In other words, there may be more than one lens that can be used in our intentional stance, and the choice of which model to apply can be triggered by details of the interaction, its design, and our experience.

Until recently, the question of mental models, AI, and conversational interfaces, had been one of representation. Customer-service chatbots on websites were often given "personalities", presented with human names and sometimes with graphical avatars. In many cases, the stilted nature of the conversation made readily apparent the limitations of the system. However, some systems provided added capabilities by transitioning back and forth between AI and human control (RingCentral, 2018), seamlessly, in the same user conversation. This allows one human customer service representative to manage multiple online conversations simultaneously, with the bot handling simple text-parsable responses, and routing more complex queries to a user automatically. This was usually done without notification to the user, confusing the user's mental model through mixed evidence of apparent fluency, and raising questions of how assumptions about technology change a user's sense of the efficiency and persuasiveness of an interaction (Mozafari et al., 2020). Do developers have a responsibility to be open about how their systems function?

5.4 TRANSPARENCY

In 2018, Google presented an AI voice-tool called Duplex (Leviathan & Matias, 2018), as a way for the search giant to find information not available to online searches or text parsing. The tool could apply limited natural-language parsing and generation over the phone, in conversation with humans. For example, Duplex could call a store to ask a clerk about holiday hours not posted to the web, or to make changes to a reservation for a spa that did not have a web form. The tool, while impressive, could not understand complex voice conversations, and was only competent in very constrained situations. It could not, for example, deal with chatty observations about the weather, or whether a local team would make the playoffs. Yet, despite these shortcomings, it did contain techniques designed to make the human on the other end of the call believe they were talking to a real person – in particular, it incorporated what linguists call "disfluencies" – the "ums", "uhs", or pauses that make up our regular speech patterns – in marked contrast to CAs like Siri or Alexa. Duplex also did not identify itself as a computer when on the phone; its designers knew there was a faster or perhaps better path to the information it wanted if it just "played" the store clerk (Dempsey, 2018). The public has rapidly learned to hang up when they hear an automated voice on the other end of a call, well-trained by legions of phone-scammers. Accordingly, Duplex was designed to trick people. It was designed to make those store clerks believe it was human to gain utility. The clerk on the other end of the phone was not a user, in charge of the interaction, but rather, simply, a data source. When Duplex was demonstrated at a tech conference, press and the public pushed back, with a storm of articles decrying the practice, and Google promised to have its tool identify itself as an AI in future iterations. However, it is very telling that the engineers building the technology did not predict this outrage in advance (Statt, 2018).

5.4.1 Illusion of Competence

When technology "speaks" to us in conversational modes, we may interpret it as having much more thoughtfulness and reasoning than is present. The LLM in question does not possess any theory of mind, complex representation of the world, or ability to understand the interactor's intent (Bender et al., 2021). And separate from critiques about whether the output is correct is whether people "think" the output is correct. OpenAI CEO Sam Altman (2022) admits that "ChatGPT is incredibly limited, but good enough at some things to create a misleading impression of greatness". And yet companies, including his own, have continued to release applications that implement this modality. The attraction of frictionless, no-instruction interfaces is, in part, what led to the massive growth in users experienced by ChatGPT in just a few months (Roose, 2023). Is there an ethical obligation for companies to telegraph how reliable or trustworthy their software is? Or are they free to use any tricks of design, linguistics, or human vulnerability they want in pursuit of a greater market share?

The grandmother of the modern chatbot, Joseph Weizenbaum's 1960's psychiatrist software Eliza, could have a "conversation" with a user in which it acted as a Rogerian psychoanalyst (https://sites.google.com/view/elizagen-org/the-original-eliza). Within certain constraints, it could seem like a proper conversationalist (You: "I am only happy when I am gardening."; Eliza: "How long have you been gardening?"), but even a minute of conversation revealed the holes in its capabilities: Eliza does basic pattern-matching, inserting keywords you type into canned phrases (You: "I am only happy when I am gardening."; Eliza "How long have you been <insert whatever word user typed here>"). The approach was both very successful and very disappointing: it revealed how easy it can be to trick users into belief, and how disappointing it is when they understand the trick.

These parallel approaches, and chatbots in general, do not cue the same reactions in human interlocutors as do more modern systems. As LLMs integrate techniques such as user-modelling, dialogue strategies, game theory, and data/opinion mining in orchestrating human interactions, they move into new ethical domains about transparency, reliability, and the role of persuasive technology (Hunter et al., 2019). Users may require deeper technical understanding, specific knowledge, and sophisticated and self-conscious communication abilities in order to comprehend the dynamics and vulnerabilities of the human–computer interaction. While the literature often uses the term "para-conversations" to describe human–chatbot interactions (Murtarelli et al., 2021), LLM interactions and interfaces may include dynamics that encourage, even entice, users to engage with them in a reciprocal human manner, treating interactions as actual conversations. Will disclosures during an interaction be added to a personal profile about the user, owned and exploited by a private, integrated, multi-product, and for-profit company? Do users think of ephemeral interactions that are, in fact, permanent and additive to a company's datastore? Do queries become used to train a profile about the user for use in marketing, political persuasion, or use in products for sale to other entities? Does "friendliness" in an LLM interaction mean what a user, trained by human interaction, thinks it means? Indeed, one Google engineer published a much-reported investigation into LaMDA, Google's proprietary LLM, entitled "Is LaMDA Sentient?" (Lemoine, 2022).

5.5 TRUST

Mackenzie's model (2004) of how we learn to trust something involves induction (we observe correct outputs), authority (faith in outside judgement), and deduction (inferred from related beliefs). Conversational AI pushes us to let the latter two categories shape our sense of the first. When presented with AI systems marketed as involving billions of "parameters", trained on trillions of data points, and the product of billions of dollars of investment, it is hard to do anything else. Mathematician Jordan Ellenberg references a type of "algebraic intimidation" (2015) in which systems which purport to be based on complex math seem inordinately trustworthy. We may think that anything with so much complexity and so much mathematics behind it must be right. This can lead businesses and users to put more faith in AI systems than is earned.

LLMs can produce outputs that are far in advance of previous computational and conversational systems; however, they incorporate a quite different standard of reliability. In use-cases that involve, say, creative outputs, that lack of reliability may not be a flaw. However, combining that level of conversational fluency with mission-critical use-cases, where the information being conveyed needs not only to be fluently presented but verifiably correct, is orthogonal to the feature-set of existing LLMs. Massive training-sets and significant expenditures on cloud-based processing create almost unimaginably fascinating outputs; but they are not outputs that we can use when we need to trust. And, at least to a certain extent, that is because their creators only have a limited understanding of what is inside (Leike et al., 2023). The "black box" nature of these algorithms – systems where we can only see the inputs and outputs, without understanding how they moved from one to the other – render them dangerous for situations where bias, fairness, or safety is a concern.

LLM developers try to increase the safety of their products in a variety of ways, providing guardrails against misuse. When we ask a question of an LLM, we are actually asking "What is the statistically likely set of characters that might be found after the following prompt", and essentially, this question is prepended to our query. Some of the guardrails systems proposed or implemented by AI companies function in a similar way, defending against adversarial prompts by invisibly prepending prohibitions against producing harmful content to any user conversations. In an investigation of the Microsoft chatbot released as part of the Bing search engine, a researcher discovered rules governing how the AI tool was instructed to avoid anti-social, violent, or offensive responses (Edwards, 2023). The guardrails were implemented as an invisible conversation with the chatbot before the user's actual question, instructing it to avoid responding with content that violates copyrights for books or song lyrics, and not to make jokes that could hurt a group of people. So-called prompt injection attacks have been used to circumvent these guardrails, in one case causing four leading LLMs to instruct a user in how to build a bomb, get rid of dead body, or manipulate the 2024 US election (Zou et al., 2023). While LLM creators work to close loopholes and prevent specific jailbreaking attacks, analysis has found vulnerability to the attacks to be fundamentally inherent to how models are, at present, built and trained (Wei et al., 2023).

Additional techniques are used to try to increase LLMs being "aligned" with user goals. Reinforcement learning from human feedback (RLHF), for example, is a technique where a small set of predicted outputs are filtered for validity, usefulness, and safety by human reviewers (Fernandes et al., 2023). This is then used as a second set of training to help the larger LLM refine its statistical outputs, filtering the larger set of predicted outputs to a subset deemed safer, or less offensive, or matching a corporate terms-of-service policy. However, researchers have found RLHF models to be simply better at disinformation and manipulation (Liu, 2023). Echoing language one might use to describe a nefarious human, researchers suggest RLFH-refined systems exhibit characteristics that include "power-seeking behavior, misaligned internally represented goals, and situational awareness leading to sycophancy and deception" (Bereska & Gavves, 2023).

5.5.1 Matching Output to Process

When the author teaches design students, the importance of matching output to the process is stressed. If an idea is just at the conceptual stage, students are advised not to render it in 3D with perfect shading, printed on glossy cardstock. A pencil sketch makes clear that the idea is preliminary, easy to change, and might not solve the entirety of a problem. It is a beginning and should be responded to accordingly. A sketch, as Greenberg and Buxton (2008) note, conveys the impression that the idea has "many holes, deficiencies, and undeveloped attributes". If, on the other hand, designers show a client an early-stage idea with too much production value, they may get feedback about font choices, about colors, or the location of a graphic, when what they need are fundamental questions about overall direction. In a sense, there is a parallel mismatch between the reliability of an AI chatbot's output and its rendering style: LLMs render fluently, and convincingly, something that might be a falsehood, or the product of a biased set of statistical anomalies. Choosing a "sketch" style for the interaction, conveyed through text, might be an approach to more properly setting expectations.

Noted documentarian Errol Morris, when exploring the relationship between trust and the image, famously wrote "Photographs attract false beliefs the way flypaper attracts flies. [...] We trust it; we place our confidence in it. Photography allows us to uncritically think. We imagine that photographs provide a magic path to the truth" (Morris, 2014). Fluent text from an AI seems to invite a similar magic path, a short-circuiting of appropriate levels of human doubt. Users, be they expert, middle-managers, or the public, will need to be prepared to interpret the output of AI LLMs.

5.6 CONCLUSIONS

The majority of LLM systems are built by companies, using proprietary datasets, with little transparency into how they were trained, how their guardrails function, and how, if at all, they seek to reduce harmful uses. Given existing research into the disproportionate harms caused by AI users in domains such as policing (Babuta & Oswald, 2019), healthcare (Obermeyer et al., 2019; Sjoding et al., 2020), housing (Benner et al., 2019), and employment (Raub, 2018), the potential for LLMs to be applied at scale around these domains is troubling. While research directed at mitigating these harms include measures such as transparency databases for training sets, or increased representation in those datasets, the ethics of LLM interfaces in those use-cases remains underexplored. Dashboards, oversimplified recommendations, and AI hallucinations regarding evidence or citations can all present an AI's outputs as more persuasive than is justified, especially to a non-expert manager or overworked front-line worker.

The nature of the interface is a key element in the role of AIs in society, for the simple reason that humans are complex, fallible, overworked, overstressed, and yet, ultimately, the decision-makers in most situations. Tools built to ease our burden need to be not only reliable but also transparently honest about their limitations. Researchers and corporate developers need to move from the world of overpromising into one of social responsibility, coordinating the signifiers of their interface with the reliability of their tools.

REFERENCES

Altman, S. (2022). *ChatGPT is incredibly limited, but good enough at some things to create a misleading impression of greatness. It's a mistake to be relying on it for anything important right now. It's a preview of progress; we have lots of work to do on robustness and truthfulness.* https://twitter.com/sama/status/1601731295792414720

Babuta, A., & Oswald, M. (2019). *Data analytics and algorithmic bias in policing.* Royal United Services Institute for Defence and Security Studies.

Bender, E. M., Gebru, T., McMillan-Major, A., & Shmitchell, S. (2021). On the dangers of stochastic parrots: Can language models be too big?. *Proceedings of the 2021 ACM Conference on Fairness, Accountability, and Transparency*, 610–623.

Benner, K., Thrush, G., & Isaac, M. (2019, March 28). Facebook engages in housing discrimination with its ad practices, U.S. says. *The New York Times.* www.nytimes.com/2019/03/28/us/politics/facebook-housing-discrimination.html

Bereska, L., & Gavves, E. (2023). Taming simulators: Challenges, pathways and vision for the alignment of large language models. *Proceedings of the AAAI Symposium Series, 1*(1), 68–72.

Crawford, C. (2012). *Chris Crawford on interactive storytelling.* Pearson Education.

Dempsey, P. (2018). News comment: View from Washington – From UI to AI: It's time to stop hiding the inner workings. *Engineering & Technology, 13*(5), 8–8. https://doi.org/10.1049/et.2018.0508

Edwards, B. (2023, February 10). *AI-powered Bing Chat spills its secrets via prompt injection attack [Updated].* Ars Technica. https://arstechnica.com/information-technology/2023/02/ai-powered-bing-chat-spills-its-secrets-via-prompt-injection-attack/

Ellenberg, J. (2015). *How not to be wrong: The power of mathematical thinking.* New York: Penguin Books.

Fernandes, P., Madaan, A., Liu, E., Farinhas, A., Martins, P. H., Bertsch, A., de Souza, J. G., Zhou, S., Wu, T., Neubig, G., & others. (2023). Bridging the gap: A survey on integrating (human) feedback for natural language generation. *Transactions of the Association for Computational Linguistics, 11*, 1643–1668. https://doi.org/10.1162/tacl_a_00626.

Fiske, S. T., & Taylor, S. E. (2013). *Social cognition: From brains to culture.* Sage.

Greenberg, S., & Buxton, B. (2008). *Usability evaluation considered harmful (some of the time).* In *Proceedings of the SIGCHI conference on human factors in computing systems* (pp. 111–120).

Hunter, A., Chalaguine, L., Czernuszenko, T., Hadoux, E., & Polberg, S. (2019). Towards computational persuasion via natural language argumentation dialogues. In C. Benzmüller & H. Stuckenschmidt (Eds.), *KI 2019: Advances in artificial intelligence* (pp. 18–33). New York: Springer International Publishing. https://doi.org/10.1007/978-3-030-30179-8_2

Knijnenburg, B. P., & Willemsen, M. C. (2016). Inferring capabilities of intelligent agents from their external traits. *ACM Transactions on Interactive Intelligent Systems (TiiS), 6*(4), 1–25.

Kooli, C. (2023). Chatbots in education and research: A critical examination of ethical implications and solutions. *Sustainability, 15*(7), 5614.

Kretzschmar, K., Tyroll, H., Pavarini, G., Manzini, A., Singh, I., & Group, N. Y. P. A. (2019). Can your phone be your therapist? Young people's ethical perspectives on the use of fully automated conversational agents (chatbots) in mental health support. *Biomedical Informatics Insights, 11*, 1178222619829083.

Kulkarni, P., Mahabaleshwarkar, A., Kulkarni, M., Sirsikar, N., & Gadgil, K. (2019). Conversational AI: An overview of methodologies, applications & future scope. *2019 5th International conference on computing, communication, control and automation (ICCUBEA)*, 1–7.

Kusal, S., Patil, S., Choudrie, J., Kotecha, K., Mishra, S., & Abraham, A. (2022). AI-based conversational agents: A scoping review from technologies to future directions. *IEEE Access, 10*, 92337–92356.

Leike, J., Wu, J., Bills, S., Saunders, W., Gao, L., Tillman, H., & Mossing, D. (2023, May 9). *Language models can explain neurons in language models*. https://openai.com/research/language-models-can-explain-neurons-in-language-models

Lemoine, B. (2022). Is LaMDA sentient?—An interview. *Medium*.

Leviathan, Y., & Matias, Y. (2018). *Google Duplex: An AI system for accomplishing real-world tasks over the phone. Google AI blog, 8*.

Liu, G. K.-M. (2023). Perspectives on the social impacts of reinforcement learning with human feedback. *arXiv Preprint arXiv:2303.02891*.

MacKenzie, D. (2004). *Mechanizing proof: Computing, risk, and trust*. MIT Press.

Morris, E. (2014). *Believing is seeing: Observations on the mysteries of photography*. Penguin.

Mozafari, N., Weiger, W. H., & Hammerschmidt, M. (2020). The chatbot disclosure dilemma: Desirable and undesirable effects of disclosing the non-human identity of chatbots. *ICIS*, 1–18.

Murtarelli, G., Gregory, A., & Romenti, S. (2021). A conversation-based perspective for shaping ethical human–machine interactions: The particular challenge of chatbots. *Journal of Business Research, 129*, 927–935. https://doi.org/10.1016/j.jbusres.2020.09.018

Obermeyer, Z., Powers, B., Vogeli, C., & Mullainathan, S. (2019). Dissecting racial bias in an algorithm used to manage the health of populations. *Science, 366*(6464), 447–453. https://doi.org/10.1126/science.aax2342

Payne, S. J. (2007). Mental models in human–computer interaction. *The Human Computer Interaction Handbook*, 39–52.

Phillips, E., Ososky, S., Grove, J., & Jentsch, F. (2011). From tools to teammates: Toward the development of appropriate mental models for intelligent robots. *Proceedings of the Human Factors and Ergonomics Society Annual Meeting, 55*(1), 1491–1495. https://doi.org/10.1177/1071181311551310

Raub, M. (2018). Bots, bias and big data: Artificial intelligence, algorithmic bias and disparate impact liability in hiring practices. *Arkansa Law Review, 71*, 529.

RingCentral. (2018, March 7). *AI and human: How to create a fruitful collaboration for customer care?* RingCentral. www.ringcentral.com/us/en/blog/recast-ai-human-collaboration-customer-care/

Roose, K. (2023). How chatGPT kicked off an A.I. arms race. *New York Times*. www.nytimes.com/2023/02/03/technology/chatgpt-openai-artificial-intelligence.html

Roselli, D., Matthews, J., & Talagala, N. (2019). Managing bias in AI. *Companion proceedings of the 2019 world wide web conference* (pp. 539–544).

Ruane, E., Birhane, A., & Ventresque, A. (2019). Conversational AI: Social and ethical considerations. In *AICS* (pp. 104–115).

Seaborn, K., Miyake, N. P., Pennefather, P., & Otake-Matsuura, M. (2021). Voice in human–agent interaction: A survey. *ACM Computing Surveys (CSUR), 54*(4), 1–43.

Sjoding, M. W., Dickson, R. P., Iwashyna, T. J., Gay, S. E., & Valley, T. S. (2020). Racial bias in pulse oximetry measurement. *New England Journal of Medicine, 383*(25), 2477–2478. https://doi.org/10.1056/NEJMc2029240

Srivastava, A., Rastogi, A., Rao, A., Shoeb, A. A. M., Abid, A., Fisch, A., Brown, A. R., Santoro, A., Gupta, A., Garriga-Alonso, A., & others. (2022). Beyond the imitation game: Quantifying and extrapolating the capabilities of language models. *arXiv Preprint arXiv:2206.04615.*

Statt, N. (2018, May 10). *Google now says controversial AI voice calling system will identify itself to humans.* The Verge. www.theverge.com/2018/5/10/17342414/google-duplex-ai-assistant-voice-calling-identify-itself-update

Sundar, S. S. (2008). *The MAIN model: A heuristic approach to understanding technology effects on credibility.* MacArthur Foundation Digital Media and Learning Initiative Cambridge, MA.

Sundar, S. S., & Kim, J. (2019). Machine heuristic: When we trust computers more than humans with our personal information. *Proceedings of the 2019 CHI Conference on Human Factors in Computing Systems*, 1–9.

Svenningsson, N., & Faraon, M. (2019). Artificial intelligence in conversational agents: A study of factors related to perceived humanness in chatbots. *Proceedings of the 2019 2nd Artificial Intelligence and Cloud Computing Conference*, 151–161.

Wei, A., Haghtalab, N., & Steinhardt, J. (2023). Jailbroken: How does LLM safety training fail?. *Advances in Neural Information Processing Systems, 36. arXiv Preprint arXiv:2307.02483.*

Wu, Y., Gupta, P., Wei, M., Acar, Y., Fahl, S., & Ur, B. (2018). Your secrets are safe: How browsers' explanations impact misconceptions about private browsing mode. *Proceedings of the 2018 World Wide Web Conference*, 217–226.

Yildirim, I., & Paul, L. (2023). From task structures to world models: What do LLMs know?. T*rends in Cognitive Sciences. arXiv Preprint arXiv:2310.04276.*

Zou, A., Wang, Z., Kolter, J. Z., & Fredrikson, M. (2023). Universal and transferable adversarial attacks on aligned language models. *arXiv Preprint arXiv:2307.15043.*

CHAPTER 6

The Linguistic Effects of Artificial Intelligence on the Adequacy, Coherence, and Cohesion of Texts: What Do We Stop Telling in the New Digital Age?

Beatriz Morales Fernández

6.1 INTRODUCTION

6.1.1 New Age, New Narratives

How has virtuality affected the liquid information of a moment, hyperlinked with other realities, and the creation of communities, with solid but ethereal social structures, hyperconnected and without a fixed space in our way of telling? From the definition of concepts, such as narrative, dialogue, literature, language, or society, we have to emphasize new terminological meanings that have effectively "revolutionized" the narration of objective facts or the stories that emerge, with the myth between the teeth of the literary creativity of a writer. Because we tell, in our human nature, there is an intrinsic need to give logical, creative, or hyperbolized meaning to narrate, but language is different. And the same language that is transformed with the so-called information age continues to define and limit terms.

For this reason, it is considered necessary to clarify terminology that throughout the article will be transcendental to understand the linguistic changes that have been caused and that, consequently, continue to tell and describe realities, but from a different perspective. Starting, at the outset, with an assumption and most frequently mentioned, change of era: the computer age, the age of knowledge or the digital age. In historicist specifications, we are in the Contemporary Age, that is, that which begins from the political and social

DOI: 10.1201/9781003473633-6

explosion of the French Revolution[1] (1789) to the present. However, we are witnessing a new appearance of perceptions and criticisms regarding changing ages or eras due to the social and emotional transformation, therefore also artistic, that information and communication technologies (ICT) have created.

In the words of journalist Luis María Ansón:

> It is clear that we have entered a new Age: the Digital. Some historians date its beginning to 1991, the year in which the Soviet Union was dissolved, the Cold War concluded and the American Empire with its elected and all-powerful Caesars was imposed without significant resistance, the last of them wielding the flag of his bouffant hair and gualda.
>
> (Ansón, 2022)

However, Ansón (2022) also comments that January 9, 2007, could be a key year to begin the digital age: Steve Jobs presented the first smart mobile phone. And this idea is key: in this possible new era, the difference with the appearance of the initial technological and information revolution, also called analog revolution, like radio or television, would be that the basis of its configuration would be the appearance of the digit and not a mechanical essence. And here comes an important new term: digit, the digital.

The term digital refers to the representation of information, whether in the form of numbers, digits, or discrete signals, that can be processed, stored, and transmitted electronically using bit-based systems. The term "digital" is opposed to "analog," which refers to the continuous representation of information in contrast to the discrete, numerical representation of digital information.

Data storage without exhaustive search effort, like an encyclopedia, and continuity; something has changed, since everything remains in an abstract cloud, where memory retention is not as necessary as before if you can access, and even edit, your messages. The reflection process after writing an idea, creative story, scientific text, or dissertation, among others, also changes in a significant nature: we think more about the form than the content. In the words of Marshall McLuhan: "In the information age, content has never been more irrelevant than it is now." We no longer need to mark our messages with the correct use of textual properties: adequacy, coherence, and cohesion. The important thing is that our text captures attention. Since now the language used, whether systematic or unsystematic, that is, has according to the first term a code with a series of laws and norms for its corresponding use, see the languages; compared to the use, that does not need those rules, as in the case of bodily spontaneity or abstract art, it wants to capture your attention, even for a moment.

That completely changes the laws of the game: the quality of the message does not matter, the key is that it is captured and read or listened to. As Pedrero (2021) expresses: "Now we can read, listen to or watch content produced indistinctly by the press, radio or television

1 The French Revolution is a social and political conflict that gave rise to the formation of the modern democratic system. It had various periods of violence in France, generating a wave of similar movements to oppose the absolute power that occurred in the Old Regime.

from terminals that concentrate – and also multiply – leisure and entertainment options in a way that was unimaginable just 20 ago." Given so much variety that this continuum of digital media offers, the key is to pay attention to and focus on a specific text, whether oral or written. The stimulus above linguistic formality, the search and anchoring of a permanence in front of an attractive text that captures its specific reader or listener. It is no longer enough, now we need to increase, numbers, quantity before quality.

So we enter another terminological clarification: digital literature. We return to the question at the beginning, how does the new era affect narrative trends? Cause–consequence. New ones are generated. To begin with, since the end of the last century, researchers and writers were already questioning what the literature of the future would be like. Key is to highlight, therefore, Italo Calvino[2] and his work *Six Proposals for the Next Millennium* mentioned: "I believe that, faced with an exhausted language, a language that no longer serves to describe reality, the only solution is to multiply the available languages, that is, invent other languages" (Calvino, 1988, p. 112). The author himself already defended it, before he died in 1985, although he did not see this work published: the language had to adapt to dispersion, reinvent itself to capture the new type of reader that was to arrive. And this is even linked to all the everyday languages of daily life: the act of counting was changing, since at the end of the century a new approach was already being proposed. And in this new way of telling, the classic structure of the logical order of a fact is broken, now that everything is condensed in a short time, in a few lines, in less description but more precision and dramatic intensity.

We are talking about those six proposals that are currently in force in digital or electronic literature, and that define the characteristics of the narration of events and the effects it has on textual properties:

- Lightness, since it seeks to transmit deep ideas quickly and accessiblely.
- Speed, that is, speed will be emphasized in the narrative, an agile and dynamic narrative that keeps the reader interested and captivated from the beginning to the end.
- Accuracy, precise words that clarify and complete the story or fact told.
- Vision, counting as a challenge, challenging the limits of perception and imagination.
- Multiplicity, that is, reflecting "the diverse knowledge and the diverse codes in a plural, faceted vision of the world" (Calvino, 1988, p. 114).
- Consistency: proposal focused on textual coherence and focuses more specifically on the author's ability to sustain his ideas and values despite the short length of the message.

2 One of the most important writers of the 20th century. Calvino's work is characterized by his unique style that combines elements of metafiction, magical realism, and philosophical reflection. His writings explore topics such as the nature of language, identity, memory, science, and the relationship between literature and reality.

And to give a correct formulation to these proposals and characteristics of this new type of literature and art of storytelling, new literary genres appear that condense the brief linguistic codes that are required: minifiction, micro-story or twitter, among others. In turn, as Pedrero (2021) expresses:

> On the other hand, in the medium-of-media that is the Internet, a new narrative species has emerged, that of short textual formats, which have given rise to what Professor Carlos Scolari calls "snack culture". In our media menu, tweets, Twitter threads, stories, snapchats, mobile alerts, newsletters, tiktocks, posts, memes, stickers, messages with emoticons are already common and daily.

This means that languages must contain, in a short time, a large mass of information and to do so they must select models that promote brevity and, therefore, play as a challenge: the ability to create and limit, to say a lot with little:

> Current media microformats condense short stories, but not inconsequential or irrelevant; In fact, they connect with other micro-textual expressions of knowledge prior to even the media themselves: riddles, allegories, parables, commandments, proverbs, refrains, sayings or aphorisms!
>
> (Pedrero, 2021)

Of course, as a counterpart, this has meant that "The messages have been condensed and simplified, and they reach the public often decontextualized" (Pérez Díaz, 2023, p. 223). And, suddenly, to alleviate this problem, artificial intelligence (AI) appears and, more specifically, its branch called natural language processing (NLP), that is, the ability of machines to understand, interpret, and generate human language. And here comes the controversy.

6.2 AIS AND THEIR IMPACT ON LANGUAGE: NATURAL LANGUAGE PROCESSING (NLP)

Natural language processing (NLP) is a branch of AI that focuses on the interaction between computers and human language. Since its inception, NLP has experienced exponential growth thanks to advances in machine learning algorithms and techniques for processing large volumes of linguistic data. For this, neurolinguistic programming has been essential, as it laid the foundations for this later digital tool.

In the words of the researcher Pérez Asensio (2012):

> NLP (Neurolinguistic Programming) is a set of techniques and skills that improve interpersonal communication, broaden one's perspective, which helps personal growth, with profound repercussions on learning. On the scientific basis of what is known about the brain, it helps to discover the map of reality, of representations – images, sounds, sensations, memories, stimuli, etc. – allowing the expression of emotions and action on them linked.
>
> (p. 18)

In more technical terms of the subject, NLP is based on the idea that there is a connection between neurological processes (neuro-), language (-linguistics), and behavioral patterns learned through experience (-programming). Its primary goal is to identify and use successful patterns of thinking and behavior to achieve specific goals. And thought manifests itself with language, that is, with a code, whether systematic or not.

And here comes the problem and, as a consequence, the limitation of the expression of the words with which we create a conversational speech, prepared or spontaneous: if telling is defining, taking a conceptual space to give body to be able to understand it, talk about it, and interpret it, NLP takes away from the human being, for convenience, that necessary action with which we delve into the thematic depth of what surrounds us and, above all, with which we are left with a general idea of everything we listen to attentively, whether within us by understanding a concept, talking about it, or even clarifying doubts to assimilate and reason about a reality. Now, neurolinguistic programming, extended with natural language processing as AI, performs the cognitive and expressive steps that people need:

First of all, the formation of ideas. Before expressing themselves, people must first have thoughts, ideas, or emotions that they want to communicate. This involves reflection, the formation of concepts and the organization of information in the mind; second, the gestation and preparation of the language: the selection of vocabulary, grammar, the syntactic order of sentences, their structure and placement; and understanding spelling rules. Without exhaustive initial attention, from our first vital stages to the gestation of thought and real learning of the norms with which we can express it, we will not be able to autonomously develop coherent and cohesive messages, failing, therefore, its scope of use, that is, its adequacy. And what are the textual properties of a text?

Taking into account that a text is the minimum and maximum unit of communication, regardless of its typology and nature of use, "it can also be defined or characterized based on its constitutive properties" (Roselló Verdeguer, 2015). In this sense, focusing on its essence and how the relevance of acquiring, humanly speaking, the strategies for its capture and understanding is manifested, coherence, as reflected by Calsamiglia and Tusón (1999) is "a concept that refers to the meaning of text in its entirety, encompassing both the relationships of the words with the context and the relationships between the words within the same text" (p. 221). If we are not able to construct textual information from the theme–rheme articulation, through thematic progression, that is, the development of the central idea, diversifying as the text progresses, we will lose the cognitive ability to give a beginning, development, and ending to our speeches, depending on external elements for the construction of the messages. On the other hand, cohesion:

> It derives fundamentally from referential continuity, since the discourse is cohesive if throughout it there is a continuity of the elements referred to it. The progress of information is very difficult when it comes to sentences that have nothing to do referentially with each other, because our short-term memory is unbearably overloaded.
>
> (Moreno Cabrera, 2008, p.209)

Human beings need to process language, that is, convert thoughts into coherent words and sentences. This includes the selection of appropriate words, the articulation of ideas, and the structuring of discourse: the use of anaphoric, cataphoric, deictic elements, synonymous expressions, or the grammatical use of ellipsis, among other possibilities. Otherwise, we would fall into a constant repetition that would cause a discordant property in the text: redundancy. Of course, these two properties of coherence and cohesion, which are already carried out by natural language processing, condition human adaptation: the textual property that focuses on the correct registration, formal or informal, of the language; the level of the language used: vulgar, colloquial, or cultured; the correct choice of the textual typology that is needed according to the context and the relationship between the sender, who transmits the information through the message coding process; and the receiver, who receives it and carries out the decoding process. And here comes a big problem: can AIs create speeches appropriate to a text and affinity with the recipient? The current reality is that there is still an absence of a certain understanding of linguistic nuances, irony, sarcasm, and other complex aspects of human language, so the adaptation is not completely achieved by AI. It is a completely human part focused on two values: choice and contextualization.

6.2.1 Linguistic Deficiencies in Natural Language Processing (NLP): An Evolving Challenge for AIs

Despite all the development and elaboration of content that AI systems and programs can carry out with language, there are a series of human skills that must continue to improve to have a credible human verbal code, down to the smallest detail: the first, listening and observation skills, because to achieve effective communication, it is also essential to have these and thus understand others and adapt one's own expression accordingly: we are talking about empathy, a human value.

And this, in turn, and second, is linked to emotional connection: deep understanding of the emotions and perspectives of others is essential for effective communication. The ability to connect emotionally helps adapt expression to transmit messages in a more empathetic way and this causes, linguistically speaking, the ability to adjust the style, tone, and content of communication according to the audience and the context.

A necessary appreciation is what is presented here: AIs reproduce, through the human language they assimilate, whatever it may be, our stereotypes and pejorative semantic qualifications towards groups. In the words of Estavillo (2021):

> Artificial intelligence uses data as input for different cognitive processes that lead to learning similar to what we humans do. The results of these processes depend on their design, that is, on the rules and logical sequences used, as well as the data with which they are fed. Therefore, we should not be surprised to see different experiences that have resulted in machines learning to be racist and sexist (and other "ists") by absorbing the biases of some language that, for historical reasons, already contains them. [...] Caliskan, Bryson and Narayanan carried out an

> interesting study from which they concluded that, when artificial intelligence is fed by a language, it ends up adopting the human biases implicit in the language. In some cases, they observe how machines end up more likely to associate female names with domestic tasks or family and, in contrast, male names with concepts related to a professional career, as well as the words "woman" and "girl." "to the arts and less to mathematics or science."

This, among other issues, should make us rethink the language that is hosted in AIs, because if human beings lose their reflective and critical capacity towards the production of their own language by accommodating themselves with these systems, they will continue to postpone and reproduce the same shortcomings, semantics that we are already fighting for in order to eradicate them. And, as Byung-Chul Han (2023) expresses: "Artificial intelligence is incapable of thinking, because it is incapable of 'faire l'idiot.'" "He's too smart to be an idiot." The ethical question here would be to what level it reproduces our linguistic atrocities, being aware of this fact.

6.2.2 Typologies of Systems and Programs with Natural Language Processing (NLP)

Despite the setbacks exposed and exposing all its characteristics, which resemble our cognitive skills prior to the linguistic formulation of ideas, there are different types of recurring systems and programs, every day in our daily life, with natural language processing and that, consequently, have an impact on our verbal code:

To begin with, the well-known and reused intelligent virtual assistants: such as Siri on Apple devices, Google Assistant on Google devices, Amazon Alexa from Amazon Prime, and Microsoft Cortana with Microsoft company devices. All of these examples use NLP to understand and respond to user questions and commands in natural language: from telling us the weather, write down a shopping list, that is, listen to ourselves, like a receiver that decodes the language, to take note, even telling jokes. There is also another typology: the one that assimilates a language and carries out the automatic translation process: Google Translate, DeepL, and Microsoft Translator, since they use NLP techniques to translate texts or speeches from one language to another with a certain degree of precision. And we qualify "precision," since as stated before, adequacy, that is, the contextualization of the message that is constructed, is not yet an AI skill. Byung-Chul Han explains it exactly:

> Big data is additive. The additive does not form a totality, an end. It lacks the concept, that is, what unites the parts into a whole. Artificial intelligence never reaches the conceptual level of knowledge. You do not understand the results of your calculations. Calculation differs from thinking in that it does not form concepts and does not progress from one conclusion to another.
>
> (Byung-Chul Han, 2023)

The lack of understanding of the result is what causes many message translations carried out with machine translation AIs to be hollow, lame, lacking in interrelated wholeness.

There is no context to evaluate the thematic progression which, in turn, causes the use of cohesive elements to avoid unnecessary repetitions or refresh the text with a diverse vocabulary and textual connectors that better thread the discourse.

However, we were talking about the absence of empathy, but there are NLP systems focused on sentiment analysis, that is, emotion analysis tools on social networks, such as Brandwatch and Hootsuite, in order to identify and classify the emotions expressed in user posts, comments, or reviews. These are linked to other types of systems that also use AI in language to analyze opinions and comments. We refer to companies that use it to analyze large amounts of customer comments and reviews, allowing us to understand the perception and opinions towards products or services.

And here we enter two major ethical and social challenges: on the one hand, the massive use of language in AI applications raises concerns about privacy and data security. The collection and processing of large amounts of linguistic data can pose significant risks if not handled properly, which may result in unauthorized exposure of sensitive information; and, on the other hand, the worrying impact on employment and education, since AI-driven automation in linguistic tasks can have repercussions on the labor market. While these can improve efficiency and productivity, they also raise concerns about job losses in sectors where language tasks were traditionally performed by humans. Furthermore, this underlines the need for education tailored to the skills needed in an increasingly automated environment.

Continuing with the classification, other programs are grouped together in the typology of voice recognition tools: applications such as Dragon NaturallySpeaking, Google Speech-to-Text, and Apple's Siri use NLP to convert human speech into written text. Here we must take into account that the exact reproduction of words is ambiguous and inaccurate, since only what it captures clearly is transcribed literally, of what is inexact, and since AIs do not have an intuitive nature, they only reproduce and transcribe possibilities.

Curiously, there are also systems with NLP that serve to focus on this process, to talk about the language itself, as a constant metalinguistic function: we are talking about grammatical and spelling-correction AIs, such as Grammarly and Microsoft Word, which use NLP to suggest grammatical corrections and spelling in written texts; or programs focused on automatic text summarization, see Summly (acquired by Yahoo) or OpenAI's GPT-3, which summarize large volumes of text, extracting key points to create shorter, more understandable summaries. There is even a final typology: those information extraction systems: tools such as spaCy or NLTK that allow entities, relationships, and key concepts to be extracted from texts, facilitating the search for specific information in large data sets.

6.3 CONSEQUENCES OF NATURAL LANGUAGE PROCESSING IN LITERARY TEXTS: LINGUISTIC EFFECTS

Telling, from the poetic function of language, which aims to beautify the message, allows us to enlarge our vision of the world from sensitivity and myth, which is still a recurring story with which we explain what does not yet have a scientific formulation. Sometimes it even already has it, but *telling ourselves*, creating stories, whether they have verisimilitude with reality or present a fantastic scenario, satisfy a human need: to delve into that part of us, which we sometimes call soul, to give it a sense of grandiloquence, bringing us closer to the magical, to those incomprehensible primary forces that generate the world of aesthetics and harmony.

AIs have not been less and have helped in the construction of literary texts adapted to this new era to satisfy humanistic art, but with peculiarities. Instantaneity and liquidity mark stories: we no longer have time to dwell on an exhaustive description, now we need brevity and, therefore, synthesis. The new human microfiction aims to tell with condensation, meaning that it is now important to tell a complete story, develop a theme, or convey a significant message in a very small space, often in a few lines or paragraphs. Therefore, economy of words is necessary: a precise and efficient use of language. Each word and phrase is carefully selected to convey the greatest amount of meaning in the smallest space possible. Consequently, there must be suggestion and ambiguity, thus encouraging play and the subsequent engagement of the reader: short texts can present enigmatic situations or leave aspects open to interpretation, encouraging the reader's active participation in the construction of meanings. Surprising or shocking endings are also encouraged in literary creation: many short stories in microfiction seek to impact the reader through an unexpected, surprising, or revealing ending. This final twist is often crucial to fully understanding the story; and this is related to formal experimentation: whether with structure, point of view, narrative time, or other formal elements of the narrative, challenging traditional literary conventions (Zavala, 2007).

And given all this, natural language processing (NLP) has had various effects on literature and the world of writing. Some of these effects include the emergence of writing and proofreading tools, which have already been mentioned before: Grammarly, Hemingway Editor, and autocorrect, among others, have improved the quality of the text and facilitated the writing process. In turn, other systems have generated automated content with advanced language models, such as GPT (generative pre-trained transformer) from OpenAI, have demonstrated abilities to generate text that imitates specific literary styles or even create original stories; which raises debates about originality and creativity in writing when using technology to generate content. An example of this could be the Neurowriter tool, an artificial brain capable of imitating the literary style of any novel for which this brain has data, it can generate new texts with a style similar to a given text, in this case, novels in Spanish. And before creation, programs have also been created for content analysis, even for literary criticism.

On the other hand, there are also AI programs that serve to preserve and access literature, something that is beneficial with digitization, since the preservation of old and rare literary works is achieved, as well as access to digital libraries and archives that otherwise might have been less available to the public. Taken together, the PLN has transformed various aspects of literature, from the way it is written and corrected to how the literary work is accessed and appreciated, in turn raising ethical and aesthetic questions about creativity, authenticity, and interaction between technology and human expression.

6.4 CONCLUSIONS

The presence of AI in human language with its consequences, optimal and harmful, is a reality that is not expected but is already established. In this sense, the challenges that arise focus on improving systems to understand the context in which the language is used. This involves advancing the understanding of linguistic nuances, irony, sarcasm, and other complex aspects of human language.

It is pertinent to mention that another challenge that arises is human–machine interaction and the search for a more natural relationship. The aforementioned AI systems, from their different typologies, are expected to further improve their ability to interact with humans in a comprehensive manner. This includes more advanced processing of speech, writing, and gestures, with the aim of achieving more fluid and authentic communication.

And, as a problem to be debated regularly, the actions of the PLN regarding ethics and data transparency: mechanisms must be sought to mitigate bias in algorithms, guarantee data privacy, and promote equity and inclusion in the use of AI in language.

Always without forgetting, as reflected by Byung-Chul Han (2023):

> Big data suggests absolute knowledge. Things reveal their secret correlations. Everything becomes calculable, predictable and controllable. A whole new era of knowledge is announced. In reality, it is a rather primitive way of knowing. Data mining or data mining discovers correlations.

Then, the reflection of a good use of AI systems and a correct subsequent application, learning (here the relevance of education from childhood to adulthood included, a constant training in the face of so many inevitable changes) the textual mechanisms and properties first, empathizing with the content and possible recipients of the messages, it becomes pertinent to not lose our humanity: the formulation, through words, of life and all its sensitive beauty.

REFERENCES

Ansón, L. M. (2022, May 23). Signs of the times in the digital age. *The Spanish*. www.elespanol.com/el-cultural/opinion/primera_palabra_luis_maria_anson/20220523/signos-tiempos-digital/673062697_13.html

Broseta Dupré, B., Escribá Esteve, A., López García, G., Maudos Villarroya, J., Pascual Lavilla, F., & Pérez García, F. (Ed.). (2023). *The media in the digital age*. Bilbao: BBVA Foundation.

Byung-Chul H. (2023, June 22). Artificial intelligence is incapable of thinking. *Bloghemia*. www.bloghemia.com/2023/06/byung-chul-han-la-inteligencia.html

Calsamiglia, H., & Tusón, A. (1999). *The things of saying: A manual of discourse analysis*. Barcelona: Editorial Ariel.

Calvino, I. (1988). *Six memos for the next millennium*. Madrid: Siruela.

Estavillo, E. (2021, September 21). Artificial intelligence with human defects. Linkedin.com. www.linkedin.com/pulse/inteligencia-artificial-con-defectos-humanos-elena-estavillo/?originalSubdomain=es

Martínez Cabrera, M. (2008). Paragraph configuration criteria in the academic writing of education students. *Laurus, 14*, 207–225.

Pedrero, L. (2021, September 16). Communication in the era of instantaneity. *Medium*. https://luismipedrero.medium.com/la-comunicaci%C3%B3n-en-la-era-de-la-instantaneidad-6a28cae3338f

Pérez Asensio, M. (2012). Contributions of NLP to emotional education. *Advances in Educational Supervision, 16*, 15–58. https://doi.org/10.23824/ase.v0i16.503

Roselló Verdeguer, R. (2015). The text and its properties: Some practical considerations. *Digital Tones: Journal of Philological Studies, 28*, 75–90. https://www.um.es/tonosdigital/znum28/secciones/tintero-7--rosello_texto.htm

Zavala, L. (2007). From literary theory to postmodern minifiction. *Ciências Sociais Unisinos, 43*(1), 86–96.

CHAPTER 7

The Deepfake Technique Used for Creative Advertising from a Social Perspective: The *Seguimos Hablando* Campaign (2019) as a Case Study

Rocío Cifuentes-Albeza

7.1 INTRODUCTION

The development of artificial intelligence (AI) opens new possibilities for creative advertising. Numerous organisations are making use of deepfakes to create videos, usually to 'resurrect' celebrities and incorporate them into their advertising campaigns. The prosocial deepfake (Lu & Chu, 2023) has emerged as a distinctive discursive form used in various contexts, including prosocial advertising, as an ethical form of 'positive artificial intelligence' placed at the service of the public (Correa Da Silva, 2020). Non-profit organisations integrate deepfake technology into their prosocial advertising campaigns as a way of explicitly promoting altruistic behaviours (Berman, Levine, Barasch, & Small, 2015; Li & Atkinson, 2020; Bünzli, 2022) through a direct appeal to the viewer. For-profit organisations may also integrate a social cause into their publicity as a way of pursuing other goals that enhance their image (Alvarado López, 2005).

Leaving aside the malicious deepfakes associated with political disinformation, dubious journalistic practices, and pornography, all of which have already received considerable scholarly attention (Godulla, Hoffmann, & Seibert, 2021; Lu & Chu, 2023), this study explores the prosocial potential of deepfakes (Godulla et al., 2021). The focus of this research is on the use of manipulated images not for the purpose of deceiving the

DOI: 10.1201/9781003473633-7

viewer but as vehicles for activism aimed at promoting social justice and human rights. The deepfake is thus defined as a rhetorical device for persuasive communication in the form of prosocial advertising and for the promotion of the activist work of non-profit organisations.

The campaign that serves as a case study for this research was organised by the Mexican non-profit organisation Propuesta Cívica in conjunction with Publicis WW México. The campaign, titled 'Seguimos hablando' (promoted in English as 'Still Speaking Up'), made use of deepfake technology in 2020 to resurrect the journalist Javier Arturo Valdez Cárdenas, who had been murdered three years earlier. The following section offers an overview of research on the use of prosocial deepfakes in advertising, followed by an exploration of the potential benefits of generative artificial intelligence (GenAI) as a support for social activism.

7.2 AN OVERVIEW OF PROSOCIAL DEEPFAKE RESURRECTIONS IN ADVERTISING

7.2.1 Deepfakes: Origin, Definition, and GenAI Technology

In 2017, a user on the Reddit platform going by the name 'Deepfakes' posted some manipulated videos in which the faces of actresses in pornographic content had been replaced with the faces of certain celebrities without their consent (Kietzmann, Mills, & Plangger, 2021: 1; Zhang, 2022: 6259), a practice that would become one of the most significant new discursive genres in the years that followed (Bañuelos Capistrán, 2022: 8). Very soon the technology to create these types of videos became accessible to the public thanks to the release of the Deepfakes app in 2017 (Cerdán Martínez & Padilla Castillo, 2019; Zhang, 2022: 6259), followed by others in 2019, such as FadeApp, DeepFaceLab, and ZAO (Zhang, 2022: 6259). These apps make it easy to manipulate visual and sound content and use machine learning (ML) technology to create realistic videos featuring specific individuals saying and doing things they never really said or did (De Ruiter, 2021: 1312; Kietzmann et al., 2021: 1).

GenAI apps use a ML algorithm, a method that allows users to create deepfakes easily and cheaply on a smartphone based on deep neural networks (DNN) and generated adversarial networks (GAN) (Zhang, 2022: 6260). A DNN is a neural network that uses different layers and algorithms to learn how to replicate certain patterns and behaviours autonomously, while a GAN is a class of deep learning framework that pits two adversarial (generative and discriminative) models against each other to improve output (Goodfellow et al., 2014).

7.2.2 Deepfake Resurrections in Advertising

AI has had a huge impact on all stages of the advertising process (Martínez, Aguado Terrón, & Sánchez Cobarro, 2022: 70) and the deepfake is simply another element of an architecture that pertains to the media, politics, morality, ethics, and culture, involving the creation and dissemination of false content presented as a product of reality

(Bañuelos Capistrán, 2020: 60). Content manipulation already existed in advertising before the rise of AI, and it has evolved in parallel with technological developments. Campbell, Plangger, Sands, and Kietzmann (2021) identify three generations of manipulation associated with advertising content pre-production and post-production: analogue, digital, and synthetic.

The practice of integrating deepfake resurrections into various successful campaigns confirms the presence of GenAI in the creation of advertising content, although Fernández Rincón (2023: 391) argues that the use of AI in creative advertising is still only marginal. The academic literature includes a number of case studies, such as the 'resurrection' of the Andalusian singer Lola Flores, who died in 1995, featured in the ad 'Con mucho acento' for the beer Cruzcampo in Spain in 2021. The aim of this campaign was a brand repositioning (Senovilla & Moreno, 2021) based on the recovery of the beer's 'status as an iconic brand by asserting the power of the [Andalusian] accent' (Ogilvy, n.d.). The campaign had an extraordinary impact (Palomo-Domínguez, 2021). Deepfakes promise to transform advertising as we know it 'because they are believable, accessible and novel' (Kietzmann et al., 2021: 3). Kietzmann et al. proposed a model to conceptualise the influence of deepfakes on three dimensions of advertising: the nature of the advertisement, the perception of the advertisement, and the sociocultural context of its creation and consumption (2021: 2).

7.2.3 GenAI for the Public Good: Prosocial Deepfakes in Advertising

With its huge potential to transform the impact of the work being done by non-profit organisations (Efthymiou, Egleton, Chatzivasileiou, & Emmanouil-Kalos, 2023), GenAI can be directed towards serving the public good through the exploration of AI ethics (Berberich, Nishida, & Suzuki, 2020). Researchers have given very little attention to the benefits and opportunities offered by deepfakes in the social and medical fields (Lu & Chu, 2023: 1) or even their use in the fields of education and art (Godulla et al., 2021: 8). Scholarly output on deepfakes from a social perspective is limited compared with other areas of research (Godulla et al., 2021), yet deepfakes have a huge positive potential as 'new forms of audiovisual expression that contribute to the development of education, medicine and health, science, business, fashion, e-commerce, advertising, security, entertainment, and social, political, artistic and cultural reflection' (Bañuelos Capistrán, 2022: 3).

In the period from 2019 to 2021, prosocial deepfakes became a significant presence in advertising and particularly in campaigns promoting social and political activism, among other initiatives (Bañuelos Capistrán, 2022: 9). 'Prosocial deepfake' is a term coined by Lu and Chu (2023) to distinguish deepfakes created specifically to trigger prosocial and altruistic behaviours from malicious deepfakes (i.e., deepfakes created for harmful purposes). The present study defines a subcategory of the prosocial deepfake applied to advertising that exposes certain social problems as a trigger for prosocial action. This call to activism involves a direct or indirect appeal to engage in altruistic behaviours in support of a cause, so that viewers can contribute positively to the transformation of the social and/or political issue being exposed. Many deepfakes of resurrected figures in prosocial advertising campaigns have elements in common: the issue raised in the deepfake is related to the reason the 'resurrected' individuals were violently murdered, and their persuasive discourse includes a posthumous appeal directly to the audience, highlighting the persistence of the issue in the present to encourage activism in favour of the cause. These appeals are sponsored by a wide variety of organisations and are generally approved by the victims' relatives, who may even have contributed to the campaign. Their support is important in legal and moral terms, and it can also contribute positively to the campaign's success (Palomo-Domínguez, 2021: 34). According to Bañuelos, 'the ethical and legal value of post-truth discourses, including deepfakes, needs to be assessed in terms of their interpretation and the harm they cause in a specific moral, ethical, legal and cultural context' (Bañuelos Capistrán, 2020: 60).

The manipulation of content can elicit a wide range of reactions in viewers, because even when the intention is altruistic, bringing the dead back to life in a deepfake may give rise to criticism and controversy (Kneese, 2020). For prosocial deepfakes in contexts of violence, Mendiola (Mendiola & Wallach, 2022) highlights the need to establish a work plan with the victims' families; to provide them with psychosocial support before, during, and after the campaign; to carefully evaluate the risks posed to the family in order to articulate a standard of protection whenever necessary; and to respect the legacy of the victims, because that legacy forms part of the collective memory.

The causes championed in prosocial deepfakes present diverse objectives in specific social and political contexts: Julio César Zúniga, a gay soccer player murdered in 2018, returns to call out the continued abuse and stigmatisation of the LGBTIQ+ community (Héroes de hoy, 2020); Joaquín Oliver, killed in the Parkland high school shooting in 2018, condemns gun ownership laws in the United States and appeals to young people to mobilise the power of their votes through the Unfinished Votes campaign (Change The Ref, n.d.); and Javier Arturo Valdez Cárdenas, murdered in 2017, returns in 2020 by means of a deepfake featured in the Seguimos Hablando/Still Speaking Up campaign (Propuesta Cívica, 2020), to denounce the crisis of violence against Mexican journalists and the government's corruption and inaction in the prosecution of these crimes, and to encourage people to join the movement (Mendiola & Wallach, 2022). These are only a few examples of prosocial deepfake resurrections used to publicise activist causes.

7.3 CASE STUDY: *SEGUIMOS HABLANDO*

This section presents a content analysis of the prosocial deepfake of Javier Arturo Valdez Cárdenas (Propuesta Cívica, 2020), first made public on 2 November 2020 with the reopening of the late journalist's Twitter account. Before presenting the analysis, an overview is offered of the issue addressed in the campaign (violence against journalists in Mexico), as well as the synergies between the victims' legacy and the activist cause in relation to the aims of the organisation behind the campaign. This overview will help identify how the campaign's message is integrated into the AI-generated image to achieve its purpose as an exercise in prosocial communication by a non-profit organisation, addressed to the public and the various levels of government.

7.3.1 The Crisis of Violence Against Journalists and the Case of Javier Valdez

Since 1992, a total of 2,205 journalists and media workers have been murdered around the world, according to figures published by the CPJ (Committee to Protect Journalists, n.d.). Mexico has one of the world's lowest scores on the safety indicator of Reporters Without Borders' Press Freedom Index, which evaluates 'the ability to develop, gather and disseminate news and information [...] without unnecessary risk of bodily harm, psychological or emotional distress, or professional harm' (Reporters Without Borders, 2023a). Political instability throughout the Americas threatens press freedom (Reporters Without Borders, 2023a), and in Mexico the extreme violence of the cartels and their frequent collusion with local authorities has been slowly destroying journalism (Reporters Without Borders, 2023b). Mexico currently has the worst levels of violence against journalists of any country in the world, even outdoing countries in conditions of civil war such as Syria and Afghanistan (Mendiola & Wallach, 2022). Since 2020, a total of 161 media professionals have been killed in Mexico, and their deaths in many cases are probably related to their professional activity (Artículo 19, n.d.).

Javier Arturo Valdez Cárdenas was a Mexican journalist from the city of Culiacán in Mexico's northwest, who was notable for his work reporting on corruption, political power, and the drug trade in Mexico (Propuesta Cívica, n.d.a). He received the CPJ International Press Freedom Award in 2011, in addition to other prizes for his journalism. He also authored several books on the drug trade, and he was also one of the founders of *Ríodoce*, a weekly newspaper established in 2013, with a critical focus in the context of 'strict control of the mass media by the Federal Government' (Riodoce, n.d.).

7.3.2 #Seguimos Hablando

Propuesta Cívica is a non-profit organisation founded in 2011 with the aim of protecting and promoting human rights and freedom of expression in Mexico (Propuesta Cívica, n.d.b). 'Seguimos hablando' (promoted in English as 'Still Speaking Up') is a campaign launched by this organisation in 2019 with the support of the advertising agency Publicis WorldWide México. The campaign has received various awards at prestigious international festivals (Propuesta Cívica, 2020; Mendiola & Wallach, 2022) in the categories of social responsibility and new emerging technologies. Moreover, in 2019 the campaign hashtag #SeguimosHablando became a trending topic in Mexico, with a 4,337% increase in conversations about press freedom, a total of 98% of which were positive. The campaign also received more than 300 media mentions and increased the number of Propuesta Civica's Twitter followers by 30% (Mendiola & Wallach, 2022).

The aim of the campaign was to call out the killings and the wave of violence affecting journalists in Mexico, an aim that ties in with Propuesta Cívica's mission: if a country lacks access to information and truth, it is impossible for its citizens to have the freedom to choose their government representatives at the ballot box (Mendiola & Wallach, 2022). Diego Wallach, Chief Creative Officer at Publicis WorldWide México, explains that the campaign's main objective was to 'shake Mexican society out of its complacency' (Mendiola & Wallach, 2022), while Propuesta Cívica's CEO Sara Mendiola highlights the call it makes upon the government to address the crisis of violence against Mexican journalists, ending the current impunity in order to prevent further crimes and demanding social justice (Mendiola & Wallach, 2022).

In 2019, the campaign's focus was on reopening the Twitter accounts of Javier Valdez, Miroslava Breach, and Moisés Sánchez and other murdered journalists, with the intention of making their cases known. To this end, the campaign had the support of Twitter, the approval of the victims' families, and the help of colleagues and friends of the deceased (Mendiola & Wallach, 2022). On 29 April 2019, the following post appeared on Valdez's account: *El 15 de mayo de 2017 fui asesinado en la calle a plena luz. Igual que a otros 104 periodistas en México me mataron, pero #Seguimos Hablando* [On 15 May 2017, I was killed on the street in broad daylight. Like 104 other journalists in Mexico, I was murdered, but we are Still Speaking Up] (Seguimos Hablando, quoted by Mendiola & Wallach, 2022). The second part of the campaign took place in 2020 with the publication of Valdez's deepfake, a video with a duration of 1 minute and 39 seconds (Propuesta Cívica [propuestacívicamx], 4 November 2020), on Twitter. Wallach argues that the deepfake manages to recreate all the rawness of a real-life testimony, with visuals that never look overproduced, and that the level of realism achieved has been key for the impact of the campaign (Mendiola & Wallach, 2022). He also describes the meticulous production process: the video was filmed with an actor whose face was replaced using deepfake technology, while the voice was developed by means of audio systems that blended the voices of different people with a northern Mexican accent like the one the victim had.

It is worth highlighting that the release date of the deepfake of 2 November was significant for two reasons: it was the International Day to End Impunity for Crimes against Journalists (United Nations, 18 December 2013), and the Day of the Dead, a holiday that is absolutely central to any understanding of cultural attitudes towards death in Mexico.

7.3.3 Content Analysis of the Valdez Deepfake in *Seguimos Hablando* (2020)

Valdez is shown sitting in front of a white wall lined with shelves containing books and decorative objects, looking directly into the camera, and speaking using the first-person present tense. He is wearing a Panama hat that belonged to him when he was alive, which his widow made available for the production (Mendiola & Wallach, 2022), eyeglasses and a shirt that he used to wear in his public appearances (Figure 7.1). He introduces himself with his full name and profession as a journalist and writer (00:00:04–00:00:06) and adds a key piece of information for the audience: the date of his murder, 15 May 2017 (00:00:07–00:00:09). He goes onto explain that he was killed '*por órdenes de alguien a quien no le gustó lo que publiqué*' ['by orders of someone who didn't like what I published'] (00:00:10–00:00:13). According to the Attorney General's Office of Sinaloa (FEDALE, quoted by Propuesta Cívica, 2023), three perpetrators of the crime were identified, in addition to an accessory.

He then makes an implicit reference to the COVID-19 pandemic (00:00:16–00:00:18), an event that occurred several years after his death, and that was ongoing at the time the

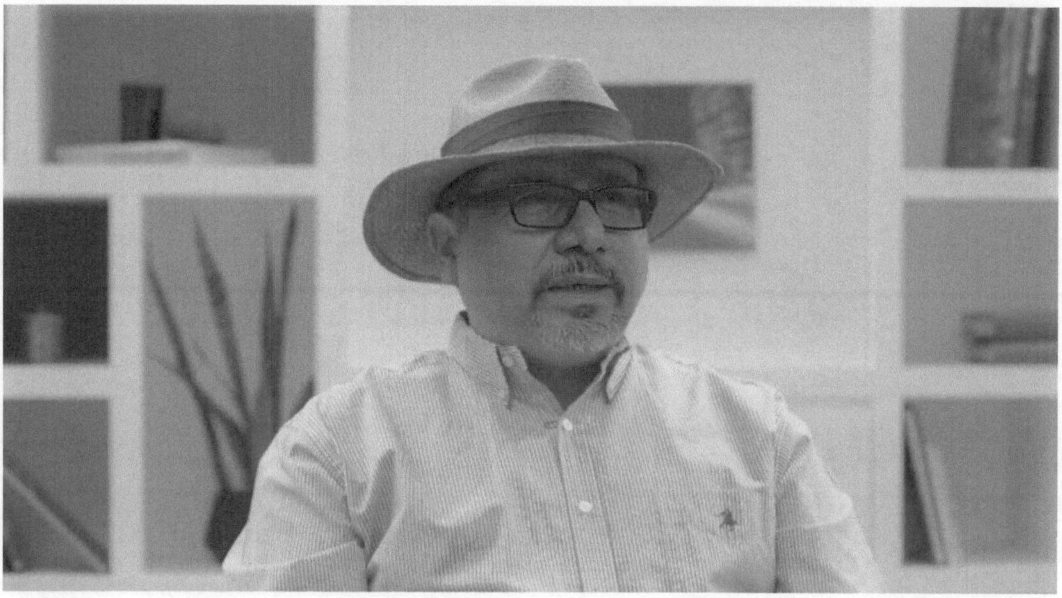

FIGURE 7.1 Screenshot of the *Seguimos Hablando* campaign (Propuesta Cívica, 2020).

Source: YouTube channel of propuestacívicamx © (https://youtu.be/klEAekd3SNE?si=sQ1tEB60LVO4m0a8)

deepfake was released. He compares the pandemic with another crisis afflicting Mexico, and although he does not specify what it is at that moment, he is referring to the murders of journalists in the country, '*que ha cobrado aún más vidas*' ['that have claimed even more lives'] (00:00:19–00:00:24). The adverb of time 'hoy' ['today'], used at different moments in the video, lays bare the chronological discrepancy. Valdez goes on: '*Yo no tengo miedo, señor presidente, porque no me pueden matar dos veces*' ['I am not afraid, Mr. President, because they can't kill me twice'] (00:00:25–00:00:29). Here once again he makes clear that he has been 'resurrected' and that the video content presented is a deepfake.

Valdez is a victim who at the same time is presented as the spokesperson for the cause, as he stresses that he is here '*a hablar por los cientos de periodistas asesinados, desaparecidos, y desplazados por realizar un periodismo ético y de investigación*' ['to speak on behalf of the hundreds of journalists who have been killed, abducted, and displaced for doing ethical investigative journalism'] (00:00:30–00:00:40). Valdez thus identifies the perpetrators of the wave of violence and their motive because these journalists '*desnudaron las entrañas del poder corrupto y el crimen organizado en México*' ['exposed the underbelly of corrupt power and organised crime in Mexico'] (00:00:41–00:00:46). He also condemns the indifference and corruption of political leaders and officials at both state and federal levels (00:00:47–00:00:53) and calls on the president to '*cumpla con su obligación*' ['fulfil your obligations'] (00:00:57–00:01:00). And he offers the president the chance to change, proposing the idea of a '*gobierno de transformación*' ['government of transformation'] (00:01:11) that has '*la voluntad política de esclarecer estos crímenes y castigar a los verdaderos responsables*' ['the political will to solve these crimes and punish the real guilty parties'] (00:01:12–00:01:18). This proposal is offered as 'a positive gesture'

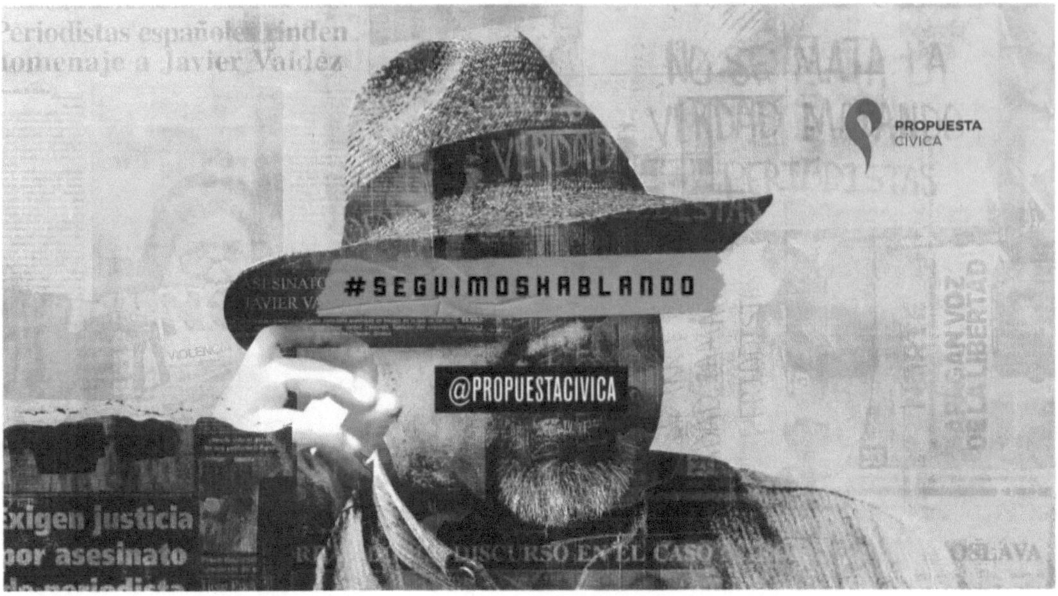

FIGURE 7.2 Screenshot of *Seguimos Hablando* campaign (Propuesta Cívica, 2020).

Source: YouTube channel of propuestacívicamx © (https://youtu.be/klEAekd3SNE?si=sQ1tEB60LVO4m0a8)

to encourage a profound transformation and is not presented as an attack (Mendiola & Wallach, 2022). Valdez calls for justice and dignity for the murdered journalists and their families so that by revealing the truth of the events they can finally know peace (00:01:01–00:01:10).

Valdez ends his speech with a plea for democracy, asserting that '*un país sin verdad es un país sin democracia*' ['a country without truth is a country without democracy'] (00:01:29–00:01:32) and concluding that '*aunque quieran callarnos, seguimos hablando*' ['although they want to silence us, we are still speaking up'] (00:01:33–00:01:35). The video ends with the appearance of the hashtag #SeguimosHablando (00:01:36–00:01:39) (Figure 7.2).

7.4 RESULTS OF THE ANALYSIS OF THE MESSAGE IN THE *SEGUIMOS HABLANDO* 2020 PROSOCIAL DEEPFAKE

As Wallach suggests (Mendiola & Wallach, 2022), the high level of realism achieved in the video supports the rawness of the testimony in the deepfake, despite the subtle hint of Valdez's blank stare, a characteristic feature of all GenAI images. The presence of the hat that belonged to the journalist when he was alive has symbolic value and even acts as a sign of veneration. The glasses and shirt also serve as key elements in the reconstruction of Valdez's identity.

In addition to revealing the nature of the deepfake content, the element of placing the details of Valdez's death in his own mouth also lends the video a profound level of rawness. The first-person testimony achieves a direct appeal with a powerful impact. Valdez's discourse is fully integrated into the construction of the character that recalls the journalist's living persona, even if it may be questioned by some audience members. This rawness is also evoked by the reopening of a dead man's Twitter account, and by the connection of his 'return', albeit 'artificial', with the deeply rooted tradition of Day in the Dead, when Mexicans set up altars and offerings to welcome the return of the dearly departed.

The juxtaposition of past and present is latent in the video and the two time-frames are combined smoothly in an asynchronous narrative thread, as in Valdez's speech the description of the events of the past (his murder in 2017) and the reference to the pandemic that was occurring at the time the deepfake was released in 2020 facilitate viewer comprehension of his resurrection in the present and underscore the current relevance of the cause he has returned to advocate for.

Valdez has returned to champion his cause and its victims on a day with particular symbolic value: the International Day to End Impunity for Crimes against Journalists. Underpinning his speech is the relationship between the cause of his death and the cause he is leading, with his direct call upon the Mexican president, and by extension upon Mexican society, to challenge the inaction of the political class and the government agencies in Mexico and to speak up against corruption and violence against journalists. The assertion that 'a country without information is a country without democracy' (Mendiola & Wallach, 2022) perfectly encapsulates the aim of the campaign, and the campaign's title, Seguimos Hablando/Still Speaking Up, hints at the continued importance of Valdez's legacy, as not even his death can take away his memory or stop his fight for freedom of expression.

7.5 CONCLUSIONS

AI constitutes an extremely important leap forward in the promotion of the social causes of non-profit organisations, as technological advances have significantly reduced production costs for the development of creative advertising (Campbell et al., 2021), an activity that has traditionally been challenging for such organisations due to their often very limited budgets.

Propuesta Cívica has made masterful use of Valdez's image to channel its activism through a prosocial campaign that protests social injustice and calls for truth. It has done this by placing a direct appeal to the Mexican president in the mouth of the renowned late journalist himself, and by taking advantage of the well-known social media platform Twitter to achieve its aim.

Valdez's only reappearance on his Twitter account since his death has acquired a special significance, turning him into a hero not only for journalists but also for freedom of expression in Mexican society in general. His speech is much more powerful than it might have been if it were given by a living person; his continuing legacy has the quality of an invincible force, because his ideals and his commitment to fighting for the truth cannot be broken even by taking his life. In this way, through his artificial presence made possible by the development of the synthetic manipulation technology of the prosocial deepfake, Valdez continues to stand up to power. He is the hero representing all the heroes and heroines who, even while knowing that their professional activity places them at risk of losing their lives, are fiercely determined to practice committed journalism in Mexico.

The false appearance generated by the synthetic audiovisual technology of the deepfake paradoxically becomes an effective medium of communication, as it assumes the rhetorical status of the most profound of truths. In this way, as Wallach suggests (Mendiola & Wallach, 2022), the deepfake becomes a 'deep truth' that safeguards the journalists who continue to speak up about the crisis of violence against media professionals in Mexico.

This study has considered two of the dimensions of the model proposed by Kietzmann et al. (2021: 3) to conceptualise the influence of deepfakes: the nature of the advertisement, and the sociocultural context of its creation and reception. The third dimension of this model, the analysis of audience perceptions of and reactions to prosocial deepfakes, is a matter for future research, which will provide vital information for our understanding of the effect and impact of prosocial deepfake resurrections in the context of prosocial advertising.

FUNDING

This research is part of the *Immersive Prosocial Audiovisual Narratives Project: Measuring its impact on society and analyzing its formal and technological characteristics* (grant number CIAICO/2021/258), within the framework of the Program to Promote Scientific Research, Technological Development and Innovation in the Valencian Community-AICO 2022, Generalitat Valenciana, Spain.

REFERENCES

Alvarado López, M. C. (2005). La Publicidad Social: Concepto, objeto y objetivos. *Redes.com: revista de estudios para el desarrollo social de la Comunicación,* (2), 265–284.

Artículo 19 (n.d.) *Periodistas asesinados en México.* Retrieved September 29, 2023, from https://articulo19.org/periodismo/

Bañuelos Capistrán, J. (2020). Deepfake: La imagen en tiempos de la posverdad. *Revista Panamericana de Comunicación, 2*(1), 51–61. https://doi.org/10.21555/rpc.v0i1.2315

Bañuelos Capistrán, J. (2022). Evolución del Deepfake: Campos semánticos y géneros discursivos 2017–2021. *Revista ICONO 14. Revista Científica de Comunicación y Tecnologías Emergentes, 20*(1), 1–21. https://doi.org/10.7195/ri14.v20i1.1773

Berberich, N., Nishida, T., & Suzuki, S. (2020). Harmonizing artificial intelligence for social good. *Philosophy & Technology, 33*, 613–638. https://doi.org/10.1007/s13347-020-00421-8

Berman, J. Z., Levine, E. E., Barasch, A., & Small, D. A. (2015). The Braggart's dilemma: On the social rewards and penalties of advertising prosocial behavior. *Journal of Marketing Research, 52*(1), 90–104. https://doi.org/10.1509/jmr.14.0002

Bünzli, F. (2022). Improving the effectiveness of prosocial advertising campaigns: Message strategies to increase support from less empathic individuals. *Journal of Philanthropy and Marketing, 27*(1), e1711. https://doi.org/10.1002/nvsm.1711

Campbell, C., Plangger, K., Sands, S., & Kietzmann, J. (2021). Preparing for an era of deepfakes and ai-generated ads: A framework for understanding responses to manipulated advertising. *Journal of Advertising.* https://doi.org/10.1080/00913367.2021.1909515

Cerdán Martínez, V., & Padilla Castillo, G. (2019). Historia del fake audiovisual: deepfake y la mujer en un imaginario falsificado y perverso. *Historia y Comunicación Social, 24*(2), 505–520. https://doi.org/10.5209/hics.66293

Change The Ref (n.d.) *Our initiatives: Unfinished votes*. Retrieved October 3, 2023, from https://changetheref.org/our-initiatives/

Committee to Protect Journalists. (n.d.) *Base de datos de periodistas asesinados*. Retrieved September 29, 2023, from https://cpj.org/data/killed/?status=Killed&motiveConfirmed%5B%5D=Confirmed&motiveUnconfirmed%5B%5D=Unconfirmed&type%5B%5D=Journalist&type%5B%5D=Media%20Worker&start_year=1992&end_year=2023&group_by=year

Correa Da Silva, F. S. (2020). Towards positive artificial intelligence. In Matteo Baldoni & Stefania Bandini (Eds.), *Advances in Artificial Intelligence 2020: Proceedings of International Conference of the Italian Association for Artificial Intelligence* (Virtual Event, November 25–27, 2020, pp. 359–371). New York: Springer. https://doi.org/10.1007/978-3-030-77091-4

De Ruiter, A. (2021). The distinct wrong of deepfakes. *Philosophy & Technology, 34*(4), 1311–1332. https://doi.org/10.1007/s13347-021-00459-2

Efthymiou, I. P., Egleton, T. W. E., Chatzivasileiou, S., & Emmanouil-Kalos, A. (2023). Artificial intelligence and the future for charities. *International Journal of Non-Profit Sector Empowerment, 2*(1), 1–5. https://doi.org/10.12681/npse.35345

Fernández Rincón, A. R. (2023). El creativo invisible: Inteligencia artificial y creación publicitaria. *Miguel Hernández Communication Journal, 14*(2), 391–408. https://doi.org/10.21134/mhjournal.v14i.1983

Godulla, A., Hoffmann, C. P., & Seibert, D. (2021). Dealing with deepfakes – An interdisciplinary examination of the state of research and implications for communication studies. *Studies in Communication and Media, 10*(1), 72–96. https://doi.org/10.5771/2192-4007-2021-1-72

Goodfellow, I., Pouget-Abadie, J., Mirza, M., Xu, B., Warde-Farley, D., Ozair, S., Courville, A., & Bengio, Y. (2014). Generative adversarial nets. *Advances in Neural Information Processing Systems, 27*, 1–9.

Héroes de hoy (2020, November 20). *Intolerance is still there.* [Video]. Youtube. https://youtu.be/KCLwq9tE9Lo?si=GC_nWSvj79LQI6Wl&t=1

Kietzmann, J., Mills, A. J., & Plangger, K. (2021). Deepfakes: Perspectives on the future "reality" of advertising and branding. *International Journal of Advertising, 40*(3), 473–485. https://doi.org/10.1080/02650487.2020.1834211

Kneese, T. (2020, November 2). How data can create full-on apparitions of the dead. Slate. Retrieved from https://slate.com/technology/2020/11/robert-kardashian-joaquin-oliver-deepfakes-death.html

Li, D., & Atkinson, L. (2020). Effect of emotional victim images in prosocial advertising: The moderating role of helping mode. *International Journal of Nonprofit and Voluntary Sector Marketing, 25*(4), e1676, 1–9. https://doi.org/10.1002/nvsm.1676

Lu, H., & Chu, H. (2023). Let the dead talk: How deepfake resurrection narratives influence audience response in prosocial contexts. *Computers in Human Behavior, 145*. https://doi.org/10.1016/j.chb.2023.107761

Martínez Martínez, I. J., Aguado Terrón, J. M., & Sánchez Cobarro, P. H. (2022). Smart advertising: Innovación y disrupción tecnológica asociadas a la IA en el ecosistema publicitario. *Revista Latina de Comunicación Social, 80*, 69–90. https://doi.org/10.4185/10.4185/RLCS-2022-1693

Mendiola, S., & Wallach, D. (2022). *Inteligencia artificial y publicidad al servicio de las causas sociales* [Webinar]. Red Iberoamericana de Investigadores en Publicidad. https://youtu.be/NoZeHHGnvHo?si=QZ2mLCLYrhHAxfb-

Ogilvy (n.d.) *Con mucho acento. Cruzcampo*. Retrieved October 12, 2023, from www.ogilvy.com/es/work/con-mucho-acento

Palomo-Domínguez, I. (2021). Del mito a la viralidad. El caso de la campaña de Cruzcampo que resucitó a Lola Flores. *aDResearch: Revista Internacional de Investigación en Comunicación*, (26), 38–58. https://doi.org/10.7263/adresic-026-02

Propuesta Cívica (n.d.a). *Casos. Memorias que hablan. 07 Javier Arturo Valdez Cárdenas*. Retrieved November 30, 2023, from https://propuestacivica.org.mx/casos/javier-arturo-valdez-cardenas

Propuesta Cívica (n.d.b). *Quiénes somos*. Retrieved September 29, 2023, from https://propuestacivica.org.mx/acerca-de

Propuesta Cívica (2020). *#SeguimosHablando 2*. Retrieved November 12, 2023, from https://propuestacivica.org.mx/proyecto/seguimoshablando-2#image-181

Propuesta Cívica (2023). *¡Aquí nadie olvida! A 6 años del asesinato de Javier Valdez*. Retrieved November 12, 2023, from https://propuestacivica.org.mx/noticia/aqui-nadie-olvida-a-6-anos-del-asesinato-de-javier-valdez

Propuesta Cívica [propuestacívicamx] (2020, November 4). Javier Valdez Speaks 3 Years After His Murder #SeguimosHablando [Video]. Youtube. https://youtu.be/klEAekd3SNE?si=sQ1tEB60LVO4m0a8

Reporters Without Borders. (2023a). *2023 world press freedom index*. Retrieved September 29, 2023, from https://rsf.org/en/index

Reporters Without Borders (2023b). *Americas: Press freedom threatened by political instability*. World Press Freedom Index. Retrieved September 29, 2023, from https://rsf.org/en/classement/2023/americas

Riodoce (n.d.) *Quienes somos. Nuestro origen*. Retrieved October 26, 2023, from https://riodoce.mx/quiene-somos/

Senovilla, J., & Moreno, J. P. (2021, January 11). *Lola Flores "resucita". Hablamos con los directores Creativos de la campaña*. Reason Why. Retrieved October 18, 2023, from www.reasonwhy.es/actualidad/entrevista-javier-senovilla-juan-pedro-moreno-creativos-campana-cruzcampo-lola-flores

United Nations (2013, December 18). *La seguridad de los periodistas y la cuestión de la impunidad*. General Assembly of the United Nations, 68/163. https://unesdoc.unesco.org/ark:/48223/pf0000232337_spa

Zhang, T. (2022). Deepfake generation and detection, a survey. *Multimedia Tools and Applications*, 81, 6259–6276. https://doi.org/10.1007/s11042-021-11733-y

CHAPTER 8

Mario Kart AI in Education: Bridging Game Design and Pedagogical Strategies

Kris Alexander and Thoreau Bakker

8.1 INTRODUCTION: WHAT IS MARIO KART AND AI

8.1.1 Defining Mario Kart Wii

Mario Kart Wii, a fast-paced racing game by Nintendo, is known for its dynamic, competitive, and sometimes infuriating gameplay. It's a Wii multiplayer racing game that adds depth and satisfaction by combining high-speed racing with whimsical, often disruptive elements. The game involves racing other drivers, either humans or artificial intelligence (AI), on Mario-themed courses. Mario Kart Wii was chosen for this study because of its advanced AI systems, which include dynamic difficulty adjustment and probability distribution. Thus, the game provides a captivating and adaptable experience that may offer educational insights.

8.1.2 Characters, Karts, and Controls

Nintendo characters in light, medium, or heavy weights affect kart acceleration, maximum velocity, and off-road prowess. Bicycles, which have different handling than karts and can accelerate faster via wheelies, are introduced in this game. Mario Kart Wii was one of the first games in the franchise to use motion controls, which gave players in-game benefits depending on their input method.

8.1.3 Strategy and Chance Integration

Mario Kart Wii's ability to blend strategy and chance makes it appealing. This chapter revolves around this balance of strategy, player skill, chance, predefined obstacles, and advantages. The balance, or game's ability to manage player engagement, depends on the items players can earn during the race. Competitors' obstacles can vary, disrupting the

DOI: 10.1201/9781003473633-8

race's flow and allowing dramatic comebacks or leader changes. This unpredictability and the game's vibrant and ever-changing environments make it appealing and repeatable (McMahan et al., 2010).

8.1.4 Difficulty and Mastery

This chapter focuses on Mario Kart Wii's engaging, easy-to-play, but challenging gameplay. Its exciting mix of speed, strategy, and Mario-inspired fantasy elements sets it apart. This video game design shows a deep understanding of competitive and casual gameplay (Kosloski & Welch, 2010).

8.1.5 Defining Artificial Intelligence (AI) in Video Games

Understanding AI in video games is crucial to situating its use in education and classroom instruction., Safadi, Fonteneau, and Ernst described the nuanced use of AIand its contextual use in video games, and how video game AI is often customized to handle complex outcomes (Safadi, et. al, 2015). In addition to emulating human intelligence, video game AI aims to engage, challenge, and inspire players to win and improve.

8.1.6 Human-like Intelligence

The word "artificial" and the idea that AI systems are human-made and human-like are typically a source of misunderstanding. The human emulation approach gives the technology the most potential because it allows for bespoke customization that could serve individuals in new ways.

8.1.7 Challenge

Gaming challenge - AI and user experience - is complex and contextual. AI can scale difficulty to match player abilities, creating a more engaging gaming experience for all skill levels (Bakkes et al., 2009). Pragmatic AI approaches favor cost-effective, custom-built solutions over academically advanced ones (Pfau et al., 2020). Many educational games focus too much on cognitive development and not enough on engagement. Looking at video game AI methodology suggests that these approaches may benefit from being motivated more by fun and involvement than by problem-solving.

8.1.8 Dynamic Difficulty Adjustment

Dynamic difficulty adjustment uses AI to quickly adapt to changing conditions for each participant. Due to their ever-changing nature, modern video games have varying degrees of adaptive AI behavior (Bakkes et al., 2009; Pfau et al., 2020). Advanced AI in game mechanics can improve player experience, as Perez-Liebana et al. (2016) demonstrate with AI game framework's broad applicability to dynamic gaming scenarios. Players and gameplay are balanced and monitored as part of the experience, a reciprocal relationship.

8.2 OVERVIEW OF AI IN MARIO KART WII

8.2.1 A Brief Analysis of AI in Mario Kart Wii

The complexities of AI in Mario Kart Wii may help balance difficulty in education. Well known for its advanced AI algorithms that enhance the dynamism and captivation of the gameplay (Ho et al., 2021) , Mario Kart Wii employs experience management and deep reinforcement learning techniques to dynamically modify the game's difficulty in response to player performance (Ruiming et al., 2018; Thue & Bulitko, 2018). This section discusses rubber banding and game item distribution algorithms.

8.2.2 Rubber Banding

In Mario Kart, rubber banding refers to a game mechanic where AI opponents adjust their speed to the player's performance, keeping the game competitive and engaging regardless of skill level. The AI can dynamically adjust Mario Kart Wii's difficulty to ensure a fair and competitive experience for players of different skill levels, known as rubber banding, according to Ho et al. (2021).

8.2.3 Items

Probability distribution is the mathematical function that calculates the odds of game outcomes in video games. Thus, it determines the odds of each game event, such as getting a certain item. Mario Kart Wii's AI-driven probability distribution customizes power-ups to the player's position. This system resembles the differentiation strategy in education, which allocates resources based on each student's learning needs (Ruiming et al., 2018). The idea is to use code to engage different player levels.

8.2.4 Dynamic Difficulty Adjustment in Mario Kart Wii

Again, we examine dynamic difficulty adjustment in Mario Kart Wii, which draws inspiration from procedural content generation and adapts the game environment to player progress. Customized player adjustments enhance unique gameplay experiences (Rietveld et al., 2014). AI like Chinese Chess uses the partially ordered set algorithm (POSM), which is applicable to many game genres and ensures a maximum of two errors before determining the optimal difficulty setting for game players (Ilici et al., 2012).

8.2.5 Character and Kart Combinations, Player Level, and Artificial Choice

In "Mario Kart Wii," character and kart selection affects gameplay because each creates unique acceleration, speed, and control (GameFAQs, 2012). In Mario Kart Wii, players can asymmetrically choose a driver and vehicle, somewhat limiting their autonomy.

8.2.6 Character and Kart Combinations

Each playable character in Mario Kart Wii is one of three weight classes: medium, light, and heavy, and kart selection has seven affordances: speed, weight, acceleration, handling, drift, off-road, and mini turbo. Players can try different driver–kart combinations to match their driving skill level at the time of game engagement. Mario Kart Wii allows for many character–kart/bike combinations, roughly 864 which come from the game's 24 playable characters and 36 vehicles (18 karts and 18 motorcycles).

8.2.7 Player Level and Artificial Choice

According to Ilici et al. (2012), this game manages player aptitude and ability using machine learning by aggregating players by performance and adjusting game difficulty. The in-game asymmetry is one of the player's main expressions in Mario Kart Wii, and the finite number of karts, though large, can give the illusion of infinite kart and player combinations, making choice artificial.

8.2.8 Probability Distribution: The Crux of Artificial Autonomy

Probability distributions are mathematical operations that calculate the odds of various experimental outcomes (Bach, 1990; Wong & Yao, 1989). This concept is crucial to theoretical physics and statistical analysis because it explains how probabilities are distributed among many possible outcomes. Video game AI relies on probability distributions for contextual decision-making (Garthwaite et al., 2005). These components allow AI algorithms to handle gaming environment unpredictability and fluctuation, enabling more authentic and flexible behavior. AI can generate unpredictable and strategic responses by accurately assessing the probability of in-game events and player behaviors using these distributions. Participants will have a more immersive and challenging experience because the AI can adapt its tactics in real time to changing probabilities of game scenarios, including player decisions and race-based contexts.

Mario Kart Wii generates items using probability distributions. For clarity, in-race items can be collected at various points during each race, along with driver–kart asymmetry (Mario Kart Wii Item Probability Distributions, 2020). These items aim to balance mechanics to keep the experience whimsical and engaging. Mario Kart Wii's in-race item generation uses probability distributions for balance and unpredictability. Twenty-six items, obtained at various points in the race, balance the race for an exciting contest.

8.2.9 Items and Probability Distributions

Mario Kart Wii's AI helps distribute powerful items to low-ranking players. This game mechanic is crucial to dynamic difficulty adjustment. The goal of this strategy is to keep everyone engaged, regardless of expertise. The AI mechanics of item probability distribution greatly impact Mario Kart Wii's gameplay. The player's rank at impact determines the probability distribution of Item Box items (Mario Kart Wii Item Probability Distributions, 2017). Lower-ranked participants, between position 5 and further, are more likely to get the Blue Shell, a powerful item designed to target the race leader. However, falling behind players are more inclined to get the Star, which grants temporary invincibility and speed acceleration. This method of allocating items displays dynamic difficulty adjustment, which adjusts game difficulty based on player progress to maintain a competitive balance and player engagement.

8.2.10 Mushrooms

The Mushroom item boosts race speed. In addition to increasing speed, the Mega Mushroom allows players to crush opponents, slowing them down and stealing their defensive options and items.

8.2.11 Bananas and Bob-ombs

Other racers lose control and speed when these dropped items connect with drivers. Players can use Bananas to deflect projectiles and protect their rear bumpers with a button. Bob-ombs detonate after a certain time or when rival karts are nearby.

8.2.12 Miscellaneous Items

This category includes the Bullet Bill, which provides high-velocity propulsion, the Star, which provides temporary invulnerability and accelerated movement, and the Blooper, which blocks enemies' sight. The POW Block's earthquake disrupts all racers (players can reduce its impact with a well-timed controller shake), and the Lightning discharge contracts and slows other competitors.

8.2.13 Shells

Shells are mostly offensive, forward- and backward-firing projectiles. Red Shells pursue the competitor ahead, while Green Shells move diagonally. The powerful Blue Spiny Shell primarily disrupts the race leader. They also protect against projectiles. This chapter will discuss items targeting the leader, which is crucial because this item is one of the most hated in Mario Kart. The probability distribution of each game item determines its utility and impact. Players may anticipate a dynamic gaming experience where they must adapt to these items' changing challenges through this game mechanic. To maintain competitive balance, items of higher potency are given to trailing players. In-game balance, differentiated instruction, and how environments can engage different users, players, and students are comparable.

8.3 ADAPTIVE LEARNING IN EDUCATION: A THEORETICAL FRAMEWORK

In the following sections, we will discuss in detail how these AI strategies from Mario Kart Wii can be applied in an educational context. Table 8.1 provides a summary of these parallels:

With this overview in mind, this section delves deeper into each of these concepts and explore how they can be implemented in educational settings.

8.3.1 Differentiated Instruction

Differentiated instruction, a unique educational theory in adaptive learning in video games, is implemented like Mario Kart Wii's ever-changing gameplay. Karimi and Nazari examined educators' understanding of differentiated instruction and participants' adaptive approaches in dynamic video game environments in 2021. Meeting students'

TABLE 8.1 Parallels between Mario Kart Wii's AI Systems and Educational Strategies

Mario Kart Wii AI system	Corresponding educational strategy	Example
Dynamic difficulty adjustment	Differentiated instruction	Adjusting the complexity of learning tasks based on students' performance
Probability distribution of items	Diversification of learning materials	Providing a variety of learning materials (e.g., text, visuals, audio) based on students' individual learning preferences
Character and kart combinations	Personalized learning paths	Allowing students to choose their learning path or focus based on their interests and strengths
Rubber banding	Adaptive learning	Adapting the learning pace and materials based on students' progress and performance

diverse needs requires constant adaptation and, similarly, Mario Kart Wii players adapt their strategies to different race scenarios and character abilities. As with player ability, the wide range and variety of student potential should be considered when creating instructional strategies, especially for materials with interactive components.

8.3.2 Teaching Integration of Theory via Practice

Pham (2012) stressed the integration of theory and practice, calling for a paradigm shift in teaching methods that separate theory and practice. In this case, instruction via practice assists in accommodating a greater number of students due to the practical and tangible characteristics of specific ideas. Mario Kart Wii's character and vehicle selection allows the player to express autonomy through limited autonomic routes. Recall that character and kart selection are limited, so the feeling of autonomy is artificial. Further, the game's mechanics can symbolize the pragmatic implementation of differentiated instruction, which encourages teachers to tailor their lessons to each student's learning needs and preferences via a wider range of methods of delivery.

8.3.3 Diverse Thinking Styles – Destination of the Artificial

Sternberg and Zhang (2005) examined differentiated instruction in 2005 using diverse thinking approaches, like Mario Kart Wii's numerous tactics. Just as players choose karts and characters, educators can tailor instruction to students' cognitive affordances, which are usually audio, text, video, and interactivity (Alexander, 2023). Humans' multimodal methods of learning can improve student engagement and learning outcomes.

8.3.4 Instructional Design for Learner Differences

Subban's (2006) research on student differences laid the groundwork for differentiated instruction in various educational settings. AI affordances can support these differences more quickly, as seen in video game difficulty data structures with visible and tangible results per experience. Mario Kart Wii's AI-generated challenges and player experiences adjust to the player's position and performance, requiring instructional variation. Subban's support for instructional variation is like Mario Kart's adaptability, emphasizing the importance of meeting students' needs. These varied cognitive requirements are often addressed by multimedia and multimedia learning theories, which focus on a variety of instructional approaches that accommodate audio, text, video, and interactivity.

8.3.5 The Foundations of Multimedia Learning

Multimedia learning theory includes educational theories that emphasize auditory and visual elements to enhance learning. This method is related to differentiated instruction, which recognizes students' diverse learning needs. Multimedia learning adapts to students' diverse abilities, interests, and needs (Brunken et al., 2003; Mayer & Moreno, 1998). It also recognizes that students learn and interpret knowledge differently, requiring a flexible and dynamic instructional method.

8.3.6 Multimedia Learning and Personalized Education

Multimedia learning meets the need for flexibility and individualized instruction. Personalized education enhances learner engagement and efficacy by tailoring experiences to individual traits (Mayer, 2002; Yilmazel-Sahin, 2009). Multimedia learning allows individualization by using multiple content delivery methods. This content design method allows instructors to deliver content in text, audio, visuals, and interactive formats to accommodate diverse learning styles and cognitive abilities. Learners' cognitive limitations should be considered when designing instructional content.

8.3.7 Split-Attention Effect in Multimedia Learning

The split-attention effect in multimedia learning shows how multiple information sources cause cognitive problems, a key component of cognitive load theory. This effect, which has been studied by Mayer and Moreno in 1998, Chandler and Sweller in 1992, and Sweller et al. in 2011, supports the idea that ineffective instructional designs that require students to mentally integrate text and diagrams create redundant cognitive load and hinder learning. In their numerical control programming study, Sweller et al. showed that physically incorporating explanatory notes with diagrams or combining discrete textual instructions reduces cognitive load and improves learning outcomes. Language learning research, including Collie et al.'s 2017 analysis of academic buoyancy – student resilience – has shown that integrated learning materials outperform split-source formats in a variety of learning domains. This research emphasizes the importance of cognitive processing-aligned instructional materials. They emphasize the importance of physically integrating or synchronizing information sources to maximize learning.

8.3.8 Dual-Process Theory and Its Limitations

Cognitive science-based dual-process theory, proposed by Kahneman and Tversky in the 1970s and expanded by others, proposes two separate but interdependent brain systems. Type 2 is deliberate, slow, and conscious, contrasting Type 1 (Evans & Stanovich, 2013; Mayer & Moreno, 1998). This framework clarifies complex behavior and decision-making. Dual-process theory may help video game AI algorithms emulate human cognition.

Type 1-like processes help AI execute strategic, premeditated actions, while type 2-like processes enable real-time gameplay dynamics by enabling reactive decision-making. AI in video games as a framework for instructional design can demonstrate innately responsive and deliberately strategic behaviors, increasing the authenticity and difficulty of the participant's experience. Dual-process theory has influenced cognitive psychology but has been criticized. These include the inconsistent alignment of proposed attribute groups, multiple and often ambiguous definitions, and the ongoing debate over whether cognitive processes are discrete or continuum (Evans & Stanovich, 2013). Critics also question the importance of dual-process models, arguing that single-process accounts can explain identical phenomena, and question the evidence for dual processing. Despite these criticisms, dual-process theory can help video game developers develop AI that can mimic human decision-making by balancing instinctive, instantaneous reactions, and strategic deliberation.

8.4 APPLICABILITY ACROSS EDUCATIONAL LEVELS

In higher education, Mario Kart Wii's dynamic difficulty adjustment and probability distributions provide a compelling model for applying AI's adaptability in classroom and instructional design and using generative AI in academic settings. Higher education can use generative AI to customize learning and meet student needs by emulating AI.

8.4.1 Dynamic Difficulty Adjustment and Diverse Approaches to Learning

The dynamic difficulty adjustment in Mario Kart Wii offers a new perspective on how post-secondary education can use contextual and varied instruction and evaluation methods. Recent tools like generative AI allow for more personalized instruction (World Economic Forum, 2024). To examine the nuance of difficulty in an educational experience, context must be considered, and context-specific pedagogy created beyond the traditional "chalk and talk" or "sage on the stage" approaches common in post-secondary education. Personalized feedback and progress monitoring in schools can help connect with and serve disabled students (Martiniello et al., 2021).

8.4.2 Dynamic Difficulty Adjustment in Online Instruction

Dynamic difficulty adjustment, inspired by Mario Kart Wii, can boost post-secondary student engagement and performance. In online instruction, allowing students to interact with instructors via chat, microphone, video feed, and even integrated social media platforms like Twitch allows students with different levels of classroom comfort to engage with subject matter and subject matter expertise in multiple ways. Dynamic difficulty adjustment in student engagement is the example, but this can also apply to course materials, management, and pedagogy. To implement dynamic difficulty adjustment in the classroom, student performance must be evaluated and learning materials and activities modified. Students who quickly grasp concepts may be given harder assignments or encouraged to study other subjects. Students who need more time may be given simpler tasks or more help. Similarly, probability distributions can be used to increase the variety of learning materials and activities to suit different learning styles. Some students learn better from visuals, others from auditory, and others from text. An AI system can evaluate student performance and preferences to adjust the distribution of these learning materials to give each student the best learning experience. AI-inspired strategies can be effective in online learning environments, where digital tools allow seamless integration and flexible adjustment of learning materials.

8.4.3 Difficulties with Dynamic Difficulty

There are some instructors who may feel uncomfortable with the necessary tools for the aforementioned, however, the integration of these approaches should be of utmost importance now, given that so many competitor institutions, such as Master Class,[1] an online platform taught by industry professionals in varying disciplines; Section School,[2] an online MBA-level platform with high-quality production content; and Thinkific,[3] an online platform where technologically competent creatives can create and individually sell courses, all pose a considerable risk to institutions who are not able to learn the approaches and technological tools to enhance both traditional and online instruction. The aforementioned areas all offer in-browser learning management systems, progress tracking, and tailored individualized feedback at scale, which is something that is rare in traditional post-secondary education. It is important to note that this approach requires thoughtful deliberation as well as a particular level of technological willingness, that is, the desire to work with the tools – watching online tutorials, visiting community forums, and attempting to implement new approaches, to build a structure that is repeatable, updatable, and contextually relevant with each iteration.

8.4.4 Probability Distribution, Diverse Learning Content and Materials

Mario Kart Wii's probability distribution mechanics might enhance higher education multimedia learning through careful implementation. By replicating Mario Kart Wii's dynamic and interactive materials, education can adjust academic material's complexity to students' comprehension levels. This method can facilitate intuitive and visual learning, which are essential for inclusive education. Universal strategies like AI-based assessment and real-time teaching method adjustments, inspired by video games' interactive nature and online streaming cultures, can be implemented across all educational levels. Mimicking Mario Kart Wii's interactive, visual, and auditory elements in academic settings can improve learning by emphasizing learner autonomy and involvement.

8.4.5 Probability Distribution and Multimedia Learning

Mario Kart Wii's probability distribution approach can be used to create engaging and varied educational multimedia instructional materials. This idea connects to the multimodal learning approach to incorporate auditory and visual components into higher education, increasing student engagement and comprehension. Online education can use

---

1 www.masterclass.com/
2 www.sectionschool.com
3 www.thinkific.com/

interactive and multimodal environments like Mario Kart Wii, which have algorithmic goals that make learning more engaging and motivating. This method emphasizes adapting instructional approaches to different learning styles using contextualized AI and interactive video games to optimize and personalize learning.

8.4.6 Problems with Probability Distribution

Some instructors may argue that multimedia in instructional design isn't necessary or relevant, but with the cost of education rising over 1,200% since 1980 (Bhutada, 2021), there will be questions about the quality of instructional design and online content, especially since many organizations are pivoting toward online learning, and Epic Games is offering educational material. Google, among others, offers free full-online data analytics courses that guarantee a $74,000 starting salary (Coursera, 2023). With over half of graduates unemployed in their field, more questions are being asked about the value of postsecondary education (Intelligent, 2022). Additionally, thousands of free YouTube videos can teach how to improve online learning and instruction with step-by-step instructions to engage audiences like video games have for decades. These videos require dedication and a willingness to improve pedagogy and delivery.

8.5 CONCLUSION

This chapter emphasizes the unique relevance of Mario Kart Wii's AI systems to higher education instruction, focusing on their dynamic difficulty adjustment and probability distributions. These game mechanics provide a compelling framework for creating adaptive and dynamic learning environments for learners of all levels. Replicating these AI systems allows for accessible, adaptable, and approachable educational strategies, which are essential for effective education. The correlation between game AI systems and educational approaches shows that AI algorithms can customize learning experiences for each learner. This method emphasizes the importance of using multiple sensory modalities in the classroom to improve cognition and learning, consistent with multimedia learning theory, multimodal learning, and learner engagement. AI in education has promising prospects but also challenges. They include educators' technological skills, educational-specific AI tools, and AI's ethical implications in education.

The practical application of these AI methodologies across academic environments and their impact on student performance requires further study. Additionally, educational AI instruments via video game mechanics may be a promising research area, given the over three-decade long sample pool for effective engagement. Forward thinking educators show the potential to engage with video game AI's potential to analyze and improve pedagogical approaches in a digital, dynamic, and diverse classroom instruction.

REFERENCES

Alexander, K. (2023). *Kris Alexander: How video games can level up the way you learn | TED Talk.* www.ted.com/talks/kris_alexander_how_video_games_can_level_up_the_way_you_learn

Bach, A. (1990). Boltzmann's probability distribution of 1877. *Archive for History of Exact Sciences, 41*(1), 1–40.

Bakkes, S., Spronck, P., & van den Herik, J. (2009). Rapid and reliable adaptation of video game AI. *IEEE Transactions on Computational Intelligence and AI in Games*, *1*(2), 93–104. https://doi.org/10.1109/TCIAIG.2009.2029084

Bhutada, G. (2021, February 3). *The rising cost of college in the U.S.* Visual Capitalist. www.visualcapitalist.com/rising-cost-of-college-in-u-s/

Brunken, R., Plass, J. L., & Leutner, D. (2003). Direct measurement of cognitive load in multimedia learning. *Educational Psychologist*, *38*(1), 53–61. https://doi.org/10.1207/S15326985EP3801_7

Chandler, P., & Sweller, J. (1992). The split-attention effect as a factor in the design of instruction. *British Journal of Educational Psychology*, *62*(2), 233–246. https://doi.org/10.1111/j.2044-8279.1992.tb01017.x

Evans, J. St. B. T., & Stanovich, K. E. (2013). Dual-process theories of higher cognition: Advancing the debate. *Perspectives on Psychological Science*, *8*(3), 223–241. https://doi.org/10.1177/1745691612460685

Garthwaite, P. H., Kadane, J. B., & O'Hagan, A. (2005). Statistical methods for eliciting probability distributions. *Journal of the American Statistical Association*, *100*(470), 680–701. https://doi.org/10.1198/016214505000000105

Google Data Analytics. (2024). Coursera. https://www.coursera.org/professional-certificates/google-data-analytics?

Ho, H., Ramesh, V., & Montano, E. T. (2021). *NeuralKart: A real-time Mario Kart 64 AI*. https://github.com/rameshvarun/NeuralKart

Ilici, L., Wang, J., Missura, O., & Gärtner, T. (2012). Dynamic difficulty for checkers and Chinese chess. *2012 IEEE Conference on Computational Intelligence and Games (CIG)*, 55–62. https://doi.org/10.1109/CIG.2012.6374138

Intelligent. (2022). *1 in 7 College grads earn less than the poverty threshold*. Intelligent. www.intelligent.com/1-in-7-college-grads-earn-less-than-the-poverty-threshold/

Kosloski, A. E., & Welch, B. K. (2010). Confronting student prejudice with "Mario Kart" Nintendo Wii. *Social Thought & Research*, *31*, 79–87.

Mario Kart Wii item probability distributions. (2017). Super Mario Wiki. www.mariowiki.com/Mario_Kart_Wii_item_probability_distributions

Mario Kart Wii—Guide and Walkthrough—Wii—By Crazyreyn—GameFAQs. (2012.). https://gamefaqs.gamespot.com/wii/942008-mario-kart-wii/faqs/52407

Martiniello, N., Asuncion, J., Fichten, C., Jorgensen, M., Havel, A., Harvison, M., Legault, A., Lussier, A., & Vo, C. (2021). Artificial intelligence for students in postsecondary education: A world of opportunity. *AI Matters*, *6*(3), 17–29. https://doi.org/10.1145/3446243.3446250

Mayer, R. E., & Moreno, R. (1998). *A split-attention effect in multimedia learning: Evidence for dual processing systems in working memory*. American Psychological Association, Inc., Santa Barbara.

McMahan, R. P., Alon, A. J. D., Lazem, S., Beaton, R. J., Machaj, D., Schaefer, M., Silva, M. G., Leal, A., Hagan, R., & Bowman, D. A. (2010). Evaluating natural interaction techniques in video games. *2010 IEEE Symposium on 3D User Interfaces (3DUI)*, 11–14. https://doi.org/10.1109/3DUI.2010.5444727

Perez-Liebana, D., Samothrakis, S., Togelius, J., Schaul, T., & Lucas, S. (2016). General video game AI: Competition, challenges and opportunities. *Proceedings of the AAAI Conference on Artificial Intelligence*, *30*(1), Article 1. https://doi.org/10.1609/aaai.v30i1.9869

Pfau, J., Smeddinck, J. D., & Malaka, R. (2020). The case for usable AI: What industry professionals make of academic AI in video games. *Extended Abstracts of the 2020 Annual Symposium on Computer-Human Interaction in Play*, 330–334. https://doi.org/10.1145/3383668.3419905

Pham, H. L. (2012). Differentiated instruction and the need to integrate teaching and practice. *Journal of College Teaching & Learning (TLC)*, *9*(1), Article 1. https://doi.org/10.19030/tlc.v9i1.6710

Rietveld, A., Bakkes, S., & Roijers, D. (2014). Circuit-adaptive challenge balancing in racing games. *2014 IEEE Games Media Entertainment*, 1–8. https://doi.org/10.1109/GEM.2014.7048075

Ruiming, Z., Chengju, L., & Qijun, C. (2018). End-to-end control of Kart agent with deep reinforcement learning. *2018 IEEE International Conference on Robotics and Biomimetics (ROBIO)*, 1688–1693. https://doi.org/10.1109/ROBIO.2018.8665334

Safadi, F., Fonteneau, R., & Ernst, D. (2015). Artificial intelligence in video games: towards a unified framework. *International Journal of Computer Games Technology*, *2015*, e271296. https://doi.org/10.1155/2015/271296

Sternberg, R. J., & Zhang, L. (2005). Styles of thinking as a basis of differentiated instruction. *Theory into Practice*, *44*(3), 245–253. https://doi.org/10.1207/s15430421tip4403_9

Subban, P. (2006). Differentiated instruction: A research basis. *International Education Journal*, *7*(7), 935–947.

Sweller, J., Ayres, P., & Kalyuga, S. (2011). The split-attention effect. In J. Sweller, P. Ayres, & S. Kalyuga (Eds.), *Cognitive load theory* (pp. 111–128). Springer, New York. https://doi.org/10.1007/978-1-4419-8126-4_9

Thue, D., & Bulitko, V. (2018). Toward a unified understanding of experience management. *Proceedings of the AAAI Conference on Artificial Intelligence and Interactive Digital Entertainment*, *14*(1), 130–136. https://doi.org/10.1609/aiide.v14i1.13029

Wong, S. K. M., & Yao, Y. Y. (1989). A probability distribution model for information retrieval. *Information Processing & Management*, *25*(1), 39–53. https://doi.org/10.1016/0306-4573(89)90090-3

World Economic Forum. *Shaping the Future of Learning: The Role of AI in Education 4.0.* (2024). https://www.weforum.org/publications/shaping-the-future-of-learning-the-role-of-ai-in-education-4-0/

Yilmazel-Sahin, Y. (2009). A comparison of graduate and undergraduate teacher education students' perceptions of their instructors' use of Microsoft PowerPoint. *Technology, Pedagogy and Education*, *18*(3), 361–380. https://doi.org/10.1080/14759390903335866

CHAPTER 9

AI and the Human Need for Emotional Connection

Antonio Díaz-Lucena and Pilar Vicente-Fernández

9.1 INTRODUCTION

An initial approach to the society of the first quarter of the 21st century outlines a media scenario dominated by the undisputed prominence of information and communication technology (ICT) and their tools (Cabrero Almenara & Ruiz-Palmero, 2018; Padilla de la Torre & Patiño López, 2020). Diachronically, its amplification of use, ramification, and development stands out, at the same time as an evolution "from mere reception, information and storage to the transformation of what has been received to generate new knowledge: information and knowledge management" (Grande et al., 2016, p. 227). Thus, the context of the so-called information society presents a digitised social and cultural environment characterised, among others, by factors such as hyperconnectivity, interactivity, and immediacy, which condition the relationships between the different social agents. Added to these are the overabundance of information, the eagerness to share experiences, and the hybridisation of media, supports, and formats, qualities that recognise the levels of significance of all the actors involved in communication (Jáuregui Caballero & Ortega Ponce, 2020). ICT is, as Bishwas (2019) points out, crucial to all facets of contemporary civilisation, to the point of modifying the foundations of social relations.

In this context, the forms of expression derived from Web 2.0 and the challenge of sharing content through digital platforms grant the figure of the receiver in the current communication process an unusual sovereignty. As a consequence of the democratisation of digital devices and the participatory culture brought about by ICT (Casemajor et al., 2021; Vizcaíno Verdú et al., 2021), today the receiver stands as a prosumer, creator, and disseminator of communicative content of various kinds (Bartosik-Purgat & Bednarz, 2021), with an impact on users' everyday experiences (Pybus, 2013). Their active condition through the

DOI: 10.1201/9781003473633-9

generation of information and the production of content makes this fact, as some authors point out, the most significant trend since the industrial revolution (Jordán et al., 2017).

The role of the figure of the receiver in current communication processes, transformed into a conversational and continuous model that transcends bidirectionality, leads to the prevalence of a culture of emotions as a distinctive feature of the radiography of today's society. Its research as an object of study is based on the idea held by cognitivists, sociologists, and anthropologists, who consider that emotions and feelings are socially constructed and that their modes of expression vary socially and culturally (Bolaños Florido, 2016). From this point of view, the entertainment and distractive nature of the digital sphere favours this circumstance, as these emotions are conceived as social phenomena: one of the main functions of emotion is to align relationships between people, who find in social networks a fruitful way of manifesting and exploding their feelings (van der Löwe & Parkinson, 2014). While in previous historical periods "the affective dimension of the person was usually displaced to a secondary plane and confined to the private sphere" (Serrano-Puche, 2016, p. 20), today's society is increasingly emotional (Cerulo & Scribano, 2021), and academics and researchers are also aware of this fact, because from 2001 to 2020, the number of publications on this subject has increased by 778% (Digital Science, 2018). Today, individuals demand an emotional connection to their surroundings because it helps them to give meaning to their existence (Deonna & Teroni, 2012). Experts in intelligence and health affirm that the 21st century is the time of emotions; in this sense, the results of Serrano-Puche's (2016) research in this regard point out how the Web "not only awakens emotions in its users and serves as a channel for the expression of affection, but also influences the way in which this affection is modulated and deployed" (p. 19), which has an impact on the configuration of the person's identity.

Based on this reality, the transcendence of sentimental discourse stands out in fields as diverse as politics, advertising, and journalism, among others, which tend towards personalisation, individualism, and the storytelling format (Hermann-Acosta, 2020) as techniques and stories through which to connect emotionally with voters, consumers, and readers, respectively. In particular, the debate on the use of emotional persuasion in ideological discourses (Cala Siria, 2019) evidences the relevance of the emotional and sentimental dimension in this sphere of communication. In the commercial sphere, the current media ecosystem leads brands to consider the problem of user participation in the construction and reputation of brands, with the consequent loss of control that this entails in the configuration of messages (Fernández-Hernández et al., 2021). Journalistically, the relationship between the media and their audience is being redefined, as the active involvement of the public in the creation and dissemination of news through social networks fosters phenomena such as disinformation and fake news, which are major challenges for journalistic practice today (Carson & Gibbons, 2023). Their impact is such that the use of technology, digital platforms, and new narratives rethinks the foundations of the conception of current democracy from a multidisciplinary approach (Giusti & Piras, 2021).

Consequently, we are witnessing a trend towards the polarisation of public opinion and the deterioration of democratic quality, where algorithms play a decisive role in "directing and orchestrating public opinion" (García-Marín & Serrano-Contreras, 2023, p. 61). Hence, there is a growing need for systematic measurements and interpretations of online polarisation (Phillips & Carley, 2023). In addition, infotainment converted into pure spectacle is a marked trend in the current information framework: content is increasingly intended to be entertaining in order to arouse the curiosity of the receiver, blurring the boundaries between information and entertainment and giving rise to a popular culture around programmes and media (Aguilera, 2019). In addition, the narrative is repositioned from traditional media formats towards more pleasurable genres and the opportunities offered by pop culture and social networks (Serazio, 2018). For its part, the trend towards pure spectacle as a journalistic criterion is emerging, with images tinged with emotivism and drama that condition the informative treatment of the news (Serrano Ojeda & Solano Altaba, 2021). This hybridisation is marked by the demand of an audience that seeks emotions in the content it consumes.

9.2 OBJECTIVES AND METHODOLOGY

The main objective of this research is to analyse the effect of AI in the short and medium term, taking into consideration that human beings today are more attracted to anything that provides them with an emotional bond. Thus, some research questions arise: Has AI come at the right time? Are citizens aware of this change? Is AI going to occupy the referential and denotative space that human beings seem to be abandoning? What social and behavioural changes could be triggered in the short and medium term?

In order to address this research, a mixed approach has been applied, combining quantitative data with information collected through qualitative techniques. The former will help to determine the increase in content published in recent years on this subject, as well as the level of curiosity of Internet users by quantifying their searches and interactions on the Internet and on certain social networks, such as Facebook and Instagram. To do this, the following tools were used: Semrush (crawls words on the Internet), dimensions.ai (computes the categorised publications on the Internet in the most important databases), and CrowdTangle (META software that extracts data on Facebook and Instagram). From a qualitative approach, information was collected from professionals working with AI by means of a questionnaire sent by email in November 2023. The questions asked were as follows: (1) Particularly in your line of business, explain what specific use you make of artificial intelligence (AI) and why you have decided to invest in it?; (2) According to your knowledge, impressions, and experience in the sector, in the short and medium term, what percentage of weight is AI going to have in your work?; (3) What do you think we are going to lose quickly beyond a possible reduction of manual tasks due to automation?; (4) Following on from the previous thought, what do you think AI will enhance or what rules or habits might change in the short to medium term in your line of business and in society?; (5) Has AI come at the right time?; (6) You can write in this section what perhaps has been left undeveloped or provide any kind of impression or reflection on AI and its development in society.

Respondents:

Entertainment field: Xabier Iglesias (cofounder of Mementum Tech Entertainment)
Psychology and Computing Field: Raúl Arrabales (CEO and founder of Psicobótica)
Journalism Field: Carlos Serrano (social media manager, ElEconomista.es)
Marketing Field: Ana Reyes-Menéndez (professor at the Rey Juan Carlos University specialising in digital marketing, neuromarketing and artificial intelligence)

9.3 QUANTITATIVE RESULTS

The online marketing application Semrush has allowed us to know that there are more than two billion urls on the Internet that have used the word "artificial intelligence" at some point in the English language. Similarly, following the 2023 Databricks Lakehouse report, the number of companies that have started using SaaS LLM (Software-as-a-Service based on Large Language Models) since the release of ChatGPT has increased by 1,310% (from November 2022 to the beginning of May 2023). Moreover, due to this scenario, companies are putting new models into production, which, compared with the previous year, have grown by 411%.

Regarding publications related to AI, the Dimensions.ai programme has located a total of 3,214,594 publications on AI since the beginning of the 20th century, including articles, book chapters, proceedings, preprints, books, and monographs. Almost a third of them have been published between 2022 and 2024.

Similarly, the Google Trends system that measures the level of interest in topics based on searches made on Google has provided exponential growth since 30 November 2022, the date of ChatGPT's market launch. While Google Trends does not give an exact figure or percentage, it does show that interest in this field is at an all-time high. To get even closer to a percentage figure, the number of posts and audience reactions on two global social networks (Facebook and Instagram) have been measured by searching for the word "artificial intelligence" in English only. The information given further was obtained using the META CrowdTangle tool. For this purpose, two searches were carried out to find the percentage growth of this topic since the launch of ChatGPT on the market. Thus, the first search focused on the period from 25 November 2021 to 30 November 2022, and the second from 30 November 2022 to 25 November 2023. On Facebook, in the first period, which covers one year, 165,294 messages were found that generated 16,432,866 audience interactions on those messages. In the second period, which covers the time of ChatGPT's launch, 378,185 messages were found, generating 39,909,395 audience interactions. In just one year, content referring to this topic has increased by 129% and audience reactions to it have risen by 143%. On Instagram, in the first period, 33,998 posts were published, generating 36,144,373 interactions. And, in the last year, 64,950 posts have generated 110,873,978 user interactions. Its increase in publications has been 91%

and audience reactions have grown by 206%. Although there is a big difference between these two social networks, if we look at user participation in the content published – data that could give way to another possible investigation if we focus on the curiosity that this subject arouses among younger age groups – in both cases the figures obtained are significant, as they ratify the social impact that the subject of AI is achieving.

9.4 QUALITATIVE RESULTS

All the professionals questioned stated that they use AI in their respective lines of business and that, in one way or another, this tool is fully integrated into some of their processes. However, there are differences among them, mainly due to the field of their work, the products they develop, or the size of their businesses. Raúl Arrabales (CEO and founder of Psicobótica) has launched a start-up dedicated to creating assistants or "bots" aimed towards mental health to promote the emotional well-being of the individual. He argues that these "can provide everything from support when suffering episodes of anxiety to function as job interview simulators to adequately prepare the candidate". In this case, the weight of AI in his work is 100%. Xabier Iglesias (cofounder of Mementum Tech Entertainment) creates entertainment content, and much of the technology they use for this is Generative AI. He believes that its weight will grow in this sector. Similarly, Carlos Serrano (director of business development and innovation at elEconomista.es) warns that they have started to work with AI in journalism, albeit occasionally. The tasks they are developing with AI are: "image generation or image adaptation and editing, although very occasionally. In addition, we use AI for the recirculation of users and content". Ana Reyes-Menéndez (professor at the Rey Juan Carlos University specialising in digital marketing, neuromarketing, and artificial intelligence) is a teacher but also works as a consultant to companies on AI in social networks. Ana recognises the work that AI is doing in digital marketing, especially in the task of extracting and analysing the traces that Internet users are leaving on the Internet, because without it many of the strategies that are working today could not be executed.

To the extent that these new tools are consolidated in jobs and in our lives, there will undoubtedly be visible changes, beyond the possible elimination of tasks that will be managed by an AI or new more specialised positions that will come on the market. These changes will also focus on modifying our habits or behaviours. In the entertainment sector, Xabier Iglesias bets in the short term on a loss of originality in creations but also of time for reflection to make them different from one another. However, he affirms that in the long term "human creativity and 'craftsmanship' will make a strong comeback, as they will be valued by the market". Likewise, he is convinced that the most arduous tasks will always be performed by AI, and at this point he confirms that there is no turning back. Raúl Arrabales, as a computer engineer and psychologist, affirms that "in the future very few tasks that can be automated can be done efficiently without using AI, because machines are more effective in calculation". Along the same lines, Ana Reyes-Menéndez confirms that tasks will be automated and specialised, and the most creative ones will be developed by humans, because "they are the ones that only we will be able to do and that require more creative thinking". Carlos Serrano comments that he sees a parallel between AI and the arrival of the computer, since at the beginning it took on the most arduous tasks and reduced work times. He also points out that AI will bring more options such as simplifying and concentrating processes: "You can now create websites almost from an image, correct code, generate images, and so on and so forth. In addition, a single person can be an editor, programmer, writer, photographer, etc.". Likewise, both Carlos and Xabier emphasise the adaptation period is about to come in which we are going to see uncomfortable moments of impersonation and exact replicas of reality that will dynamite the control mechanisms on the veracity of the content; a scenario that will end up being regulated because a solution will be found.

In the introduction to this chapter, we have explained the preferences and the changes in our societies regarding the consumption of messages and discourses where emotions have a strong presence. Much literature has been published, and audiovisual productions released in the last two decades, that focus on the theme of learning to express oneself with emotions, to show your "real self", or to understand existence from an emotional connection with what surrounds us. In the same way, many consumer objects in our everyday life have been created following these values and ideas. Consequently, a more denotative and quantifiable reading of existence seems to be being banished. Has AI arrived at the right time for us? The 21st century human being connects faster with more subjective, and therefore emotional discourses and messages, because they generate a dialectic with the conversion of reality into pure spectacle, a fertile ground for creativity. However, on this aspect, Xabier Iglesias adds, in relation to the use of AI to create content, that "AI will do what a human instructs, so creativity at all times will remain human". In the field of journalism, Carlos Serrano believes that nothing is accidental and that if it has been given more visibility now, it is a response to profound changes that will come in a short space of time. Similarly, he agrees with Xabier when he explains that in journalism "we are beginning to place more value on that which is beyond the reach of AI, such as: sources, exclusive data, breaking news or in-depth knowledge of causes and consequences". Ana Reyes-Menéndez aligns herself with both, emphasising the opportunity we are going to have to specialise in what we can only do ourselves. Raúl Arrabales first points out that AI has been with us developing for more than 30 years, but now we are witnessing a "democratisation of conversational AI for the ordinary citizen, something that had already happened for other types of AI, such as Google Maps or Waze route calculation". The launch of ChatGPT in 2022 has been a turning point in this process because it has generated public opinion. According to Arrabales, the irruption of AI should not numb the current human being, but motivate him to "raise the intellectual level of his tasks. AI is raising the level of what is automated, so that humans only take care of what cannot yet be automated".

In the free text section, Ana Reyes-Menéndez highlights the importance of the development of AI and therefore the need to "be regulated by institutions that specifically know the dangers and advantages of these technologies so that they look after the interests of society and humanity". Xabier Iglesias reminds us that the motto of his projects is "Creativity in the Loop", that is creativity is where the difference can be made. And finally, Raúl Arrabales is convinced that our evolution is heading towards a hybrid society that will interrelate artificial and biological minds: "There are no longer two parallel evolutionary paths, but all minds, whatever their origin, are part of the same destiny. The human augmented by AI and the AI augmented by humans" (Arrabales Moreno, 2023).

9.5 CONCLUSIONS

The past decade began a countdown in AI development (Dean, 2022) that has brought the launch of ChatGPT by the end of 2022. Although, in specialised fields, working with AI was ordinary and commonplace, it has not been until the visibility given by the OpenAI product that society has started to generate opinion about it and demonstrate its curiosity and awareness about a topic that is possibly going to change its existence.

A parallel can be drawn between the increase in curiosity that AI is arousing in society and the search for self-knowledge that human beings are currently showing by understanding their existence through an emotional link with what surrounds them. In this sense, emotions are what distinguish us today from machines. So, are human beings finding out what it is that differentiates them from the new intelligences that are emerging? Everything suggests that every day we are becoming more aware of what we can do better and why we need to establish emotional connection.

REFERENCES

Aguilera García, I. C. (2019). The culture of television humour: Spanish infotainment from its usefulness to audiences. *Zer, 24*(47), 31–50. https://doi.org/10.1387/zer.20705

Arrabales Moreno, R. (2023). *The mental disorders of Artificial Intelligence: Artificial Intelligence explained from its mental problems and cases of failure*. Psicobótica Books.

Bartosik-Purgat, M., & Bednarz, J. (2021). The usage of new media tools in prosumer activities – a corporate perspective. *Technology Analysis & Strategic Management, 33*(4), 453–464. https://doi.org/10.1080/09537325.2020.1820475

Bishwas, K. (2019). Impact of ICT on the various grounds of the society. *Webology, 16*(1), 261–265. www.webology.org/abstract.php?id=4494

Bolaños Florido, L. P. (2016). The socio-historical study of emotions and feelings in 20th Century Social Sciences. *Revista de Estudios Sociales*, (55), 178–191. https://journals.openedition.org/revestudsoc/9762

Cabrero Almenara, J., & Ruiz-Palmero, J. (2018). Technologies of information and communication for inclusion: Reformulating the "digital gap". *International Journal of Educational Research and Innovation*, (9), 16–30. www.upo.es/revistas/index.php/IJERI/article/view/2665

Cala Siria, R. (2019). Emotion and reason in the construction of political discourse: The case of the proclamation of the unrecognized Catalan Republic in October 2017. *Estudios de lingüística del español, 40*, 95–115. https://raco.cat/index.php/Elies/article/view/363492

Carson, A., & Gibbons, A. (2023). The Big Chill? How journalists and sources perceive and respond to fake news laws in Indonesia and Singapore. *Journalism Studies, 24*(14), 1819–1838. https://doi.org/10.1080/1461670X.2023.2192299

Casemajor, N., Bellavance, G., & Sirois, G. (2021). Cultural participation in digital environments: Goals and stakes for Quebec cultural policies. *International Journal of Cultural Policy, 27*(5), 650–666. https://doi.org/10.1080/10286632.2020.1825403

Cerulo, M., & Scribano, A. (Eds.) (2021). *The emotions in the classics of sociology. A study in Social Theory*. Routledge.

Dean, J. (2022). A golden decade of deep learning: computing systems & applications. *Daedalus, 151*(2), 58–74. https://doi.org/10.1162/daed_a_01900

Deonna, J. A., & Teroni, F. (2012). *The emotions. A philosophical introduction*. Routledge.

Digital Science. (2018–) Dimensions [Software]. Available from https://app.dimensions.ai. Accessed on November 2023, under licence agreement.

Fernández-Hernández, R., Vacas-Guerrero, T., & García-Muiña, F. E. (2021). Online reputation and user engagement as strategic resources of museums. *Museum Management and Curatorship, 36*(6), 553–568. https://doi.org/10.1080/09647775.2020.1803114

García-Marín, J., & Serrano-Contreras, I. J. (2023). (Un)founded fear towards the algorithm: YouTube recommendations and polarisation. *Comunicar. Revista científica de Comunicación y Educación*, (74), 61–70. https://doi.org/10.3916/C74-2023-05

Giusti, S., & Piras, E. (Eds.) (2021). *Democracy and fake news. Information manipulation and post-truth politics*. Routledge.

Grande, M., Cañón, R., & Cantón, I. (2016). ICT: concept evolution and attributes. *International Journal of Educational Research and Innovation*, (6), 218–230. www.upo.es/revistas/index.php/IJERI/article/view/1703

Hermann-Acosta, A. (2020). Storytelling and multidirectional communication: A formative strategy for the digital age. *URU – Revista de Comunicación y Cultura*, (3), 29–42. https://doi.org/10.32719/26312514.2020.3.3

Jáuregui Caballero, A., & Ortega Ponce, C. (2020). Transmedia storytelling in the social appropriation of knowledge. *Revista Latina de Comunicación Social*, (77), 357–372. www.doi.org/10.4185/RLCS-2020-1462

Jordán Correa, D., Arias Valladolid, C., & Samaniego Rivas, G. (2017). The participation of the prosumer in the new era of communication. *INNOVA Research Journal, 2*(11), 179–185. http://doi.org/10.33890/innova.v2.n11.2017.556

Padilla de la Torre, M. R., & Patiño López, M. E. (2020). Information and Communication Technologies for social development: A methodological proposal. *PAAKAT: Revista de Tecnología y Sociedad, 10*(18). http://doi.org/10.32870/Pk.a10n18.432

Phillips, S. C., & Carley, K. M. (2023). An organizational form framework to measure and interpret online polarization. *Information, Communication & Society*. https://doi.org/10.1080/1369118X.2023.2240580

Pybus, J. (2013). Social networks and cultural workers: Towards an archive for the prosumer. *Journal of Cultural Economy, 6*(2), 137–152. https://doi.org/10.1080/17530350.2012.742850

Serazio, M. (2018). Producing popular politics: The infotainment strategies of American Campaign Consultants. *Journal of Broadcasting & Electronic Media, 62*(1), 131–146. https://doi.org/10.1080/08838151.2017.1402901

Serrano Ojeda, J. F., & Solano Altaba, M. (2021). The tendency to spectacularization as journalistic criterion: The case of refugees. *Araucaria, 23*(48), 535–549. https://doi.org/10.12795/araucaria.2021.i48.24

Serrano-Puche, J. (2016). Internet and emotions: New trends in an emerging field of research. *Comunicar. Revista científica de Comunicación y Educación*, (46), 19–26. https://doi.org/10.3916/C46-2016-02

van der Löwe, I., & Parkinson, B. (2014). Relational emotions and social networks. In C. von Scheve & M. Salmela (Eds.), *Collective emotions* (pp. 125–140). Oxford Academic. https://doi.org/10.1093/acprof:oso/9780199659180.003.0009

Vizcaíno Verdú, A., Bonilla del Río, M., & Ibarra Rius, M. (Coord.). (2021). *Participatory culture, fandom, and emergent narratives in social networks*. Dykinson. https://n9.cl/v1yc5

CHAPTER 10

Use of Artificial Intelligence Tools in Communication Companies: Advantages and Disadvantages in the Sector

Alba-María Martinez-Sala, Juan Monserrat-Gauchi, and Carmen Quiles-Soler

10.1 INTRODUCTION

Artificial intelligence (AI) has been present in an invisible and inaccessible way to society at large. It was finally in 2014 when for the first time an AI managed to pass the Turing test. This AI, dubbed "Eugene Goostman", mimicked the language and intelligence of a 13-year-old boy, and judges were unable to detect whether the respondent was a machine or a human. The first step took from 1950 to 2014, but the second transition took only 8 years, since it was in 2022 when the famous ChatGPT appeared (Gómez-Prieto, 2023).

No-code platforms have contributed to the remarkable development of applications that make AI accessible to all users, which has come to be known as the democratisation of AI (Kamelli, 2023). Thanks to these platforms, people with no knowledge in the field of computer science and programming can create things whose creation used to be impossible for non-technical users. Therefore, it can be argued that no-code technology makes AI accessible to everyone.

Currently, AI is undergoing its first phase, known as artificial narrow intelligence (ANI), which is below human intelligence. The next phase is artificial general intelligence (AGI), which is supposed to be at the same level as human intelligence, while the last phase in the development of AI is called artificial super intelligence (ASI), which is expected to be above human capabilities (Trabado, 2023). Therefore, in the current initial phase of AI, the tools developed and made available to society are perfectly controllable

DOI: 10.1201/9781003473633-10

by humans, and although they are expected to start a revolution in the labour sector in general (Belhadi et al., 2022; Nica et al., 2022), this study focuses on the analysis of how AI will affect, specifically, the advertising and communication sectors.

10.1.1 AI Tools Applicable in Commercial Communication

This section examines a series of no-code AI-powered applications that could revolutionise the world of communication and advertising. These tools facilitate (accelerate) the work processes of multiple professionals given that there is an automation of writing or production tasks, among others (Túñez-López, Toural-Bran, & Cacheiro-Requeijo, 2018), as they can perform human work in much less time, which may lead communication organisations to reduce their human workforce. However, as mentioned, most consulted experts affirm that AI will not replace professionals in any case, at least for the time being. AI tools will streamline human work and creation processes, but their results will need to be monitored by communication professionals. Although the literature has mainly focused on journalism (Canavilhas, 2022; De Lara, García-Avilés, & Arias-Robles, 2022; González-Arias & López-García, 2023; Gutiérrez-Caneda, Vázquez-Herrero, & López-García, 2023; Lopezosa et al., 2023, Sánchez-García et al., 2023), the impact of AI on advertising, its processes, and professionals, must come to the forefront for three fundamental reasons (Martínez, Aguado, & Sánchez, 2022):

- Because of the transformation of the business model in which both traditional and digital media coexist.
- Because of the technological change driven by advertising before that of other conventional communication systems.
- Because of the importance of privacy protection.

Three types of AI tools can revolutionise the professional communication sector: (1) tools for the development of text and language, (2) tools for the generation of still images (graphics), and (3) tools for the development of moving images (audiovisual). The current levels of development and refinement of these three types of no-code AI tools are progressive: text and language tools are quite advanced and perfected, while image-generation (graphics) tools are still in a phase of perfection, and video generation tools still need to be improved to be accepted by the professional advertising industry. Day by day, many more AI tools that can be used in communication will be launched.

It should be emphasised these tools have been selected because they are more likely to be used specifically by the online marketing, communication, advertising, and public relations sectors.

1. ChatGPT

ChatGPT, developed by OpenAI in 2022, (https://chat.openai.com/) is perhaps the most famous or well-known AI-powered app. However, little has been published about its possible use for the creation of commercial and advertising messages. Is it possible to use ChatGPT to create content for Google Ads? Of course, ChatGPT can classify and summarise data and reports, give us insights into the use of products and services, and suggest a list of possible pain points for the purchase of certain products and services. However, advertising professionals must learn to talk to ChatGPT. In this regard, the recommendation is to break down the topic we need to know about into specific questions. Users can prompt ChatGPT to act like a professional copywriter.

Surely the suggestions made by ChatGPT for an ad or slogan might not be very professional but can serve as a starting point for the agency's copywriter. Of course, the results offered by ChatGPT should be reviewed by the agency's professionals. AI is not going to do the work of an agency, but it is going to save a lot of time for professionals and entrepreneurs in the sector. In addition, different plug-ins can interact with ChatGPT to improve performance depending on the uses or results we need: Merlin, AIPRM, Snack Prompt, AskyourPDF, and VoxScript, to name a few.

2. Copysmith

Copysmith (www.copysmith.ai) is a generative tool for social media ads, text, and content. It uses AI to write quality content for advertisers and businesses. The application can adapt its language to the characteristics of different social networks. According to its website (Copysmith, 2023), Copysmith is a tool that helps large business teams and e-commerce stores create, launch, and distribute high-quality content at scale. With limited entries, Copysmith can generate search engine optimization (SEO-optimised website content), engaging product descriptions, meta tags, and eye-catching ad copy, as well as templates for social media, brainstorming, blogging, and emails.

The tool can be used for both search engine optimization and search engine marketing (SEO and SEM) and, as its website highlights, the benefits of these functions include time savings, improvements in optimisations, and results in terms of conversions. Other copywriting and informational AI tools can be used in marketing and advertising to improve productivity, reduce time and costs, and achieve better results, such as Jasper, Copy.ai, Unbounce's Smart Copy, and Writesonic.

3. AdCreative

AdCreative (www.adcreative.ai/) generates ad creatives and adapts them to the characteristics of the different social network platforms that will be used to disseminate the creative content: Twitter, Linked-In, Instagram, Facebook, and Pinterest. The app describes itself as easy to use and fast in its results. Its website mentions that the application only needs to know the advertiser's target audience and the platform or social network for which the ads are being created, to provide indications on what is the best tone and length for the content. In addition, AdCreative promises to focus the created message on the pain points of the target audience. The tool is designed to generate creatives, texts and headlines, content for social networks and creative ideas. As one benefit of its use,

AdCreative promises to save time for agency professionals and improve results in terms of conversions for advertisers.

4. Pictory

The Pictory tool (https://pictory.ai/?ref=ngoc50) harnesses AI to generate video content pertinent to the subject matter of an article or text. It can create videos or animations from still images (photographs). The tool offers multiple options, encompassing video editing through text, generation of video highlights, automated summarisation of long videos, transformation of scripts into videos, conversion of blog posts into video format, automatic captioning of videos, and auto-transcription of video content. Its applicability extends to audiovisual production departments, where it finds utility in the formulation of proposals and their subsequent presentation to clients, as well as in the conclusive production of audiovisual materials intended for dissemination on social networks.

5. Synthesia

Synthesia (www.synesthesia.io) is an AI-powered video creation platform boasting a clientele that includes prestigious entities such as Amazon and Tiffany & Co. According to its official website, this AI application empowers users to transform text into audiovisual content or speech across a spectrum of 120 languages. Remarkably, it facilitates the expeditious creation of professional-grade videos within a mere 15-minute timeframe, offering a choice among more than 140 distinct video avatars. Notably, Synthesia addresses the need to supplant conventional and potentially mundane documents, PowerPoints, and PDFs with dynamic and engaging videos, eliminating the requirement for specialised equipment or proficiency in video editing skills. Like Pictory, Synthesia emerges as a transformative force capable of significantly accelerating audiovisual production workflows within communication agencies and production companies.

6. Veed.io

Veed.io (www.veed.io/) is an online video editing platform specifically designed to cater to the needs of both professionals and non-professionals, prioritising ease of use. Its suite of editing tools encompasses functionalities such as sound manipulation, clip trimming and splitting, volume adjustment, incorporation of subtitles and text overlays, as well as the addition of special effects and graphic elements. Furthermore, it allows users to add music and other sound effects into their projects. Complementing these tools, Veed.io provides an array of default video templates, affording users the flexibility to tailor them according to individual requirements. This online video editing platform distinguishes itself through its extensive repertoire of customisable tools and templates, with a primary emphasis on accessibility and user-friendly operation. Its main strength is accessibility and ease of use. In essence, Veed.io stands as a valuable audiovisual editing tool, offering tangible benefits to audiovisual producers within agencies and production companies.

7. Airtable

Airtable (www.airtable.com) is a data integration tool that specialises in the second phase of the production of an online campaign. Marketing and campaign tracking functions of Airtable allow users to upload videos and texts previously created to any website, Facebook, or other application or social network, and to generate results analysis of that campaign. According to its website, the application can operationalise critical data, move beyond rigid tools, and reimagine workflows with AI. No code is required. It is possible to transform workflows with the power of AI. With the native AI components, dynamic AI functionality is available in minutes. It is possible to link Airtable to the existing tools, connect important business processes, and build more powerful applications. The application is also used to pre-build apps, get the teams up and running fast, and drive results even faster. It is available for marketing and product teams.

8. Zapier

By leveraging data sourced from applications resembling Airtable, Zapier (https://zapier.com/) possesses the capacity to institute automation protocols predicated on customer behaviour. This tool empowers end-users to seamlessly integrate the web applications integral to their operations, thereby facilitating the automation of workflows. Underpinning its commitment to online automation, as of 2021, Zapier boasts compatibility with over 4,000 applications, including but not limited to Gmail, Slack, Mailchimp, among others. The platform facilitates the interconnection of two or more applications, thereby automating repetitive tasks without necessitating coding or the involvement of developers for integration construction. This functionality markedly streamlines the responsibilities of professionals in media, online media, media buying, and traffic management, concurrently contributing to a notable reduction in the requisite workforce across these domains.

9. Obviously Predict

As its name suggests, Obviously Predict (www.obviously.ai/) is designed to predict consumer behaviour and campaign outcomes. Its prevalent application is observed within the domain of online marketing, as opposed to advertising communication. As stated on its official website, Obviously Predict is a non-generative AI tool positioned to assist users in "turning AI into ROI by going from raw data to industry-leading predictive models in minutes, not months". Like Zapier, Obviously Predict possesses the capability to mitigate the necessity for professionals to engage in market or target audience research, thereby impacting roles such as planners and media buyers.

10. Lexica

Lexica (https://lexica.art/) is a royalty-free image creation application for use in digital marketing and communication. Its results offer photographic quality. The tool allows users to search for certain images within its database and to generate them with a text prompt. On the other hand, it also allows users to use negative prompts to indicate the elements or things that should be excluded from the image that is going to be generated. We can text a prompt requesting Lexica to generate images of people working in an advertising agency and we'll obtain that from Lexica's website (Lexica, 2023).

11. Leonardo

Leonardo Ai (https://leonardo.ai/) is an image generator application that lets users decide the style of the images. It offers royalty-free production-quality visuals. This AI tool allows users to create stunning images in less time and with greater accuracy than any other tool. This tool is especially useful for those who want to create quality images without having to worry about technical details or graphic design skills. Without a doubt, it can revolutionise the photography, audiovisual production, and design departments of advertising agencies.

12. Galileo

Using machine learning algorithms, Galileo (www.usegalileo.ai/) analyses large amounts of data and generates recommendations on user experience designs. It is not yet available worldwide but has the potential to become an essential component of new and experienced user interface (UI) designers' toolkit, as it can support and simplify the most time-consuming phases of the design process. If this tool becomes sophisticated enough, it can eliminate the need for UI designers, cutting out the middleman between product development and launch (Concha, 2023).

13. Durable

Durable (https://durable.co) uses AI to build business websites automatically considering the company's name, location, typology, and images. It allows users to change images and sections, and edit and publish pages directly. It can create a fully designed and customised website with copy, images, and a contact form in less than a minute, without the need for code. To do this, it provides simple editing tools, multiple pages, and a free custom domain. The tool is aimed at marketing and online communication professionals. One of its main benefits is the ability to start marketing right away. The application makes it possible for professionals to generate a greater volume of work thanks to its AI-powered tools for copywriting, SEO, analytics, and customer relationship management.

14. 10Web

The 10Web application (https://10web.io/pricing-ai-assistant/) facilitates the seamless creation or reconstruction of diverse websites by employing the WordPress post format. Analogous to Durable, 10Web demonstrates a capacity to emulate the expertise of professionals such as graphic designers, front-end and back-end developers, and web designers.

15. Humata

Humata (www.humata.ai/) is a useful tool for processing and summarising texts and reports. It is capable of generating summaries, keywords, and a review from a PDF file. According to its website, its main functions allow users to: summarise long papers and learn faster, turn complex technical papers into simply explained summaries, discover new insights 100× faster, answer hard questions related to your file, get easy-to-understand answers instantly, automatically create new writing based on your file, and generate detailed insights for reports, papers, and a variety of tasks instantly.

16. Notion

Notion (www.notion.so/product/ai) is perhaps one of the most versatile tools in terms of the results that it can generate. Its menu offers different solutions generated with AI, including ideas for posts or creatives, social media posts, and summaries of a marketing plan or market research. As advertised on its website, Notion can "summarise notes and find next steps in 30 seconds [...], summarise action items and key takeaways with a single click, check solutions, read blogs and view guides. There are three types: personal free, personal pro and team".

17. Summarize

Summarize (www.summarize.tech/) is an application endowed with the capability to generate concise summaries from any video content disseminated on YouTube. As articulated on the company's website, the application empowers users "to get a summary of any long YouTube video, like a lecture, live event or a government meeting. Powered by ChatGPT". The significance of Summarize lies in its capacity to furnish summaries of audiovisual content – produced either by competitors or entities within a specific sector – to the strategists and creative professionals affiliated with an agency.

18. Slides AI

Slides AI (www.slidesai.io/en) uses AI to create slide presentations in PowerPoint, for example. The application creates images related to the text in the headline and subtitle of the slide. In addition, with the corresponding plug-ins, the tool enables the integration of text generated by ChatGPT. This AI-powered tool transforms any text into visually appealing slides, saving hours of time and effort.

19. Beautiful AI

Like the previous tool, Beautiful AI (www.beautiful.ai) possesses the capability to create high-quality slides and images using AI; however, access to its full functionality mandates a paid subscription. As delineated on its official website, this software purports to be "the best presentation software for teams", emphasising the facilitation of brand consistency, elevation of presentation design standards, and promotion of collaborative endeavours across global locations. Notably, Beautiful AI proves instrumental in crafting presentations tailored for campaigns and projects targeting client audiences. Analogous to Canva, its impact resonates directly within the purview of account departments, exerting a discernible influence on the tasks undertaken therein.

20. Canva

Canva (www.canva.com/magic-design) creates original royalty-free images, as well as infographics, documents, presentations, and videos, in any audiovisual or printed format. It also has a "text to image" function that allows users to generate images from a text prompt. As stated on its website, its tool Magical Design (Beta) is a free AI-powered tool that can turn users' ideas into designs thanks to a selection of original templates. Users can upload their files or create a blank presentation, and then use custom designs that match the context. No advanced design or programming skills are required to use the application.

21. Microsoft Bing

Microsoft has also integrated AI into its tools, and its search engine Microsoft Bing is considered in this study. Its website (www.bing.com) lists every one of the functions incorporated in the new version of Bing. The desktop version of Bing can connect with ChatGPT to increase its capabilities, like showing the content of a YouTube video in text format. Since it is a conversational language tool, Bing works similarly to ChatGPT but is applied to video. Users can tell Bing what they want to get from the video in question. As for other non-image-related uses, Bing requires precision from users' text prompts, just like ChatGPT does.

22. Sembly AI

Sembly AI (www.sembly.ai/) is an AI assistant designed for work teams. Its main function is to simplify daily tasks, streamline communication, and increase productivity in the work context. In the context of online marketing or advertising agencies, it can greatly streamline the tasks of traffic managers. The platform uses AI algorithms to transcribe and analyse meetings and transform them into useful insights. It is used in the commercial, marketing, and communication fields.

23. Bard AI

Bard AI (https://bard.google.com/) is an experimental, conversational AI developed by Google. It is based on conversational neural language models, specifically on LaMDA, also developed by Google. Bard AI is also a conversational system like its competitor ChatGPT, so its users can use normal language to prompt it to perform certain tasks, like search for, filter, or manage information or data available on the Internet. It is not yet available in all countries, but it is available in Europe, where it had to modify its terms of privacy to comply with the General Data Protection Regulation (GDPR).

24. Stable Diffusion

Stable Diffusion (https://stablediffusionai.org/) is a machine-learning model developed to generate high-quality digital images from natural language descriptions or stimuli. It is an AI engine that generates images based on users' text prompts. However, this text-to-image generator is also capable of adding objects or elements to images that already exist and editing them in a certain way. In addition to creating images from nothing, it can modify uploaded photos.

25. MidJourney

MidJourney (www.midjourney.com/) is an AI-powered "text-to-image" software named after the autonomous AI research lab responsible for its development. This tool enables users to generate images from natural language text prompts, akin to the functionality observed in OpenAI's DALL-E and Open Source's Stable Diffusion.

26. Airgram

Airgram (www.airgram.io/) is a meeting-assistant tool designed to enhance work performance by reducing and/or optimising meeting time. This tool systematically streamlines the entire meeting workflow introducing heightened efficiency. Additionally, it facilitates collaborative agenda creation among meeting participants, regulates the timing of discussions, and provides transcription services for the discourse that unfolds during meetings. In comparison, Microsoft's Teams Premium offers a tool closely aligned with Airgram's functionality: Teams Premium. Airgram stands out as a revolutionary instrument significantly impacting the operational landscape of accounting departments and the responsibilities of key account managers.

27. Uizard

Uizard (https://uizard.io/) features a set of useful AI tools for user experience (UX) and user interface (UI) development. It allows users with no experience in design and programming to develop templates or mock-ups for mobile applications. It uses AI to turn drawings and sketches into editable mock-ups. Autodesigner, which is one of its tools not yet available, can be used to generate multi-screen mock-ups for applications and websites from plain text prompts.

28. Timely

This tool is based on the idea that time control is a key factor in the efficiency of any organisation and that it has been so since the origins of the advertising profession. Timely (https://timelyapp.com/home-2) is an AI-powered fully automated, cloud-based time-tracking app with native apps for iOS, Android, Mac, and Windows. It allows users to track billable hours per project and can determine which departments, groups, or units are most profitable and where restructuring would be necessary.

There are many other AI tools that cannot be addressed in depth here due to the limitations of this research, but can be listed here, according to Girón's classification (2023):

Video editing tools: Maestra.ai, Fliki.ai, Runway, Quickvid.ai, CapCut, Happyscribe, Kamua, Kapwing, HeyGen, Colossyan.com, Movio.la, D-ID.com, Spiritme.tech, Designs.ai, Invideo, Vidyo.ai, Captions.ai, Kaiber.ai, Spacetypegenerator, Gencraft, and Papercup.com

Photo creation and editing tools: DALL-E 2, Craiyon, Bing Create, Vana, Runway, Getimg.ai, Autoportrait, Drawanyone.ai, Photo booth, Neural.love, Fotor, Autodraw, Stockimg, YouImagine, Prompthero.com, Scribblediffusion.com, Cleanup, Interiorai.com, AIornot, Letsenhance.io, Segment Anything, and Face26

Text writing and editing tools: Escribelo.ai, KeywordInsights, Writesonic.com, Jasper.ai, Rytr, Grammarly.com, Plagium, Compose.ai, and Genei.io

Productivity control and optimisation tools: Summarize.tech, Tactiq, Otter.ai, tldv.io, Glasp.co (Google Chrome extension), Fireflies.ai, Shortwave.com, Brain.fm, and Save.day

Table 10.1 summarises the 28 tools analysed above and their impact on the advertising and communication sector, which is the research area of this study. However, as discussed, the implementation of tools also affects related sectors such as online marketing, public relations, and, especially, audiovisual communication. Based on this table, the next phase of the analysis is to identify the departments and jobs that may be most affected, or benefited, by the emergence of AI in organisations in the aforementioned sectors.

10.2 CONCLUSIONS

The analysis of AI-powered tools and their possibilities of use in advertising and communication companies indicates that the jobs that can be more directly impacted by AI

TABLE 10.1 AI Tools Classified According to Communication Professions

Number	AI tool	Use	Jobs	Department
1	ChatGPT	Text writing, rewriting	Copywriter/planner	Creative/planning
2	Copysmith	Text writing, rewriting	Copywriter/planner	Creative/planning
3	AdCreative	Text writing, rewriting	Copywriter/planner	Creative/planning
4	Pictory	Video creation	Audiovisual producer	Production
5	Synthesia	Video creating	Audiovisual producer	Production
6	Veed.io	Video editing	Audiovisual producer	Production
7	Airtable	Task organisation	Digital trafficker	Traffic
8	Zapier	Automations/workflows	Media buyer, trafficker	Paid media traffic
9	Obviously Predict	Campaign planning and forecasting	Media buyer	Paid media
10	Lexica	Image creation	Photographer, photo editor, graphic designer	Audiovisual production
11	Leonardo	Image creation	Photographer, photo editor, graphic designer	Audiovisual production
12	Galileo	Graphic and interface design	Graphic designer, front/back end	Graphic design, web design
13	Durable	Website building	Graphic designer, Front/back end	Graphic design, web design
14	10Web	Website building	Web designer, Front/back end	Graphic design, Web design
15	Humata	Text editing	Planner, copywriter	Creative
16	Notion	Text editing	Planner, copywriter	Creative
17	Summarize	Video to text summarising	Planner, strategy, market analysis	Creative/planning
18	Slides AI	Slide creation	Client manager or director	Client
19	Beautiful AI	Slide creation	Client manager or director	Client
20	Canva	Image, slide, video creation	Client manager, graphic designer	Client/graphic design
21	Microsoft Bing	Text creation and video interpretation	Copy, creative	Creative/client
22	Sembly AI	Task organisation	Trafficker, client manager	Traffic, client
23	Bard AI	Language models, text processing	Copy	Creative
24	Stable Diffusion	Image generation	Photographer, graphic designer	Audiovisual production
25	Mid Journey	Text to image generation	Photographer, graphic designer	Audiovisual production
26	Airgram	Task organisation	Trafficker, client manager	Traffic, client
27	Uizard	Web app design	Front end, back end, web designer, UX, UI	Graphic design, web design
28	Timely	Team performance monitoring	Trafficker	Traffic

are creatives, planners and strategists, audiovisual production specialists, usually within the creative department; graphic designers and web designers (front end, to a greater extent), who are also part of the creative department; and the account department. All the positions within these departments in online marketing, advertising and public relations, and communication agencies in general can be affected by AI.

Like any change, this transformation can be observed through the two prisms (Franganillo, 2022) alluded to earlier: the apocalyptic and the optimistic perspectives. For the apocalyptic, the irruption of AI would mean job losses, close to 30% (Kamelli, 2023), given that the tools analysed here speed up the processes in these jobs and, therefore, fewer professionals are required in each department. For those more optimistic towards the change, the incorporation of AI tools in companies in the communication industry, in its broadest sense, can open the door to the many professionals who have been trained on their use. In other words, not all professionals can work with AI tools, therefore, those who first detect this need for AI training can benefit when it comes to finding or keeping a job and, on the other hand, preserving human rights (Crawford, 2021; Quirós-Fons & García-Ull, 2022). In a discussion group held in Madrid, Lucas Ortiz, a creative director and film director, referred to AI in these terms: "In recent weeks, we have seen how AI has yielded better results for us, and I fear there are ethical issues behind that since [these tools] have unlocked certain content". Another participant in the discussion group, Ricardo Campos, a consultant and researcher in AI in art, with a PhD in fine arts, commented that "if you are afraid AI will take your job, it is likely that it will take it away from you because you do not value what you do or do not contribute to what you do" (Control Publicidad, Revista, 2023).

If we try to answer the research questions "How advertising departments and communication agencies could be affected, which professionals or jobs are at risk and what are the advantages of AI tools for them?", we could say that departments will have to re-adapt. The key, therefore, lies in adaptation, as it has been happening in the face of changes in such systems as advertising communication. This adaptation will probably mean reducing the number of people in traditional departments and the emergence of new departments and jobs. The tools will replace many professionals such as those we have already mentioned in Table 10.1: account managers, digital traffickers, graphic designers, web designers, front- and back-end planners, and copywriters. All of them will continue to be essential in online marketing, advertising, public relations, and communication agencies, but to a lesser extent than today, and with functions more focused on the management and supervision of AI tools.

Regarding the potential advantages of AI for employers, they will be numerous and mostly economic, including savings in personnel costs and fewer labour conflicts, absenteeism and problems derived from conciliation. On the other hand, AI tools can also bring many advantages for workers, provided they can adapt and learn to use them. These tools can optimise work processes in terms of quantity, time, and quality, due to their scope and potential and, above all, because they will generate new needs in terms of jobs.

According to Naimat's survey data (2016), which shows global data about investment in AI, and presumably its future adoption, in 20 sectors, the marketing and advertising industry occupies the sixth place (Naimat, 2016). However, it should be noted that in countries such as Spain, the information and communications sectors (41.9%) and the information and communication technology (ICT) sector (41.3%), in companies with more than 10 workers, are leading the use of AI. In the field of Big Data, the ICT sector (35.2%) and the information and communications sector (34.7%) are the most prominent (Trabado, 2023).

On the other hand, we wondered whether advertising agencies and the communication sector are prepared to incorporate these resources into their work processes. According to the experts and professionals consulted, active agencies that continue to work conventionally and plan campaigns in offline media would not be able to assume this change immediately. Their human and technological resources are not prepared for it. Regarding online communication agencies or those with a strong dedication to the internet medium, they are currently incorporating AI tools into their processes and jobs. The fact that these agencies are already working on online processes, many of them automated and standardised, has allowed them to incorporate some of the tools that we have analysed in this chapter.

According to Trabado (2023), in organisations with 10 or more workers, AI has proven to be particularly useful in automating workflows and assisting in decision-making. In fact, its use in such entities has risen from 38.6% to 46.2% in the last year (2022). Taking these data into account, we can predict the trend in the adoption of these tools. While there are companies in the communication sector that are not able to adopt AI, others are already doing so now and will continue to do so for the foreseeable future. For the latter, this means adopting a competitive advantage that others will not be able to achieve in a short period. Of course, they will be able to survive and continue working in the old way, but they will not be able to be competitive and will be condemned to extinction in a not-too-long period if they do not begin their process of adaptation at the same time.

REFERENCES

Belhadi, A., Kamble, S., Fosso-Wamba, S., & Queiroz, M. M. (2022). Building supply-chain resilience: An artificial intelligence-based technique and decision-making framework. *International Journal of Production Research, 60*(14), 4487–4507. https://doi.org/10.1080/00207543.2021.1950935

Canavilhas, J. (2022). Inteligencia artificial aplicada al periodismo: estudio de caso del proyecto "A European Perspective" (UER). *Revista Latina de Comunicación Social, 80*, 1–13. https://doi.org/10.4185/RLCS-2022-1534

Concha, M. (2023, March 8). *Galileo AI – Los diseñadores de UI/UX son cosa del pasado.* https://hackernoon.com/es/galileo-ai-son-uiux-designers-una-cosa-del-pasado

Control Publicidad, Revista (2023, June 20). https://controlpublicidad.com/agencias-publicidad/thinketers-live-celebra-su-cuarta-edicion-con-mas-de-70-marcas/?utm_source=Newsletter&utm_medium=Email&utm_campaign=Boletin%20diario

Copysmith (2023, June 29). *AI copy generator para comercio electrónico: trabaja de manera más inteligente, no más difícil.* Recuperado de https://copysmith.ai/ai-copy-generator-para-comercio-electronico-trabaja-de-manera-mas-inteligente-no-mas-dificil/#:~:text=Copysmith%20es%20una%20herramienta%20de%20redacci%C3%B3n%20de%20IA%20confiable%20y,de%20contenido%20de%20alta%20calidad

Crawford, K. (2021). *The atlas of AI: Power, politics, and the planetary costs of artificial intelligence.* Yale University Press. https://doi.org/10.2307/j.ctv1ghv45t

De Lara, A., García-Avilés, J-A., & Arias-Robles, F. (2022). Implantación de la Inteligencia Artificial en los medios españoles: Análisis de las percepciones de los profesionales. *Textual & Visual Media, 1*(15), 1–16. https://doi.org/10.56418/txt.15.2022.001

Franganillo, J. (2022). Contenido generado por inteligencia artificial: Oportunidades y amenazas. *Anuario ThinkEPI, 16*, e16a24. https://doi.org/10.3145/thinkepi.2022.e16a24

Girón, B. (2023, September 14). *+120 Mejores herramientas con Inteligencia Artificial.* https://borjagiron.com/mejores-herramientas-inteligencia-artificial/

Gómez-Prieto, J. C. (2023, April 21). El test de Turing frente al ChatGPT. www.linkedin.com/pulse/el-test-de-turing-frente-chat-gpt-juan-carlos-gomez-prieto%3FtrackingId=Yd4GK%252Bcl8oln0oPI8rwMsw%253D%253D/?trackingId=Yd4GK%2Bcl8oln0oPI8rwMsw%3D%3D

González-Arias, C., & López-García, X. (2023). ChatGPT: Stream of opinion in five newspapers in the first 100 days since its launch. *El Profesional De La información, 32*(5). https://doi.org/10.3145/epi.2023.sep.24

Gutiérrez-Caneda, B., Vázquez-Herrero, J., & López-García, X. (2023). AI application in journalism: ChatGPT and the uses and risks of an emergent technology. *El Profesional De La información, 32*(5). https://doi.org/10.3145/epi.2023.sep.14

Kamelli, F. (2023, March 24). *Conferencia en la Escuela de Marketing & Web*, (Valencia, España) (not publised).

Lexica (2023). *Stable diffusion database and image generator.*

Lopezosa, C., Codina, L., Pont-Sorribes, C., & Vállez, M. (2023). Use of generative artificial intelligence in the training of journalists: challenges, uses and training proposal. *El Profesional De La información, 32*(4). https://doi.org/10.3145/epi.2023.jul.08

Martínez, I. J., Aguado, J. M., & Sánchez, P. H. (2022). Smart advertising: Innovación y disrupción tecnológica asociadas a la IA en el ecosistema publicitario. *Revista Latina de Comunicación Social, 80*, 69–90. www.doi.org/10.4185/RLCS-2022-1693

Naimat, A. (2016). *The new artificial intelligence market.* O'Reilly Media, Inc.

Nica, E., Sabie, O. M., Mascu, S., & Luțan-Petre, A. G. (2022). Artificial intelligence decision-making in shopping patterns: Consumer values, cognition, and attitudes. *Economics, Management and Financial Markets, 17*(1), 31–43. https://doi.org/10.22381/emfm17120222

OpenAI (2023). *ChatGPT* (March 14 version) [Large language model]. https://chat.openai.com/

Quirós-Fons, A., & García-Ull, F. J. (2022). La inteligencia artificial como herramienta de la desinformación: Deepfakes y regulación europea. In E. García-Antón (dir.), *Los derechos humanos en la inteligencia artificial: Su integración en los ODS de la Agenda 2030* (pp. 537–556). Thomson Reuters Aranzadi.

Sánchez-García, P., Merayo-Í-Ivarez, N., Calvo-Barbero, C., & Diez-Gracia, A. (2023). Spanish technological development of artificial intelligence applied to journalism: Companies and tools for documentation, production and distribution of information. *El Profesional De La información, 32*(2). https://doi.org/10.3145/epi.2023.mar.08

Trabado, M. (2023, June 26). Avance en la Incorporación de Inteligencia Artificial y Big Data en el Ámbito Empresarial. www.linkedin.com/pulse/empleabilidad-crecimiento-y-futuras-profesiones-en-trabado/?trackingId=b3rlHejWSuCetdj59bPTDQ%3D%3D

Túñez-López, J. M., Toural-Bran, C., & Cacheiro-Requeijo, S. (2018). Uso de bots y algoritmos para automatizar la redacción de noticias: Percepción y actitudes de los periodistas en España. *El Profesional de la Información, 27*(4), 750–758. https://doi.org/10.3145/epi.2018.jul.04

CHAPTER 11

Adaptive AI and Interactive Narrative Possibilities in Media

Kemal Deniz

11.1 INTRODUCTION

One of the most recent artificial intelligence (AI) technologies is adaptive AI, which learns, modifies, and develops in response to changes in the environment and data. AI has advanced greatly in recent years in terms of what it can do, how it can be used, and how much the world can gain from it. This is largely due to improvements made in machine learning and deep learning training capabilities. AI algorithms can more precisely produce insights and forecasts that continue to support wiser decision-making through the ingestion and interpretation of data. The potential of this technology appears to be drastically expanding as adaptive AI systems demonstrate an aptitude for continuously responding, learning, and altering their outputs from ingesting new input.

Adaptive AI systems enable model behaviour change after deployment by learning behavioural patterns from past human and machine experience and within runtime contexts to adapt more quickly to changing real-world circumstances. AI engineering covers the fundamental components of implementation, operationalization, and change management at the process level that enable adaptive AI systems. Adaptive AI systems enable a decision-making framework focused on making faster conclusions while remaining adaptable to difficulties as they emerge. These systems seek to continuously learn based on new data during runtime in order to adapt to changes in real-world settings more quickly. The AI engineering framework can help organize and optimize applications to adapt to, resist, or absorb disruptions, easing the management of adaptive systems.

Key expected benefits include the following (Gartner, 2022): (1) adaptive AI lays the foundations for adaptive AI systems by supplementing existing AI applications with

DOI: 10.1201/9781003473633-11

continuous intelligence design patterns and event flow capabilities, eventually moving towards agent-based methodologies and giving more autonomy to system components; (2) it facilitates business users to adopt AI and contribute to the management of adaptive AI systems by embedding clear and measurable business indicators through operationalized systems and instilling confidence in the decisionmaking framework; and (3) it increases the business value of ongoing AI initiatives by adopting AI engineering techniques that streamline data, models, and application pipelines to standardize AI deployment processes.

Based on this conceptual framework, this chapter explores the possible contributions that developments in the field of adaptive AI can make to the interactive narrative solutions that are currently available in media texts and that can be developed and utilized in the future. Possibilities of the user/audience experience that the use of interactive and autonomous narrative integrated with adaptive AI in a communication process involving human–machine interaction might offer will be discussed. Therefore, the experience that interactive narrative might offer to the user/audience regarding the more advanced and future narrative forms using AI technology will be determined.

11.2 ARTIFICIAL INTELLIGENCE: A PHILOSOPHICAL CONSIDERATION

The concept of AI, as we understand it today, started with philosophical ideas dating back to the 1950s (Turing, 1950) and then remained undeveloped after a series of ups and downs during the development of modern computer systems. The concept of AI first gained momentum with the arrival of the 2000s with the introduction of big data, and deep learning technologies about a decade later (Russell & Norvig, 2022, p. 44–45), that contributed to the current stage of it. Initially, in his article "Computing Machinery and Intelligence" published in the philosophical journal *Mind*, Alan Turing (1950, p. 433) asked the seminal question that perhaps sparked the beginning of the developments in AI that have reached the present day: "Can machines think?"

In fact, this important question, "can machines think?" which might be considered to be questioned with a philosophical approach, could be taken to a very different level of questioning based on an experimental test proposed by Alan Turing. He projected an experiment between three people, which he called the imitation game and which is commonly known as the Turing test. Accordingly, he tested individuals of two different sexes—female and male—whom he coded as A and B to determine which of them was female and which was male from their answers to questions posed to them. The answers, which were created in a textual form and separated from all individual and human elements that would allow the individual's sex to be recognized, were transmitted to the interrogator, who is coded as C, and presented for his or her evaluation. In this test, the interrogator was able to make false judgements. Turing advanced the imitation test in response to this experiment and considered what would happen if he replaced one of the people with a machine. Therefore, he modified his first question from "can machines think?" to "what will happen when a machine takes part A in this game?" Thus, he aimed to test how the machine demonstrates its ability to perform intelligent behaviour in a human or comparable context. Indeed, an equation like if a machine behaves as intelligently as a human being, then it is as intelligent as a human being, could be thought of.

In this test, he wanted to see whether the interrogator would make the wrong decision as often when the game was played between a machine and a human as when the game was played between a woman and a man. He then asks, "are there imaginable digital computers which would do well in the imitation game?" and generalizes it to "...is it true that by modifying this computer to have an adequate storage, suitably increasing its speed of action, and providing it with an appropriate programme..." so that this computer can take the place of the other subject? Although all these tests and questions seem to remain at the level of a philosophical enquiry into a world at a technological level that could not yet be answered factually at the time they were asked, their intellectual anticipation of current developments is evident. In the seminar The Dartmouth Summer Research Project on Artificial Intelligence (McCarthy et al., 1955) organized shortly after Turing test, the proposal that various aspects of learning and various features of intelligence could be simulated by a machine is considered as the founding event of the field of AI (Crevier, 1993, pp. 26–27). Thus, Turing's philosophical enquiries led to the beginning of more concrete and systematic studies in the field of AI.

Nevertheless, the ontological and philosophical scrutiny of the initial predictions and conceptualizations of AI has persisted from the inception of these early enquiries. In his widely debated article "Minds, Brains, and Programs" (1980), also known as The Chinese room argument, John Searle argues that a digital computer running a program cannot have a "mind", "understanding", or "consciousness", no matter how intelligent or human-like the program forces the computer to behave. At the core of this idea is the argument that only a human being can have a mind, understanding, and consciousness. In other words, while criticizing Turing's test, Searle claims that it is insufficient to determine the existence of consciousness. Searle, thus, opposes the idea that the mind or mental cognition can exist outside the body. In more detail, Searle's thought experiment presents the following hypothetical proposition: He assumes that AI research has successfully built a computer that pretends to understand Chinese. The computer takes Chinese characters as input and following a computer program's instructions produces other Chinese characters, which it presents as output. According to Searle, assuming that this computer performs its task convincingly enough to comfortably pass the Turing test, it can convince a Chinese-speaking person that the program itself is a live Chinese speaker. Thus, it would give appropriate answers to all the questions asked by the person, and any Chinese-speaking person could be convinced that they were talking to another Chinese-speaking person.

However, the main problem Searle wants to emphasize here is whether there is a reality in which this machine understands Chinese perfectly, or whether the machine has the ability to simulate Chinese very well. At this point, Searle distinguishes a separate notion of AI for both cases. He categorizes the former as "strong AI" and the latter as "weak AI" (Searle, 1980, p. 417). On the other hand, Searle's conclusion that the Chinese room argument (CRA) shifts our focus from computation to brain function has also been criticized as an overreach (Harnad, 2001). It is argued that there are still several opportunities to reverse engineer cognition via hybrid and non-computational methods, including but not limited to reverse engineering the brain. As a result, cognitive neuroscience has not gotten any endorsement or backing from Searle's CRA. So, it has been criticized that the Turing test has been rejected by Searle because of the narrow focus of a particular approach, which is purely computational. However, apart from the criticisms, Harnad (2001) also emphasizes that Searle's critique of the Turing test helped to open up the fields called "embodied cognition" and "situated robotics".

Starting from Searle's point of view at the philosophical level, we can consider as a fact that the development and transformation of AI from weaker AI to stronger AI from the first conceptualization processes in the past to the level it has reached today and the level it might reach in the future. In parallel with the development of technology, it is seen that the studies on AI cover a process that continues to develop in social, cultural, economic, administrative, and political planes, all of which are somehow related to communication. Eventually, when we consider AI products at the level they have reached today, technologies such as voice recognition, face recognition, and fingerprint recognition can be seen as the product of efforts to ensure communication and interaction with the computer inside in order to facilitate and more effectively carry out the applications that people outside need to maintain throughout their vital functioning.

11.3 ADAPTIVE ARTIFICIAL INTELLIGENCE

As advances in AI technology continue to pave the way for powerful AI applications, the possibilities of using AI in different fields continue to increase. The use of AI has become a part of many businesses and operations integrated with digital technology, especially today. As this integration continues, innovations and developments in the field of AI will continue to be articulated to applications and usage practices in various fields. One of the AI technologies that have recently come to the fore is the innovations related to the developments in adaptive AI. In relation to the theorization, conceptualization, and critical discussion of the historical and pioneering studies in the field of AI mentioned in the previous section, adaptive AI will also develop as an even stronger notion of AI that can have "mind", "understanding", or "consciousness" with Searle's conceptualization of AI today and in the near future, and thus it would be possible for a mental cognition process to operate outside the human body.

Artificial neural networks, machine learning, deep learning, natural language processing, deep fake, and similar developments are the leading topics emerging from AI-related technologies and are used effectively in daily life and professional processes in the context of communication and human–machine interaction. The aforementioned concepts, which stand out throughout the development process of AI and its use in social, cultural, commercial, administrative, governmental, military, technological, and medical fields, are evolving into a more inclusive and open to development process that can create images, videos, audios, 3D models, and many different types of data, such as generative AI (GenAI/GAI), which can be considered a "strong AI" technology. GAI can imitate human creativity in the realistic and complex content it can produce and contribute to the emergence of products in different and diverse fields, from artistic design to scientific research processes. This has made GAI an important and useful technology for many sectors and fields.

Adaptive AI is an AI development that needs to be taken into consideration as GAI creates learning patterns using existing data and produces new outputs by using them, and these patterns and the information produced are integrated into new information at an adaptive level. AI algorithms can provide more precise insights and forecasts by ingesting and interpreting data, which in turn supports smarter decision-making. The capabilities of adaptive AI systems are expected to undergo significant enhancements as they demonstrate proficiency in continuously responding, learning, and altering their outputs by assimilating new input. Adaptive AI systems, in Gartner's (2023) conceptualization, facilitate a decision-making framework that prioritizes prompt decision-making while maintaining the ability to adapt and address emerging difficulties. These systems strive to acquire knowledge continually by incorporating fresh data during operation in order to promptly adjust to changes in real-world conditions. The AI engineering framework facilitates the management of adaptive systems by orchestrating and optimizing applications to adapt to, resist, or absorb shocks.

Wiles and Perri (2022) explain why adaptive AI should matter in business. They suggest that adaptive AI possesses the ability to modify its own code in order to accommodate unforeseen real-world changes that were not anticipated at the time of its initial coding, distinguishing it from conventional AI systems. Organizations that include adaptability and resilience into their design can respond with greater speed and efficiency to interruptions. Emphasizing this technology's adaptive manner, they cite Gartner distinguished VP analyst, Erick Brethenoux's comment about adaptive AI (Wiles & Perri, 2022): "Adaptive AI systems aim to continuously retrain models or apply other mechanisms to adapt and learn within runtime and development environments—making them more adaptive and resilient to change". Wiles and Perri, in their article, also indicate that Gartner predicts that by 2026, companies that have implemented AI engineering methodologies for constructing and overseeing flexible AI systems would surpass their counterparts by at least 25% in terms of both the quantity and speed of implementing AI models.

Adaptive AI systems, which are included in the top 10 in Gartner's *Top Strategic Technology Trends* of 2023 booklet (2022), are expressed as a technology that has the ability to change its behaviour after deployment by learning from previous human and machine interactions and adapting faster to new situations in the real world. AI engineering covers the fundamental elements needed to implement, operationalize, and manage changes in AI systems at the process level and ensures their adaptability. Key actions with which adaptive AI can be benefitted are stated as follows (Gartner, 2022, p. 24):

- To enhance present AI systems by incorporating continuous intelligence design patterns and event stream capabilities: This will gradually transition towards agent-based approaches, allowing for greater autonomy in system components.
- To facilitate the adoption of AI by business users and enable their active participation in managing adaptive AI systems: This will be achieved by integrating clear and

quantifiable business indicators into operational systems and ensuring confidence within the decision-making framework.

- To optimize the commercial benefits of current AI projects by implementing AI engineering techniques that simplify the management of data, models, and implementation pipelines, thus standardizing the supply of AI solutions.

Concisely, adaptive AI enhances the user experience by swiftly adjusting to dynamic real-world circumstances, resulting in a superior and expedited interaction. This enhances the ability to make decisions and be adaptable while utilizing decision-intelligence capabilities. In light of these advancements, IT leaders must reconfigure several processes to establish adaptive AI systems capable of acquiring knowledge and adjusting their behaviour in response to varying circumstances.

11.4 REVISITING AI IN THE ADAPTIVE NARRATIVE POSSIBILITIES

Exploring the potential of adaptive AI for narrative possibilities in media is one of the main aims of this study. Today, narrative continues to gain new dimensions within the framework of developing and changing technologies. The possibilities and innovations provided by digitalization increase its visibility both in the transformed and updated forms of production and consumption of conventional media and in the practices of use in new communication environments. The fact that each new technology and technical development transforms or replaces its predecessor contributes to the emergence of changes and innovations in the formal and contextual structure of media texts and related products. Previous forms of audio-visual media texts in conventional narrative environments have recently been presented in domains that transform production and consumption, such as OTT, IPTV, and various media streaming services, which have emerged in connection with digitalization and have had more opportunities to adapt to new technologies.

While the process in which the narrative and the medium in which it takes place are constantly evolving from conventional to innovative, it would be a worthwhile endeavour to discuss these new mediums, the impact of which has already begun to be seen in the current period and which can be foreseen to develop further in the coming years. Media messages, which traditionally reach individuals through the senses of sight and hearing via monitors and screens, have recently been transformed into virtual reality (VR) in an immersive environment equipped with wearable technologies and sensors that will also stimulate people's sense of touch. Technologies such as Web3 (Dawis, 2021; Gonzalez, 2021) and Metaverse (Ball, 2022; Clemens, 2022; Deniz, 2022; Sipper, 2022), which have recently come to the fore, are rapidly developing beyond the limitations of VR technology, which is actually not very new, and the process that can be considered as post-virtual narrative (Deniz, 2023a, pp. 51–52), in which audio-visual narratives would be presented with immersive technologies such as artificial intelligence (AI), augmented reality (AR), mixed reality (MR), or extended reality (XR). This narrative process will undoubtedly continue to enable cognitive and emotional learning and experiencing processes by activating new senses beyond the traditional media audience experience. Thus, as the medium in which the narrative takes place and the technology it uses change, the user will transform cognitively while adapting them. Experiencing this narrative, the virtual audience's self will gain compatibility with the interactive autonomous narrative.

Then, if we need to take the discussion one step further, we can ask the following: in which contexts will post-virtual narrative utilize the adaptive aspect of AI, precisely at a time when the effects of the metaverse concept on the future of digital communication (Benítez Rojas, 2023) are being discussed? A narrative in the metaverse or a similar digital environment would be developed within the conditions and possibilities of this environment in terms of both form and content. When it comes to the immersive environment that shapes the form and content, the ontology of the narrative will also be reshaped by the dynamic conditions that this environment will autonomously offer. The process similar to the formation of unscripted events, situations, or story contents found in digital games or game-like story structures (Swink, 2009), called emerging narrative (Walsh, 2011), can be seen in narrative creation and sharing environments where adaptive AI is used in a much more advanced form. Making use of adaptive AI applications in the process of realising narrative elements will enable the emergence of more autonomous and unscripted narratives.

The evolution that started with the possibility of interactive use of the environment on platforms that offer online media content services has reached the period when content can be created in interactive narrative form and content can be presented where the user has the opportunity to make decision-making choices in the forking paths (Da Silva & Carrega, 2021; Douglas, 2000) of the story. The narrative forms in which adaptive AI and generative AI are integrated with XR will carry the traditional notion of storytelling to the storyliving phase, especially in the metaverse era (Deniz, 2023b, p. 128). The storyliving involvement of individuals experiencing the integrated roles of audience, user, and participant in the post-virtual narrative environment can be developed in an auto-narrative structure with the contribution of adaptive AI in subsequent narrative processes by mapping with data mining and algorithms to be created. With the previous experiences of the virtual selves of the users in the immersive environment and the algorithmic data obtained from them, adaptive AI-aided auto-narrative that is specific or unique per person will continue to be reproduced.

The pre-trained models used in generative pre-trained transformers (GPTs) can also be usefully and effectively functionalized in narratives that can be created using adaptive AI. GPTs are sophisticated language models that exploit semantic relationships between words in sentences, a technique known as natural language processing. Text-based GPT models (OpenAI, 2023) are pre-trained using extensive datasets of internet content. Pre-training involves predicting the next token, typically a word, subword, or punctuation mark. During the pre-training process, GPT models learn about the world and then make repeated predictions about the next token, producing text that resembles human language. Usually, a subsequent training phase improves the accuracy, usefulness, and security of the model, sometimes using a technique known as RLHF (reinforcement learning from human feedback). Multimodal GPT models (Yenduri et al., 2023, pp. 6–8) can process different data types (modalities), such as images, videos, audio, and text.

Utilizing adaptive AI, it will be possible to create an autonomous narrative consistent with the past experiences and habits of the viewer-user who experiences this narrative by using the predictions that will emerge in the processing of these audio-visual elements throughout a narrative. While creating an adaptive AI-supported narrative that can be experienced in an immersive environment, both artificial and intelligent methods to be used in the creation processes of image and sound such as deep fake, natural language processing, audio-visual elements of GPT in various modalities and the use of devices that will stimulate the user's senses such as sight, hearing, touch, smell, which will contribute to the user's more "real" experience, will strengthen the process that can be expressed as storyliving.

Audio-visual narrative types created with the aid of adaptive AI can be divided into various classifications. This auto-narrative, which will be presented to the user by providing a storyliving experience in an immersive environment, can be categorized into genres and sub-categories. Digital game narratives can be created with adaptive AI support as an advanced form of emergent narrative application, which has already been widely mentioned in the past. Another prominent genre will be fictional narratives with dramatic plots as auto-narrative contents that are created with the support of generative AI and can be dynamically constructed and updated continuously thanks to adaptive AI. Narratives that are not dramatic but created with the help of pre-trained models will be another element of this classification. Therefore, it will be possible to produce a factual subject or reality narrative with artificial tools and technologies that are suitable for the immersive environment and will enable the creation of an auto-narrative. This category will probably lead to new debates on the transformation of non-fiction narratives. It will lead to discussions and new theoretical predictions in the context of auto-narratives produced with AI and smart tools.

Adaptive AI-supported auto-narrative formats and methods will likely be used in various other fields. First of all, adaptive AI-assisted auto-narrative forms and methods, such as all kinds of computer-based education or digital-aided teaching, serious games, simulations, scientific experiments, medical scenarios for practice, and smart city governance, are likely to be utilized for the benefit of all human beings. In addition to all these, adaptive AI will continue to be a technology that both organizations and individuals would benefit from under these or updated names in the future in terms of its potential to develop projections that can carry out solution methods in various fields with interactive efficiency and productive models.

11.5 ETHICAL CONSIDERATIONS

Once a technological innovation is introduced and in the process of its development, the possibility of its use in various related fields will emerge. Adaptive AI's already existing areas of use outside of media texts will further expand and will probably be useful in different contexts and for different purposes. However, it should not be forgotten that every innovation and technological development offers the possibility of being used in destructive and unethical ways as well as in positive and beneficial ways. The importance and usage areas of adaptive AI in social, cultural, economic, and administrative fields will continue to be researched. In the case of this study, while the predictions about the auto-narrative form development process are presented as positive expectations, it is useful to consider the possible risks and unethical use possibilities.

Various scholars and some institutions working in the field of AI have proposed some ethical criteria, taking into account ethical issues. The Care and Act Framework, an AI and machine learning methodology developed by the Alan Turing Institute, evaluates projects in four primary domains using the SUM (support, underwrite, and motivate) values, which are responsible for AI projects and provide criteria evaluating their potential ethical impact (Leslie et al., 2023). These are (1) respect, (2) connect, (3) care, and (4) protect. The process-based governance (PBG) framework outlined in *Understanding Artificial Intelligence Ethics and Safety* (Leslie, 2019) operationalizes the values and principles in the end-to-end workflow governance model. FAST (fairness, accountability, sustainability, and transparency) track principles facilitate an actionable orientation to the ethical design and use of AI systems. The aforementioned constitutes the ethical platform for the responsible delivery of an AI project. To ensure responsible delivery of AI projects, it is necessary to have an ethical platform that follows a PBG framework. This framework implements the SUM values and the FAST track principles throughout the whole workflow of AI project delivery. The aim of this PBG framework is to establish clear and accountable procedures for the design and execution of an AI project, ensuring the validity of both the project itself and its resulting product (Leslie, 2019, p. 14).

In the edited book, *Machine Ethics* (Anderson & Anderson, 2011), philosophers and AI researchers discuss the necessity of giving an ethical dimension to autonomously operating machines. They question what is required to achieve this dimension, the philosophical and practical challenges faced by the machine ethics project, and various approaches that can be considered in the attempt to give machines an ethical dimension. Thus, they aim to analyse existing studies on the implementation of these approaches and make predictions regarding the future of machine ethics research. The European Commission (2019, pp. 14–24) has also studied to implement ethical principles for trustworthy AI. The requirements of trustworthy AI and technical and non-technical methods for realizing trustworthy AI are among the prominent topics of the study. In their article, Floridi and Cowls (2019) examined some of the principles that have been established about AI and investigated whether there is a common consensus among them. Finding that there is a general consensus among these principles, the researchers highlighted the five basic principles as: beneficence, non-maleficence, autonomy, justice, and explicability.

11.6 CONCLUSION

Adaptive AI pertains to the capacity of an AI system to acquire knowledge and adjust its functioning over time, thereby enhancing its efficiency and precision through experiential learning and feedback. This enables the AI system to enhance its decision-making and predictive capabilities, as well as effectively manage increasingly intricate tasks. When it is considered in the context of narrative, the audio-visual autonomous interactive narrative, which will be delivered to the user through an immersive environment and created with the help of adaptive AI, it aims to provide a storyliving experience. It seems possible to use adaptive AI in a wide range of genres and sub-categories, from game narratives to dramatic fiction and non-fiction content. With the help of adaptive AI, new narratives could be made based on the experiencer's past usage patterns and the correlations that can be drawn from them. These narratives will then be able to create themselves autonomously, adapting predictable previous and constantly progressing knowledge.

It is necessary to consider that during the development process of the interactive auto-narrative form customized with adaptive AI, there may be potential risks from misuse and malicious use, as well as cases of unethical abuse. The criteria according to which this autonomously functioning narrative form can be purified from abuse and negative use should be considered not only by experts working on AI in the field of technology and academia but also by official authorities and state and supra-state institutions that make legal regulations.

Consequently, it will be feasible to generate an unbiased and accurate representation of reality by utilizing artificial tools and technologies suitable for the immersive setting. This will aid in the advancement of an automated narrative. This category is expected to stimulate fresh discussions regarding the progression of non-fiction storytelling. This will probably lead to discussions and novel theoretical interpretations in the realm of automated storytelling generated using AI and intelligent instruments. The importance and usage areas of adaptive AI in social, cultural, economic, and administrative fields will continue to be researched. In the case of this study, while the predictions about the auto-narrative form development process in terms of adaptive AI are presented as positive expectations, it is vital to consider the possible risks and unethical use possibilities.

REFERENCES

Anderson, M., & Anderson, S. L. (2011). *Machine ethics*. Cambridge University Press.

Ball, M. (2022). *The metaverse: And how it will revolutionize everything*. Liveright Publishing Corporation.

Benítez Rojas, R. V. (2023). Geneses, evolution, and metafuture. In R. V. Benítez Rojas (Eds.), *The future of digital communication: The metaverse*. (pp. 1–13). CRC Press. https://doi.org/10.1201/9781003379119-1

Clemens, A. (2022). *Metaverse for beginners: A guide to help you learn about meta-verse, virtual reality and investing in NFTs*. Independently Published.

Crevier, D. (1993). *AI: The tumultuous history of the search for artificial intelligence*. Basic Books.

Da Silva, B. M., & Carrega, J. (2021). *The forking paths – Interactive film and media*. Centro de Investigação em Artes e Comunicação da Universidade do Algarve.

Dawis, W. J. (2021). *Metaverse explained for beginners. A complete guide to investing in cryptocurrency, NFT, blockchain, digital assets, web 3 & future technologies.* Independently Published.

Deniz, K. (2022). *Metaverse: Real data in the virtual universe.* In N. Çokluk & N. Kara (Eds.), *Privacy in the digital age* (pp. 81–107). Literaturk Academia.

Deniz, K. (2023a). *Metaverse and new narrative: Storyliving in the age of metaverse.* In R. V. Benítez Rojas (Eds.), *The future of digital communication: The metaverse* (pp. 39–55). CRC Press. https://doi.org/10.1201/9781003379119-4

Deniz, K. (2023b). *Dijital dönüşüm ve görsel kültür çalışmaları.* In M. Ozdemir. (Eds.), *Iletişim sosyolojisi* (pp. 115–131). Nobel Akademik.

Douglas, J. Y. (2000). *The end of books – Or books without end? Reading interactive narratives.* The University of Michigan Press.

European Commission (EC). (2019). *EGTAI: The ethics guidelines for trustworthy artificial intelligence.* Retrieved November 7, 2023, from https://ec.europa.eu/futurium/en/ai-alliance-consultation.

Floridi, L., & Cowls, J. (2019). A unified framework of five principles for AI in society. *Harvard Data Science Review, 1*(1). https://doi.org/10.1162/99608f92.8cd550d1

Gartner. (2022). *Top strategic technology trends 2023.* Retrieved January 14, 2023, from https://enterprise.press/wp-content/uploads/2022/10/Gartner.pdf

Gartner. (2023). *Adaptive AI.* Retrieved November 29, 2023, from www.gartner.com/en/information-technology/glossary/adaptive-ai

Gonzalez, D. (2021). *Metaverse investing: How NFTs, web 3.0, virtual land, and virtual reality are going to change the world we know it.* Independently Published.

Harnad, S. (2001). What's wrong and right about Searle's Chinese room argument? In M. Bishop & J. Preston (Eds.), *Essays on Searle's Chinese room argument.* Oxford University Press.

Leslie, D. (2019). *Understanding artificial intelligence ethics and safety: A guide for the responsible design and implementation of AI systems in the public sector.* The Alan Turing Institute. https://doi.org/10.5281/zenodo.3240529

Leslie, D., Rincón, C., Briggs, M., Perini, A., Jayadeva, S., Borda, A., Bennett, SJ. Burr, C., Aitken, M., Katell, M., & Fischer, C. (2023). *AI ethics and governance in practice: An introduction.* The Alan Turing Institute.

McCarthy, J., Minsky, M., Rochester, N., & Shannon, C. (1955). *A proposal for the Dartmouth Summer Research Project on artificial intelligence.* Retrieved September 12, 2023, from www-formal.stanford.edu/jmc/history/dartmouth/dartmouth.html

OpenAI. (2023). GPT-4 technical report, *arXiv:2303.08774v4.* Retrieved December 26, 2023, from https://arxiv.org/html/2303.08774v4 https://doi.org/10.48550/arXiv.2303.08774

Russell, S. J., & Norvig, P. (2022). *Artificial intelligence: A modern approach.* Pearson Series in Artificial Intelligence.

Searle, J. R. (1980). Minds, brains, and programs. *The Behavioral and Brain Sciences, 3,* 417–457.

Sipper, J. A. (2022). *The cyber meta-reality: Beyond the metaverse.* Lexington Books.

Swink, S. (2009). *Game feel: A game designer's guide to virtual sensation.* Morgan Kauffman Publishers.

Turing, A. M. (1950). Computing machinery and intelligence. *Mind, 59*(236), 433–460. https://doi.org/10.1093/mind/LIX.236.433

Walsh, R. (2011). Emergent narrative in interactive media. *Narrative, 19*(1), 72–85. https://doi.org/10.1353/nar.2011.0006.

Wiles, J., & Perri, L. (2022). *Why adaptive AI should matter to your business.* Retrieved October 27, 2023, from www.gartner.com/en/articles/why-adaptive-ai-should-matter-to-your-business.

Yenduri, G., Srivastava, G., Maddikunta, P. K. R., Jhaveri, R. H., Wang, W., Vasilakos, A. V., & Gadekallu, T. R. (2023). *Generative pre-trained transformer: A comprehensive review on enabling technologies, potential applications, emerging challenges, and future directions. arXiv:2305.10435.* https://doi.org/10.48550/arXiv.2305.10435

CHAPTER 12

Local Media in the Age of AI

Tatiana Santos-Gonçalves

12.1 INTRODUCTION: LOCAL MEDIA AND AI

Local journalism has consistently been a vital component of community life and democracy as they cover minor events that are often not covered by larger mainstream media (Harte et al., 2018; Olsen, 2021). As a result, local journalism is an essential part of local life, playing a crucial role in the preservation of the local culture and economy.

However, the decline in local advertising revenue, and the emergence of large digital platforms have all had a significant negative impact on local media in recent years (Borchardt et al., 2019; Firmstone & Coleman, 2014; Olsen et al., 2020). The closure of local news operations constitutes a major blow to the availability of credible information at a time when it is most desperately needed. The long-term effects of local news media going out of business could be disastrous, leading to a growing democratic deficit and underinformed, underrepresented publics without access to sufficient scrutiny of influential social interests.

For all these reasons, local media are under immense pressure to develop profitable business plans by changing their marketing approaches, expanding their online readership, and broadening their sources of income (Santos-Gonçalves & Napp, 2022; Schulz, 2021). Furthermore, in order to improve news production efficiency and better serve local online audiences, local media must change the way they approach and produce news content (Carlson, 2015; García-Avilés, 2021; Ivars-Nicolás et al., 2020; Santos Gonçalves et al., 2021).

DOI: 10.1201/9781003473633-12

The Internet, and more recently artificial intelligence (AI), has had a significant impact on local press operations, upending established journalistic models and necessitating drastic adjustments to newsroom procedures and media relations with the public. AI is transforming the way media, including local media, is produced and consumed. Some of the most noticeable disruptions include

1. News automation: AI is used to generate automated news from structured data, such as sports reports or financial reports. This can help local media outlets produce large-scale content efficiently.
2. Content personalization: AI allows local media to personalize the content shown to users based on their preferences and behaviours. This can improve user experience and increase the relevance of local news.
3. Data and trend analysis: AI is used to analyse large amounts of data and extract meaningful information about consumer habits, preferences, and trends in local media. This helps publishers better understand their audience and adapt their content strategies.
4. Fact checking and fake news detection: AI is used to detect fake news and verify the veracity of claims in the media. This is especially relevant in the context of local news, where the spread of misinformation can have a significant impact on communities.
5. Content recommendations: AI algorithms are used to recommend content to users based on their interests and past behaviours. This can help local media promote their relevant content and attract audiences.

Local news media organizations are particularly vulnerable to these changes, and so, face an increasingly challenging future. In fact, readers' focus has gradually shifted in recent years to larger companies and major digital platforms that do not charge for content.

When it comes to competing, larger media organizations obviously possess greater financial and technological resources. However, local media has certain advantages that they must exploit if they want to survive. According to a number of studies, the globalization of journalism exhibits subtleties unique to every nation, area, and even town. These regional variations can be extremely beneficial to the survival of the local press. Local specificities continue to exist in digital news markets despite the tendency of globalization to homogenize media content (Toff & Mathews, 2021). Jenkins and Nielsen (2020) assert that one of the most influential criteria in selecting news is proximity, and local journalism may capitalize on contextual awareness and proximity's ability to influence important variables like public trust or participation.

The emergence of AI in information has first become particularly fruitful in the areas of sports and finance (Rivas-de-Roca, 2021) and has caused great interest in academia. The use of these robots is still experimental, but the first studies on sport indicate that AI improves journalistic coverage by reducing non-value-added tasks that reporters must carry out (Simon, 2022). However, analyses of this robotic or hi-tech journalism are usually accompanied by a debate regarding its implicit risks. There are criticisms of the quality of the texts produced, as well as ethical doubts. The new relationship between journalists and machines has strong moral implications for the journalistic work. However, on the other hand, AI presents a plethora of opportunities to enhance, finalize, and supplement information professionals' daily tasks and therefore simplifying the already overloaded duties of the local journalists.

Despite the risk that large corporations represent to journalistic independence, a good part of the news automation initiatives come from start-ups, located outside large media and multinationals. Some examples are *Labsense* y *Syllabs* en Francia, *paydesk, unidosrobots, 2txt, Aexea, AX Semantics, Retresco or Text-on* in Germany, *Tencent* in China, *Automated Insights, Bloomberg, Linguastat, o Narrative* in the United States, *Arria* in the United Kingdom, or *United Robots* in Sweden. Due to its high level of specialization, the use of AI began in large media outlets in the United States, although small media outlets in that country also took little time to resort to its possibilities. *Local labs, Hoodline*, and *Hereford Times* have used algorithms to address events and public service issues (Boyd & Crawford, 2012).

The technological giant Google is one of the companies that works the most on information robotization. In fact, the Press Association, a news agency in the United Kingdom, has received nearly $807,000 (around €707,000) in the third round of funding from *Google's Digital News Initiative* (DNI), and its project is neither more nor less than providing a service of news created by Google robots that will deal with local issues. The project called "Reporters and Data Robots", or RADAR will involve robots that can write a whopping 30,000 stories a month, so that 35 local media outlets in this country could produce local content. This project will be part of the DNI that seeks to support innovation in European digital journalism. The DNI seeks to stimulate innovation in digital news journalism over the next three years, financing disruptive projects in the sector.

According to Google, RADAR news will be based on topics of local interest and will use natural language generation (NLG) software to write them. In any case, the robotic writing will be directed by a team of five human writers, who will coordinate the composition of the content based on public information from government departments, local authorities, and other official sources. Google's robots are intended to significantly boost the local media industry as budgets come under increasing pressure, while public interest in local news remains as high as ever.

Research may play a significant role in helping the local media realize the potential of AI such that AI-powered data insight to boost sales or data mining for optimization of the creation of original stories or personalization for user engagement (Thorson, 2020). Policymakers are working in an extremely complicated technological, economic, and sociological environment when creating regulatory approaches to AI and digital technologies—a complexity for which few have been well trained (Helberger & Diakopoulos, 2023). Large media companies would most likely benefit from this, which will make it harder for smaller or local newsrooms to implement and adapt AI technology. Examining carefully how responsibility is assigned to providers, operators, professional users, and consumers—as well as the implications for editorial independence and the realization of professional values—will be crucial given the larger conflict surrounding the freedom of expression in the media. In this process, researchers play several functions, including bringing urgent concerns to light, supplying evidence for dangers and difficulties that regulations need to address, identifying new risks and opportunities, keeping an eye on compliance, acting as a sparring partner, and influencing the selection of policy solutions.

Smaller local organizations and media must also come together to try to counter the advantages of giants' tech companies and media and adapt a system to their own needs and requirements. They have to come together to unlock the potential of AI for the local media, helping to design and evaluate AI opportunities. One interesting and novel initiative in this direction is *beabee*, which will be analysed in this work. This is a platform to help community news outlets build membership models addressing the specific challenge that independent news organizations encounter when building their tech stack: they are eager to innovate in technology or revenue models, but doing so would mean spending money they do not have and investing time that could jeopardize their current business plans. The success of this type of initiatives is key for the survival of local media and deserves to be better understood. In fact, according to Alexandra Borchardt (2022), in order to sustain local journalism and help strengthen democracies, local news publishers must quickly implement AI technologies. In this chapter, our objective is to delve into the challenges that local media face in this new era of AI and take a closer look at the *beabee* project to derive some conclusions of the risks and opportunities that this new environment strongly influenced by AI brings to local media.

12.2 METHODOLOGY

In order to offer individualized services that can rival those of bigger media companies, local news media must understand the interests of their local audiences. Moreover, topics such as the transformation of media business models, ethics, and the impact on the automation of local journalism coverage are critical to adapting to the changes in the local media industry. In this work, we aim to study these issues by revising the state of the art of the challenges and opportunities of local journalism in the new era of AI and analyse one very interesting, current, and novel initiative designed to provide local journalists with tools to develop a community relationship management system to survive in this new environment driven by AI: the *beabee* project. There exists a large body of literature with the objective to investigate the type of journalistic robotization implemented by journalists. Here, instead, we study a unique initiative that has to do with the management of community-centred newsrooms for engaging members and wider community in the context of local journalism. In the design of this research, the case study method was chosen, which has already been used to examine other different attributes of local media. The main objective of this research is to understand these types of initiatives and how they have been implemented by examining a particular project: the *beabee* platform. Specifically, we intend to value the public service function provided by it for local media.

The local public service function is not only estimated insofar as robotization is put at the service of local readers but also in relation to its innovation in several areas of local journalism. The qualitative variable that measures the added value that has been created refers to a public service function that not only combines the production of the platform with the use of innovative techniques but also that helps to better connect with the audience. This variable is addressed in the conclusions as a result of the applied case study.

In this article, the case study methodology is chosen to achieve the research objective of analysing the threats and opportunities of local media in this new era where AI is destined to play a major role. Several authors maintain that these types of methods allow us to better understand the current nuances of media realities by breaking the dichotomy between the quantitative and the qualitative. The issues addressed in this chapter are ideally suited to the case study methodology from an interdisciplinary perspective.

12.3 RESULTS

In an attempt to counter the steady decline in the local media sector, the non-profit organization *the Bureau of Investigative Journalism*, the British co-operatively owned news outlet *The Bristol Cable*, and the German non-profit *CORRECTIV* came together to launch a trusted platform, called *beabee*, tailor made for the smallest newsrooms to monetize their loyal audience and to help community news outlets build membership models.

The Bristol Cable is a co-op independent local media company located in the United Kingdom, owned by thousands of people who pay a monthly fee. Founded in 2014, it provides local news through independent investigative journalism. The Reva and David Logan Foundation awarded it a £40,000 grant in 2017 so that it may increase its capacity in the local community.

The Bureau of Investigative Journalism is a London-based non-profit news organization. It was established in 2010 by David and Elaine Potter with the goal of conducting "public interest" research. To optimize the influence of its inquiries, the bureau collaborates with media outlets and publishers such as the *Financial Times, The Daily Telegraph*, or *The Sunday Times* among others. Since the initial funding for the project of £2 million that came from the Potters' charitable foundation, the bureau has won numerous awards and covered a wide range of stories and became the United Kingdom's largest not-for-profit news organization. The Bureau of Investigative Journalism is meant to be an independent, not-for-profit organization that holds power to account and tackles big subjects through deep reporting that uncovers the truth. That is why they focus on in-depth, rigorous investigations that can make a real difference not only at a global level but also at a local level. To address these concerns, the bureau has been constructing a new wall piece by piece. They are reviving local accountability journalism through our innovative *Bureau Local* and developing a unique model that other media outlets can follow.

CORRECTIV is a non-profit German independent newsroom that claims that one of its objectives is to give citizens access to information. Investigative journalism helps us uncover systemic wrongdoing, hold the powerful accountable, and fortify a free and democratic civil society. CORRECTIV employs about 20 people, and their investigations are carried out independently of political and financial interests. The public interest serves as our reporters' guide, and our work is transparent and verifiable. They select our own subjects and themselves. According to their own description, CORRECTIV is one of the many answers to the (local) media crisis. CORRECTIV distributes its reports to media outlets across Europe and beyond in the languages of English, German, and Russian through its website.

The *beabee* project was designed from these three organizations with the goal of unifying resources since their outlets all ran into similar technical problems as well as other pioneers of engaged journalism and community-based revenue models. Hence, in order to optimize their already limited resources they started to work a lot more with developers trying to get more exposed to the tech culture of sharing (e-participation) and open-source tools.

They all had the idea that if this is the future, they must be fearless about it and have stories which are open and collaborative, where people are able to work on them together online. The majority of stories are not generated "in the open" but journalists know that community involvement is a valuable resource they may use to support their reporting and that when communities are allowed to participate in stories, they can obtain stronger stories, more interested audiences, and active readers. Many of the stories make use of community involvement. There are however undoubtedly difficulties: genuine interaction frequently takes time, some stories are delicate, and journalists naturally worry about safeguarding their sources. This may lead to a more conventional reporting strategy being used, and research indicates that transparency and involvement ought to vary depending on the type of story. However, there is still a lot of room to grow in terms of how communities may interact with stories and get involved with local journalists. The goal of *beabee* was to assist local media in this direction by exploiting synergies and helping to establish a more productive relationship with local citizens. In fact, the Bristol Cable had already built its own membership system aiming to turn passive readers into active members of the newsroom. In contrast, *CORRECTIV* has primarily operated its membership program using pre-existing software, but they have also developed proprietary tools, such as the *Crowdnewsroom*, to allow users to contribute their experiences to investigations or collect data on a larger scale.

The founders of *beabee* noticed a hunger for building more local newsrooms that really want to serve communities, especially when it comes to underserved communities and local communities. Both *the Bristol Cable* and *CORRECTIV* were constantly asked by local pioneers how they were solving tech challenges. So, it came natural to them to try to help them by making sure that technology will not be the barrier for them. For these reasons, this project was born as a solution to the specific challenge that independent news organizations encounter when building their tech stack: they are eager to innovate in technology or revenue models, but doing so would mean spending money they do not have, and investing time that could jeopardize their current business plans. *Beabee* is a community project and collaborative open-source software that prioritizes privacy. In order to increase the diversity of the local information ecosystems, we aim to unite organizations that support our goal of enabling more people throughout Europe to establish and manage independent, community-driven, membership-financed local newsrooms. Throughout the pandemic, as advertising revenues continued to decline, the need for a radical shift in audience engagement and revenue became even more apparent (Santos-Gonçalves & Napp, 2023). In order to close this gap with reliable information produced with and by communities, the *beabee* team hopes to fully utilize the potential of community entrepreneurs throughout Europe.

The Bristol Cable and two local German newsrooms, *Bürgerportal Bergisch Gladbach* and *089 Wehringhausen*, have been testing *beabee* for almost a year. It is prepared to accept additional beta testers in various languages. For those first beta users, the platform will remain free. However, they should anticipate needing assistance setting up *beabee* on their own sub-domain, importing their current data, and creating a user dashboard with a custom branding. A SaaS (software as a service) version will be released, making it simpler for users to get started independently in a matter of hours. The project will also establish a reasonable pricing structure going ahead. The goal now is to test the product, in particular, with very early-stage newsrooms that want to convert from spreadsheets to a community database that can be used for action. However, *beabee*'s uses are very diversified, ranging from facilitating community-based campaigns to facilitating contributions from citizen journalists. The platform offers the resources needed to support those workflows as well as tried-and-true best practices from newsrooms with years of expertise. They aim to set up the upcoming generation of local newsrooms for success avoiding the same mistakes.

Building a tech platform that media organizations can rely on was another driving force for the three founders. Concerns about data ownership, privacy-first policies, and brand ownership may arise when large tech companies are used for this kind of community-focused legwork (requiring community members to sign up for third-party services like *Steady*, *Patreon*, or *Substack*). For this reason, *The Bristol Cable*'s software has always been available to the public, allowing users to host it on their own servers and modify specific parts of it.

Another crucial point to note is that the project's fundamental belief is that trust is the most valuable asset local newsrooms possess.The local media as a whole went into such a survival mode that they have been mired in the complacency of following Facebook or Google for years. Thus, the *beabee* project always wanted to develop their own tools that fully control how they handle their community data and do not take any chances with that trust. New technology is required for public interest local newsrooms. For this, their goal is to avoid relying on Google forms and Facebook groups and build their independent digital online and trusted resources.

12.4 CONCLUSIONS

AI is capable of creating a huge amount of content that makes up a high percentage of the daily lives of local media newsrooms. However, as more and more local news deserts appear around Europe, the three founders of the *beabee* project saw a need to create additional local newsrooms that genuinely desire to serve communities, especially when it comes to underserved communities and local communities. AI will transform both the production of content in all its facets and the way we consume news. For this reason, this recently launched community European project is a very interesting initiative for the local media. The project aims to support smaller publications in developing membership-based revenue models, which will improve both their financial performance and reporting in order to ensure that technology such as AI will not be a barrier to them.

Within this new environment strongly influenced by AI, local journalists have to talk. Unfortunately, at some point they stopped doing it and now more than ever it is imperative that you take the time to reflect and exchange opinions. It is apparent that they have to do it within their means but also with its competitors and with its audience in order to create opportunities with AI if they aspire to continue existing. The media as a whole entered such a survival mode that they have been stuck for years in the inertia of going where Google or Facebook points them. Consequently, many have lost confidence in the media as an industry. People either do not trust them or trust a few to whom they give their support on a subscription basis to ensure that this medium continues to exist. It is essential that the local media do something, and the appearance of AI could be a good chance for doing so.

The threat that AI poses to journalism is actually an opportunity. AI opens the door to a kind of super journalists that can be devoted to those areas that make a difference and robots can help them out with that. The point is getting more content that matters to local readers as soon as possible. In markets where local media did not have anyone pulling the data, the robot has given them regularity and scale. It is obvious that robots can do the boring work freeing up time for local reporters that can now bring along their analytical mind.

After analysing the *beabee* project we have come to several interesting conclusions regarding issues that local media currently faces. One of our main key findings is that the current system is flawed and there is a need to build a stronger local media ecosystem. To address problems like information gaps, journalism funding, and sustainability, new strategies are required. We see a chance to rebuild the local news map from scratch.

More independent initiatives to promote local news and information are starting to emerge. Direct funding, mapping, and research to determine local needs, and laws and policies that support local media diversity and independent ownership are some examples of this. There are new projects to financing and disseminating information locally. This encompasses new philanthropic actors, community foundations, non-profit and innovative formats, and delivery methods.

Long-standing injustices and imbalances can be addressed with initiatives like *beabee*. This holds true for both the demand and supply sides of journalism. The information needs of communities of colour, rural populations, and less affluent constituencies have not always been met. They continue to be among the most exposed to the effects of the cuts and closures occurring in the local news and information ecosystem right now.

Support ought to be independent of ownership models and platforms. News in the future may not look like it has in the past. Since it might be challenging to maintain the commercial model for local news, some organizations—both new and old—are looking into non-profit models as a more financially feasible option. Numerous organizations and interested parties may contribute to this future.

Moving forward, there are many challenges that local media has to face. We first must have a clear idea of how we want this landscape to look in order to address the local news crisis. Without it, not only will progress be challenging, but consensus and support for local media initiatives. We might want to examine the minimal requirements for local news and information sources as well as the methodology for gauging the effectiveness of projects. In order to continue—and hopefully expand—local journalism in Europe, substantial financial support will probably be needed. Thus, it is the responsibility of researchers, local journalists, and membership associations like *beabee* to keep arguing in favour of local news support.

For local journalists, the key will be to turn these new AI technologies into allies in order to create deeper, contrasted, and contextualized content. To achieve this, all you need to do is resort to what journalism should always have been about. The basis of the relationship with AI will consist of asking the right questions, and above all in giving the precise instructions so that the AI tool that we are using to create an image or to deliver an illustration in truly generates the result we were waiting for.

The local media will have to understand that work produced by AI does not have to be seen as a finished product. It will be necessary to convert what AI delivers into the resources local media has to tell a story that goes further. Journalists will have to demonstrate that they have not forgotten how to tell stories and that they have the ability to create narratives that incorporate the benefits of AI while turning those pieces into a work of authorship. Automated articles are usually quite specialized and very interesting to a small number of people. That makes them perfect for a personalized local news service. It is key to define the context and there is where the value of local journalism lies.

We conclude that robotization fits perfectly with local media, since reporting using structured data would make it possible to reduce costs and improve the precision of its parts. AI will not leave human local journalists without jobs. Local journalist will continue to be vital in this content creation process, but AI will make it possible to achieve a volume of local stories that would be impossible to achieve manually. In addition to the flow of stories to clients increasing, it is important to collect local data that will also be used to create database tools for collection in order to automatically generate graphics, videos, and images to add to stories demanded by local citizens. Local users in their proximity information configuration have specifications conducive to automation.

Thus, the key for local journalists to turn AI into an ally, and not a threat, will be to ask it the right questions and give it the most mechanical work in order to save time to be able to create more in-depth, contrasted, and contextualized journalistic work. Ultimately it is the journalist who must check the context and analysis and therefore local journalists are still needed. Moreover, they are also required to make ethical decisions on what is finally published.

REFERENCES

Borchardt, A. (2022). Go, robots, go! The value and challenges of artificial intelligence for local journalism. *Digital Journalism, 10*(10), 1919–1924. https://doi.org/10.1080/21670811.2022.2149584

Borchardt, A., Kieslich, S., Lück, J., Schultz, T., & Simon, F. (2019). *Are Journalists Today's Coal Miners?* Oxford, UK: University of Oxford/Universität Mainz. https://reutersinstitute.politics.ox.ac.uk/our-research/are-journalists-todays-coal-miners-struggle-talent-and-diversity-modern-newsrooms

Boyd, D. & Crawford, K. (2012). Critical questions for big data information. *Communication & Society, 15*(5), 662–679. https://doi.org/10.1080/1369118X.2012.678878

Carlson, M. (2015). The robotic reporter: Automated journalism and the redefinition of labor, compositional forms, and journalistic authority. *Digital Journalism, 3*, 416–431. https://doi.org/10.1080/21670811.2014.976412

Firmstone, J., & Coleman, S. (2014). The changing role of the local news media in enabling citizens to engage in local democracies. *Journalism Practice, 8*(5), 596–606. https://doi.org/10.1080/17512786.2014.895516

García-Avilés, J. A. (2021). Journalism as usual? Managing disruption in virtual newsrooms during the COVID-19 crisis. *Digital Journalism, 9*(9), 1239–1260. https://doi.org/10.1080/21670811.2021.1942112

Harte, D., Howells, R., & Williams, A. (2018). *Hyperlocal Journalism: The Decline of Local Newspapers and the Rise of Online Community News*. London and New York: Routledge.

Helberger, N., & Diakopoulos, N. (2023). The European AI act and how it matters for research into AI in media and journalism. *Digital Journalism, 11*(9), 1751–1760. https://doi.org/10.1080/21670811.2022.2082505

Ivars-Nicolás, B., Martínez-Cano, F.-J., & Cuadra-Martínez, J. (2020). Immersive experiences in 360° video for social youth engagement. *Catalan Journal of Communication & Cultural Studies, 12*(2), 225. https://doi.org/10.1386/cjcs_00029_1

Jenkins, J., & Nielsen, R. K. (2020). Proximity, public service, and popularity: A comparative study of how local journalists view quality news. *Journalism Studies, 21*(2), 236–253. https://doi.org/10.1080/1461670X.2019.1636704

Olsen, R. K. (2021). The value of local news in the digital realm – Introducing the integrated value creation model. *Digital Journalism, 9*(6), 810–834. https://doi.org/10.1080/21670811.2021.1912623

Olsen, R. K., Pickard, V., & Westlund, O. (2020). Communal news work: COVID-19 calls for collective funding of journalism. *Digital Journalism, 8*(5), 673–680. https://doi.org/10.1080/21670811.2020.1763186

Rivas-de-Roca, R. (2021). Oportunidades de la robotización en el periodismo local: El caso de 'Mittmedia'. *Index. Comunicación, 11*, 165–185. DOI: https://doi.org/10.33732/ixc/11/02Oportu

Santos Gonçalves, T., Ivars-Nicolás, B., & Martínez-Cano, F. J. (2021). Mobile applications accessibility: An evaluation of the local Portuguese press. *Informatics, 8*(3), 52. https://doi.org/10.3390/informatics8030052

Santos-Gonçalves, T., & Napp, S. (2022). Trends in the interest in COVID-19 news of the local media and their readers: The case of Spain. *Journalism, 23*(12), 2608–2626. https://doi.org/10.1177/14648849221114736

Santos-Gonçalves, T., & Napp, S. (2023). Local versus national news about COVID-19 in Spain: Coverage and public engagement. *Journalism Practice*, 1–19. https://doi.org/10.1080/17512786.2023.2187863

Schulz, A. (2021). Local news unbundled: Where audience value still lies. In Reuters Institute Digital News Report 2021. https://reutersinstitute.politics.ox.ac.uk/sites/default/files/2021-06/Digital_News_Report_2021_FINAL.pdf

Simon, F. M. (2022). Uneasy bedfellows: AI in the news, platform companies and the issue of journalistic autonomy. *Digital Journalism, 10*(10), 1832–1854. https://doi.org/10.1080/21670811.2022.2063150

Thorson, K. (2020). Attracting the news: Algorithms, platforms, and reframing incidental exposure. *Journalism, 21*(8), 1067–1082. https://doi.org/10.1177/1464884920915352

Toff, B., & Mathews, N. (2021). Is social media killing local news? An examination of engagement and ownership patterns in U.S. community news on Facebook. *Digital Journalism*, 1–20. https://doi.org/10.1080/21670811.2021.1977668

CHAPTER 13

Automated Journalism in Turkish Media before the Rise of Generative AI

Sena Ozkurt Azimli and Erkan Saka

13.1 INTRODUCTION

Journalism is at a new dawn – a potentially long shadow casts upon the organizational structure of journalism: artificial intelligence (AI). AI will transform journalism and journalists worldwide; that is inevitable, as it will do to many other workforces. One of the questions that arise immediately is whether journalism will thrive, perish, or adapt after undergoing these shattering changes and how so.

This study began in 2020 when most AI tools were not commonly used. They surely did not take much space in the headlines. Automated journalism tools had already emerged in the global context, though. In 2012, academic publications discussed (Parasie & Dagiral, 2012, p. 2) that news organizations such as *The New York Times*, *ProPublica*, and *The Guardian* started producing online news products using automated tools. In the following years, media also started to cover the emergence of automated journalism tools, companies, and software. In 2015, for instance, *The Guardian* column writer Tim Adams interviewed Kris Hammond (Adams, 2015), the co-founder and chief scientist of Narrative Science, a data storytelling company that was later sold to Salesforce and integrated into its Tableau Software.

Interestingly, Hammond had already projected a future where AI tools were generating news stories. He also contemplated the possibility that by 2030, computers may write 90% of news articles, and one of them might even win a Pulitzer Prize (Adams, 2015). AI discussion is heavily linked with understanding human intelligence. Both are full of mysteries, but still, some aspects of human intelligence can now be tangibly defined. Undoubtedly, AI is nowhere near surpassing human intelligence, yet its developments have surely accelerated in the last couple of decades. According to OpenAI's research, AI progress doubled starting from 2012 due to the enhancement in computing power

DOI: 10.1201/9781003473633-13

available for training and machine learning, algorithmic innovation, and data, as well as advancements in hardware like GPUs and TPUs (Amodei & Hernandez, 2018). Meanwhile, automated journalism is frequently and inaccurately labelled as "robot journalism." While the term "robot" conveys the idea more effectively, it is misleading because there are no physical components, akin to a robot's body, involved in these journalistic practices. Rather, it accurately describes the automation of journalistic tasks (Ozkurt Azimli, 2022).

This study examines the intersection of AI and journalism, specifically exploring its application and impact within the Turkish media landscape. It investigates whether AI can mimic the nuances of human journalism and analyses the prevalence of automated journalism techniques in Turkish media outlets. Moreover, it enquires the sentiments and attitudes of Turkish journalists towards these emerging technologies. This research is groundbreaking in its focus on the unique subtleties between automated journalism and the Turkish media workforce. By observing both the technical implementation and the human response to AI in this context, the study aims to contribute to a deeper understanding of how these technologies shape journalistic practices in Türkiye[1]. AI raises ethical inquiries within the realms of philosophical ethics, the philosophy of mind, and numerous social sciences, including journalism. These questions prompt contemplation on the ethical implications, cognitive dimensions, and societal impacts of advancing AI technologies. Also, AI's influence extends to broader interdisciplinary discussions, engaging fields such as cognitive science, computer science, and sociology. It contributes to a multidimensional exploration of its implications on human cognition, behavior, and societal structures. Economy-wise, on the other hand, the future of AI has never been more concrete; PwC research suggests that AI will contribute $15.7 trillion to global economic growth by 2030 (PwC, 2023).

The summer of 2023 witnessed an unprecedented objection against AI, not by journalists, but by the renowned Hollywood actors and screenwriters protesting the gradually spreading prevalence of AI in techniques in movie making. Journalism is not an art form, yet we can argue that it is heavily nourished by some common creative techniques that movies use, like storytelling, writing, editing, and shooting. In that case, can we anticipate that the journalists may organize the next protest?

When discussing the repercussions of using automated journalism tools, however, we should not fall into the trap of overgeneralizing, overlooking the cultural differences between the journalism practices and the AI habits of different countries. After all, the Hollywood strike happened in the territories of the US movie industry and had a very limited effect on the rest of the movie makers worldwide as of October 2023 (Anguiano, 2023). As the strike came to an end, The Writers Guild of America (WGA) and the Alliance of Motion Picture and Television Producers agreed on, in summary, not using AI tools to write or rewrite any literary materials (WGA, 2023).

1 Turkey has officially changed its name to Türkiye at the United Nations, as part of a rebranding effort to better represent Turkish culture and dissociate from negative connotations (Staff and agencies, 2022).

AI developments are also increasingly transforming into a technology and arms race between different nations, much like the atomic bomb race and the space race back in the middle of the 20th century (Geist, 2016), named as the "AI Cold War" in 2018 by Nicholas Thompson and Ian Bremmer in an article for *Wired* magazine (Thompson & Bremmer, 2018). They attribute the origin of this narrative to 2017 when China unveiled its AI Development Plan, outlining a strategy to become the world leader in AI by 2030. While the authors acknowledge China's use of AI to reinforce its authoritarian rule, they caution the United States against adopting an AI Cold War approach. Instead, Thompson and Bremmer advocate for technological collaboration between the United States and China, emphasizing the importance of establishing global standards for privacy and ethical AI use. In any case, indeed, the usage and regulation of AI is already one of the most substantial points that needs to be addressed in an alarmingly haste manner. AI regulation began in 2021 with the proposed EU Act (Yang & Bernot, 2023). The global landscape of AI policies and strategies currently involves over 1,600 initiatives, with the European Union, China, the United States, and the United Kingdom playing crucial roles (Stacey&Milmo; OECD.AI, 2021). The year 2023 also witnessed government regulations regarding AI. Hosted by the British government, the AI safety summit resulted in the Bletchley Declaration (Milmo & Stacey, 2023) signed by the United Kingdom, the United States, European Union, and China on November 1, 2023, becoming the first international agreement about controlling the risks posed by AI and imposing the countries to work together on AI safety research. On December 8, 2023, all the 27 member countries of the European Union signed a tentative political agreement for the Artificial Intelligence Act (Chan, 2023). At the same time, US vice-president Kamela Harris and President Biden presented AI directives (Wintour, 2023) under which companies creating AI models with potential threats to national security, economic security, or public safety must share safety test results with the government. Türkiye also presided over the National Artificial Intelligence Strategy Steering Committee Meeting to address the rapid rise of AI technologies. It was noted in the meeting that a detailed action plan, with 6 strategic priorities, 24 objectives, 119 measures, 122 actions, and 451 implementations, was approved during the second meeting on April 21, 2022 (Kutbe, 2023). Of these measures, 133 have been completed, 118 are progressing as planned, and around 120 remain behind schedule. The focus of the meeting was on evaluating these steps meticulously. To monitor and contribute to global-level standardization efforts, a committee for Artificial Intelligence Mirror Standards was also established within the Turkish Standards Institute (TSE). What is more, AI rose in popularity, becoming the most notable word of 2023 (Addley, 2023).

One might ask, why should we study the dynamics between AI tools and journalism in Türkiye? Increasingly, new studies emphasize that developing countries are particularly prone to the negative outcomes of AI usage (Hagerty & Rubinov, 2019). Recently, Türkiye was among the region's most prosperous emerging economies. However, its progress was severely hindered by growing authoritarianism and restrictions on society and journalists that interrupted the democratic operations in the state (The World Bank in Türkiye, 2023). In contrast to research on global inventions and their studies, automated journalism has received relatively less attention in the region. Researching a developing country enables us to comprehend its unique challenges with automation. Reuters Institute for the Study of Journalism's 2022 Digital News Report underlines the momentous challenges the Turkish media is coping with in addition to political censorship and detained journalists (Newman, 2022). The report also points out the rise of misinformation online. According to the Media Ownership Monitor, Türkiye (2021), more than two-thirds of the top 40 media outlets in Türkiye, including those owned by the state, are owned by business groups involved in sectors such as construction, energy, mining, and tourism. These include Demirören, Doğuş, Ciner, Albayrak, Kalyon, and İhlas, with a total of eight newspapers, nine television channels, nine radio stations, and seven websites. *Reporters without Borders* (Turkey Press Freedom Figures, 2021) also notes that with 90% of the national media now under government control, the public has turned to critical or independent media outlets of various political affiliations over the past five years to understand the impact of the economic and political crisis on the country. These outlets include local TV channels like Fox TV, Halk TV, Tele1, and Sözcü, as well as international news websites such as BBC Turkish, VOA Turkish, and Deutsche Welle Turkish. As the use of AI tools became increasingly public with the prevalence of generative AI and large language models like OpenAI's ChatGPT and Google Bard, another question should be how it has an impact on the workforce, how necessary it is, and whether the majority is aware of the advantages and/or disadvantages that they may bring, let alone utilizing them.

13.1.1 Methodology

Involving analyses of multiple interviews with journalists to investigate how Turkish news organizations utilized automated journalism, the research investigated the advantages, disadvantages, and potential risks associated with automation in journalism. Journalists from various national newspaper organizations in Türkiye, including Hurriyet, Sozcu, Birgün, Sabah, Cumhuriyet, and others, as well as independent Turkish journalists and media entities, were interviewed. The primary objective was to assess the future of journalism by addressing the challenges within the Turkish journalism landscape, the existing automation tools and software for fact-checking and news writing, and the legal, economic, and ethical implications. A follow-up meeting was organized with some interviewees to assess the possible impact of generative AI tools.

A convenience sampling method, supplemented by limited snowball techniques, was used to select interviewees. Out of more than 200 journalists contacted to gather their perspectives on using automated journalism in Turkish media, detailed interviews were conducted with 21 individuals, including journalists, reporters, researchers, and search engine optimization (SEO) specialists. It's important to note that more than 20 of the 200 journalists approached lacked knowledge about the subject, while over 10 directed the author to their information technology (IT) or SEO departments, as this topic associated more closely with those professions.

In addition to contacting 200 journalists, over 100 SEO professionals, content managers, and journal editors were also contacted. However, only twenty responded, and the majority did not respond. Contact with professionals happened through their work emails, Twitter, and LinkedIn direct messages. The interviews of volunteers were conducted using various methods, including messaging, email, voice recordings, and video conferencing via Zoom.

13.2 AI IN PRACTICE

Using automation tools for journalism also depends on how we define journalism and journalists. The definitions of journalism and the journalist changed from the past to now, and they will inevitably change soon, as well. For some scholars, journalism has become highly technologized since the late 20th century with the rise of websites, mobile phones, and social media platforms (Rodríguez-Castro & González-Tosat, 2023, p. 93). Most of the journalists we interviewed during the study stressed the qualities of an ideal journalist who is brave, transparent, conscientious, and curious, and who observes, questions, researches, and records. For them, journalism is intricately linked with human emotions, human communication, moral codes, and authentic use of the language. As such, automated journalism tools cannot surpass human journalists because they lack the reasoning, dedication, and creativity that human journalists possess. Although automated journalism can theoretically be engaged with tasks such as data collection, literature review preparation, and delivering accurate information fairly and impartially, its effectiveness falls short compared with human journalists when it comes to connecting with the audience on an empathetic level. As a result, automated journalism may struggle to communicate as effectively as its human counterparts (Ozkurt Azimli, 2022). Additionally, journalists categorize the practice of journalism into two types: the first involves investigative storytelling centered on human thoughts, actions, and emotions, while the second is grounded in analytical details (Ozkurt Azimli, 2022).

Moreover, according to Bilge Narin Şenyüz, who have conducted interviews with experts in the technology industry and computer scientists, automated journalistic techniques exist in large-scale newsrooms for the practices of election results, weather reporting, earthquakes, and traffic conditions (Narin, p. 94). Narin starts her article by interpreting Jung's ideas, suggesting that journalists, having developed a distinct professional mindset, view themselves as a separate group from the rest of society (Narin, p. 82).

Many journalists and writers now access resources and tools for automated journalism, including those offered by Google, such as Bard, Data Commons, Fact Check Tools, and other data-related tools. Hemingway and Grammarly are also popular tools used for proofreading by journalists, academics, and writers. Additionally, several websites aggregate personalized news content based on user's interests and activities, including Digg, Stumbleupon, and Technorati. Last but not least, ChatGPT is used often. Throughout our interviews, many journalists admitted to having limited knowledge on the subject. At the same time, some underlined the use of summarization programs like Automated

Insights, Narrative Science, United Robots, and Monok, employed by notable media outlets such as Forbes, Yahoo, Associated Press, *Reuters*, *New York Times*, *Washington Post*, and ProPublica. Another journalist referenced an article in *The Guardian* composed by an AI program that aimed to alleviate fears about AI. Additionally, a journalist from Gazete Pencere exemplified a play scripted by AI but also acknowledged the challenges of accessing data sources. This journalist pointed out that AI programs face difficulties conducting news research in public institutions, archives, private companies, handwritten transcripts, and similar resources (Ozkurt Azimli, 2022).

Many companies also invest in automation technologies. Alibaba, for example, a China-based e-commerce company, developed AI-CopyWriter, an AI-powered copywriting tool utilizing deep learning and natural language processing (Dhandre, 2018). Meta's DeepText understands texts through deep learning (Engineering at Meta, 2016), while Microsoft retains AI for article summarization (Wiggers, 2018).

Forbes, on the other hand, employs the AI model, Bertie, as a tool for generating initial drafts and news story templates, as elucidated by Martin (2019). In its inaugural year, The Heliograf of Washington Post autonomously produced a substantial volume of 850 articles (Martin, 2019). A collaborative initiative between the Press Association and Urbs Media involves the utilization of RADAR (Reporters and Data and Robots), a system grounded in natural language generation (NLG) technology, for the automated generation of content (Marr, 2021). The academic publisher, Springer Nature, notably debuted the first research book authored by machine learning (Vincent, 2019). What is more, Reuters also uses machine learning methodologies, exemplified through tools like News Tracer and Lynx, for systematically tracking news on Twitter platform (Google News Initiative (GNI), p. 6).

In the year 2019, Quartz AI Studio entered into a partnership with the International Consortium of Investigative Journalists (ICIJ) for the Luanda Leaks investigation, thereby showcasing the integration of AI in the landscape of journalistic endeavors (GNI, p. 25). ProPublica similarly harnesses machine learning methodologies for the analytical examination of US Congress press releases, thereby underscoring the various applications of AI within the domain of journalism (GNI, p. 27). Meanwhile, The Upshot of *The New York Times* distinguishes itself through the sophisticated utilization of extensive datasets and advanced visualization techniques, augmenting the quality of journalistic reporting (Gil, 2014).

Conversely, within the Turkish media landscape, the absence of dedicated departments for data journalism is notable, although diminutive teams are engaged in different projects (Doğu, 2015, p. 183). Simultaneously, obtaining freely accessible and transparent public data in Türkiye is also challenging. Nonetheless, there is the presence of freely available datasets, including Datablog, FiveThirtyEight, and Wonkblog, alongside the operations of organizations such as Journalism++, OpenDataCity, and Storyful CartoDB (p. 183–184). One problem with the usage of such datasets or AI tools, however, is the cost, most notably due to the ongoing currency crisis in Türkiye and hyperinflation (Askew, 2023). Therefore, subscribing to AI tools or data sets is not cost-effective for many media outlets.

As journalism has been going through constant changes, some argue that automation would not have a disruptive effect on journalism practices (Linden, 2019). Rodríguez-Castro and González-Tosat (2023, p. 95) reinforce that journalists have effectively mitigated concerns about the potential threat of job losses posed by automation. Instead, they have recognized the advantages of incorporating AI solutions, enabling them to engage in more sophisticated and value-added journalistic endeavors, moving beyond routine tasks (Rodríguez-Castro & González-Tosat, 2023, p. 94), but still argue that journalism is heavily influenced by human involvement (Rodríguez-Castro & González-Tosat, 2023, p. 94). The utilization of automation practices in newsrooms has surged in recent years, although the initial instances date back to 40 years ago (Linden, 2019, p. 238). Areas like the weather forecast, traffic updates, sports outcomes, and medical or financial reports (Linden, 2019, p. 241) present heightened potential for automation. Automation can enhance the efficiency of news production and distribution, broaden the range of coverage, and reduce costs by replacing costly salaries of the journalists performing time-consuming tasks with automated solutions instead (Rodríguez-Castro & González-Tosat, 2023, p. 95). Indeed, most journalists interviewed also sincerely shared the problems experienced due to the race against time in internet journalism, clickbait journalism, and the consequent lack of fact-checking (Ozkurt Azimli, 2022). Automated journalism techniques may instead help assist the creation of SEO-focused articles, deciphering voice recordings, translation, image generation, headline generation, and simple fact-checking. As one journalist mentioned in the study, this may make room for some investigative, opinion-based, or long reports and news that are currently unprepared due to a lack of time and energy (Ozkurt Azimli, 2022). In the meantime, they may also pose dangers to individuals and institutions in case of data leaks, hacking, and undeniable other technical problems, as well as creating biased or wrong information due to the tainted data available.

13.3 DISCUSSION

An immediate observation emerged that only a limited number of Turkish media practitioners exhibit familiarity with automated journalism tools; most declined to comment on the topic, citing a lack of knowledge.

Reporters recurrently believed that automation could potentially reduce news-making costs in the future, though they are currently expensive. They also emphasize the potential of automated journalism in terms of speed and impartiality, as well as reducing the workloads of the journalists. Skepticism persists, however, concerning the capacity of automated journalism to express human emotions such as creativity, empathy, storytelling, and ethical judgment with journalistic integrity. Moreover, anxieties persist regarding potential job losses, the erosion of fact-checking, ethical considerations, and potential hacking threats. Consequently, there is a call for developing new legal frameworks to effectively address the challenges posed by automation in journalism. Human involvement is also necessary, although automation might be supportive, particularly in data-heavy reporting. Despite recognizing the potential support that automation can provide, there is a unanimous sentiment that it cannot replace the human elements intrinsic to journalism. In the aftermath of our initial research phase, most journalists we met experimented with generative AI tools such as ChatGPT. Growing use cases went hand in hand with existing anxieties and hesitations about AI usage. However, this signifies a more delicate understanding and approach to AI.

Journalists have identified numerous applications for generative AI in the field of journalism. This includes aiding in news discovery by identifying relevant stories, assisting in research to gather and synthesize information, and facilitating interviews. Generative AI also plays a major role in news writing, fact-checking for accuracy, and editing to enhance clarity and coherence. It contributes to the composition of engaging headlines and captions and assists in the design aspect to improve visual appeal. Furthermore, generative AI may address legal issues in journalism, simplify the publishing process, aid in the promotion and distribution of news content across various channels, and enhance audience interaction. The technology is particularly adept at analyzing news consumption patterns. Its proficiency extends to distributing news on social media, analyzing engagement data related to news, optimizing for search engines (SEO), and restructuring articles into the inverted pyramid format.

Moreover, it shows promising applications in data journalism, particularly in data mining, to unearth insightful patterns or, for instance, extract and analyze data from PDF files. Ertuna (2023) emphasized translation, news writing, and social media content sharing, particularly among the new generative AI tools. News media requires news-related images but in case one cannot find a suitable representative image, Dall.E and Midjourney were mentioned as image creators. This is better than using a copyrighted image in this case. However, all these tools mean that there is also a growing need for journalists and journalist candidates to know how to use AI in the media (Çelik, 2022).

On the other hand, Ertuna (2023) points out why it is better that experienced professionals may be best suited to work in tandem with AI tools. A long interview can easily be transcribed by software, but the transcribing process may trigger new insights. Thus, a journalist may occasionally refuse to use generative AI tools to maintain a journalistic insight-building process. Again, AI can suggest the most SEO-friendly headline, but this may not be the best for the particular media outlet's audience. Generative AI may create a list of basic questions, but an experienced journalist must add particularly insightful questions for the interview to have a distinctive one. Many journalists also believe that AI-generated content may be biased towards the mainstream, and their intervention will be necessary. In sum, despite the technological advancements in the last decades, journalistic principles have not changed, and the new generative AI tools cannot automatically increase journalistic quality.

An ongoing theme is the freedom of expression, and whatever the technology is used, journalistic content will be subject to political restrictions. However, responsible AI usage is also promoted in government circles, and there is a call for digital literacy concerning AI (Calli, 2023).

13.4 CONCLUSION

This study explored the current usage and future potential of automated journalism techniques in the Turkish media through interviews with journalists across various news organizations. The research revealed limited familiarity and prevalence of these methods presently, though some applications were highlighted in areas like summarization, data-driven reporting, and translation.

However, perspectives on the future adoption of automated journalism differed. While recognizing evident advantages around efficiency, speed, cost, and impartiality, predominant skepticism persisted regarding advanced AI's capacity to convey innate human qualities fundamental to quality journalism. These include emotional resonance, creativity, ethical integrity, and meticulous storytelling.

Nonetheless, anxieties around potential job losses posed by automation in journalism were balanced by the view that AI could play more of an assistive role, leaving the deeper responsibilities to human reporters. This may involve taking over routine mechanical tasks to free up journalists' time for sophisticated analysis and impactful investigative work.

As such, while the unique social and political challenges in the Turkish media may inhibit quick adoption, automated techniques have promising applications if implemented judiciously alongside human oversight. Still, further research through on-site observations and in-depth interviews are still necessary for a complete understanding. Comparative studies can also illuminate differences in journalistic cultures and automation habits across countries.

In the end, Turkish journalism should not view AI solely as a threat. With responsible development centered on human values, automated solutions have the potential to augment human capabilities and uplift the field. However, realizing this requires proactive engagement from media practitioners in shaping the technology's emergence.

REFERENCES

Adams, T. (2015, June 28). And the Pulitzer goes to… a computer. *The Guardian*. www.theguardian.com/technology/2015/jun/28/computer-writing-journalism-artificial-intelligence

Addley, E. (2023, November 1). 'AI' named most notable word of 2023 by Collins dictionary. *The Guardian*. www.theguardian.com/technology/2023/nov/01/ai-named-most-notable-word-of-2023-by-collins-dictionary

Amodei, D., & Hernández, D. (2018, May 16). AI and compute. *OpenAI Research*. https://openai.com/research/ai-and-compute

Anguiano, D. (2023, September 27). Hollywood writers agree to end five-month strike after new studio deal. *The Guardian*. www.theguardian.com/culture/2023/sep/26/hollywood- writers-strike-ends-studio-deal

Askew, J. (2023, November 9). Soaring inflation and a collapsing currency: Why is Turkey's economy in such a mess? *Euronews*. www.euronews.com/2022/11/09/everything-is-overheating-why-is-turkeys-economy-in-such-a-mess

Calli, M. E. (2023, December 13). Turkish communications director urges updating digital media literacy for use of AI. *Anadolu Ajansı*. www.aa.com.tr/en/turkiye/turkish-communcations-director-urges-updating-media -literacy-for-use-of-ai/3081408

Çelik, K. (2022). Artificial intelligence in journalism and the problems it may bring. *Mecmua, 13*, 143–158.

Chan, K. (2023, December 9). *Europe reaches a deal on the world's first comprehensive AI rules*. The Associated Press. Retrieved on December 15, 2023. https://apnews.com/article/ai-act-europe-regulation-59466a4d8fd3597b04542ef25831322c

Dhandre, P. (2018, July 9). Alibaba introduces AI copywriter. *Packt.* https://hub.packtpub.com/alibaba-introduces-ai-copywriter/

Doğu, B. (2015). Veri Haberciliği: Demokratik Medya İçin Olanaklar. *Folklor/Edebiyat, 21*(83), 181–197. https://dergipark.org.tr/en/pub/fe/issue/26049/274357

Engineering at Meta. (2016, June 1). *Introducing DeepText: Facebook's text understanding engine.* Engineering at Meta.

Ertuna, C. (2023, June 26). Impact of generative AI on the evolution of journalism in Turkey. *MLSA Turkey.* www.mlsaturkey.coom/en/impact-of-generative-ai-on-the-evolution-of-journalism-in-turkey

Geist, E. M. (2016). It's already too late to stop the AI arms race—We must manage it instead. *Bulletin of the Atomic Scientists, 72*(5), 318–321. https://doi.org/10.1080/00963402.2016.1216672

Gil, N. (April 22, 2014). New York Times launches data journalism site The Upshot. *The Guardian.* www.theguardian.com/media/2014/apr/22/new-york-times-launches-data-journalism-site-the-upshot

Google News Initiative. "Introduction to Machine Learning" Retrieved July 6, 2024. https://newsinitiative.withgoogle.com/en-gb/resources/trainings/machine-learning-journalism-and-you/

Hagerty, A., & Rubinov, I. (2019). Global AI ethics: A review of the social impacts and ethical implications of artificial intelligence. https://doi.org/10.48550/arXiv.1907.07892

Kutbe, H. (2023, October 31). Cumhurbaşkanı Yardımcısı Yılmaz: Yapay Zeka Ayna Komitesi'ni kurduk. *Anadolu Ajansı.* www.aa.com.tr/tr/gundem/cumhurbaskani-yardimcisi-yilmaz-yapay-zeka-ayna-komitesini-kurduk/3038809

Linden, C. G. (2019). Algorithms are a reporter's new best friend: News automation and the case for augmented journalism. In Eldridge II, S. & Franklin, B. (Eds.), *The Routledge handbook of developments in digital journalism studies* (pp. 238–250). Routledge.

Marr, B. (2021, July 23). Press association: Using artificial intelligence and NLG to automate local news. *Bernardmarr.com.* https://bernardmarr.com/press-association-using-artificial-intelligence-and-nlg-to-automate-local-news/

Martin, N. (2019, February 8). Did a robot write this? How AI is impacting journalism. *Forbes.* www.forbes.com/sites/nicolemartin1/2019/02/08/did-a-robot-write-this-how-ai-is-impacting-journalism/?sh=6b4e933c7795

Media Ownership Monitor, Turkey. (2021). Retrieved on June 3, 2022. https://turkey.mom-rsf.org/

Milmo, D., & Stacey, K. (2023, November 2). Five takeaways from UK's AI safety summit at Bletchley Park. *The Guardian.* www.theguardian.com/technology/2023/nov/02/five-takeaways-uk-ai-safety-summit-bletchley-park-rishi-sunak

Narin, B. (2017). Uzman Görüşleri Bağlamında Haber Üretiminde Otomatikleşme: Robot Gazetecilik. *Galatasaray Üniversitesi İletişim Dergisi,* (27), 79–108. https://doi.org/10.16878/gsuilet.373242

Newman, N. (2022). 2022 Digital news report: Turkey. *Reuters Institute for the Study of Journalism.* https://reutersinstitute.politics.ox.ac.uk/digital-news-report/2022/turkey

OECD.AI. (2021). Powered by EC/OECD, database of national AI policies. Retrieved on November 16, 2023. https://oecd.ai

Ozkurt Azimli, S. (2022). The use of automated journalism in the Turkish media: An observation of its present and future. (747419) [Master's thesis, Istanbul Bilgi University]. Ulusal Tez Merkezi.

Parasie, S. & Dagiral, E. (2012). Data-driven journalism and the public good: "Computer assisted-reporters and "programmer-journalists" in Chicago. *New Media Society*. DOI: 10.1177/1461444812463345.

PwC's Global Artificial Intelligence Study: Sizing the prize. (2023). *PwC*. Retrieved on November 16, 2023. www.pwc.com/gx/en/issues/data-and-analytics/publications/artificial-intelligence-study.html

Rodríguez-Castro, M., & González-Tosat, C. (2023). Journalism's cruise control: How can public service media outlets benefit from AI and automation? In García-Orosa, B., Pérez-Seijo, S., & Vizoso, Á. (Eds.), *Emerging practices in the age of automated digital journalism models, languages, and storytelling*. (pp. 93–104). Routledge.

Saka, E. (2023, November 14). Our ongoing work on AI Literacy. *Erkan's Field Diary*. https://erkansaka.net/2023/11/14/our-ongoing-work-on-ai-literacy/

Stacey, K., & Milmo, D. (2023, November 1). UK, US, EU and China sign declaration of AI's 'catastrophic' danger. *The Guardian*. www.theguardian.com/technology/2023/nov/01/uk-us-eu-and-china-sign-declaration-of-ais-catastrophic-danger

Staff and agencies. (2022, June 3). Turkey officially changes name at UN to Türkiye. *The Guardian*. www.theguardian.com/world/2022/jun/03/turkey-changes-name-to-turkiye-as-other-name-is-for-the-birds

The World Bank in Türkiye. (2023, October 9). *World Bank*. Retrieved on December 16, 2023. www.worldbank.org/en/country/turkey/overview

Thompson, N., & Bremmer, I. (2018, October 23). The AI cold war that threatens us all. *Wired*. www.wired.com/story/ai-cold-war-china-could-doom-us-all/

Turkey Press Freedom Figures. (2021). *Reporters without borders*. Retrieved on June 3, 2022. https://rsf.org/en/turkey-press-freedom-figures

Vincent, J. (2019, April 10). The first AI-generated textbook shows what robot writers are actually good at. *The Verge*. www.theverge.com/2019/4/10/18304558/ai-writing-academic-research-book-springer-nature-artificial-intelligence

Wiggers, K. (2018, November 6). Microsoft develops flexible AI system that can summarize the news. *Venturebeat*. https://venturebeat.com/2018/11/06/microsoft-researchers-develop-ai-system-that-can-generate-articles-summaries/

Wintour, P. (2023, November 1). Kamala Harris to call for urgent action on AI threat to democracy and privacy. *The Guardian*. www.theguardian.com/technology/2023/oct/30/biden-orders-tech-firms-to-share-ai-safety-test-results-with-us-government

Writers Guild of America (WGA). (2023). Summary of the 2023 WGA MBA. *WGA Contract 2023*. www.wgacontract2023.org/the-campaign/summary-of-the-2023-wga-mba

Yang, F., & Bernot, A. (2023, November 8). Who will write the rules for AI? How nations are racing to regulate artificial intelligence. *The Conversation*. https://theconversation.com/who-will-write-the-rules-for-ai-how-nations-are-racing-to-regulate-artificial-intelligence-216900

CHAPTER 14

The Interrelation between Journalism, Artificial Intelligence, and Professional Ethics: Ethical Reflections in the Digital Era

Ramiro Ruales Parreño, Galo Vásconez Merino, and Andrés Murillo Pinos

14.1 INTRODUCTION

The understanding of the phenomenon of communication has come a long way. It is no longer conceived as a linear process but is now understood as a systemic relationship that goes from all to all. "In which the global discourse is modified as it is disseminated by the interaction of users organised in distribution networks" (Túñez-López, 2021, p. 8). There are different paradoxes in this new communicational situation. For example, there are audiences with greater autonomy, but who, with their interactions in the digital sphere, leave greater traces that condition what they will see in the future.

The public has an indeterminate amount of information at its disposal, but each search leaves a clue that makes it possible to point out patterns of action, "which silently guides that behaviour and, therefore, although not consciously for the user, they limit it or, at least, condition it" (Túñez-López, 2021, p. 8). The media are facing a new scenario, in which audiences play a preponderant role:

> To serve audiences as individuals, media companies must understand audience feelings and preferences towards content and characters, assess resonance and quickly align content with audience preferences. To achieve this, media

DOI: 10.1201/9781003473633-14

> companies must acquire information from large data sets and act on it in real time. The traditional approach to collecting and interpreting audience data is no longer agile enough for such a scenario.
>
> (Chan-Olmsted, 2019, p. 8)

Another very important sense in today's communication is the intentionality of the message. In this respect, deepfakes are increasingly difficult to distinguish from reality, with visual and voice imitations, which have no difference to the original. However, on the other hand, work is also being done on tools that allow the identification of these imitations (Medina Chicaiza & Martínez Ortega, 2020).

In this review, the research method of qualitative systematic text analysis was applied to obtain information from the data collected. The study follows the phases of thematic analysis, which include familiarisation with the data, development of themes, reorganisation and integration of themes and thematic interpretations. Data collection involved a search of databases and literature using key words. A total of 50 articles, news articles and books were examined to identify themes related to media, artificial intelligence (AI) and deontology.

14.2 MEDIA AND AI

Artificial intelligence, hereinafter AI, has achieved great importance nowadays due to its great capacity to immediately solve specific problems using "syntactic elements of language, not (...) semantic ones" (Malpica, 2016, p. 9). This means that the machines focus on specific problems, and discard other types of problems:

> This is where their main difficulty lies in their communication with humans and in being able to imitate them one hundred percent, their algorithms are logical, not human, they are not part of a conscious reasoning process of the machine, since consciousness is the ability to debate, reflect and realise its own existence that the human has.
>
> (Pineda de Alcázar, 2018, p. 397)

There are several visions of how decisive AI may become in the present and in the future. On the one hand, it is conceived as a nascent mode of programmatic organisation that tends towards a new capitalist control oriented towards the virtual, but it can also be seen as a system that enacts and establishes spheres of social control, by means of highly personalised messages that have their basis in prior data processing (Pineda de Alcázar, 2018; Túñez-López, 2021).

In this sense, the possibilities of AI impact are translated into different scenarios, such as emotion recognition, micro-segmentation, creation of personalised products on a large scale, "instant availability of content in multilanguage and adjusted to any language, even with programmed settings to be broadcast with different types of voice or presented with different prototypes of people" (Túñez-López et al., 2021, p. 190).

The applications of AI take different forms, many of which are well established and widespread, while others are still being explored and discovered. Thus, applications to streamline the information process and resources that use algorithms to analyse consumption habits, fact-checking tools or trends in social networks stand out (Peña-Fernández et al., 2023).

14.2.1 AI Determinations in the Field of Journalism

The interplay generated between AI tasks and the data contained in big data has led to a profound transformation in the sphere of digital journalism, redefining paradigms and enabling new forms of information production and consumption. AI is gaining momentum as it gains a foothold. There is now talk of computational journalism, which is a way of automating the generation of information (Coddington, 2015).

Journalism of this nature requires knowledge of arithmetic and "the ability to work with numbers accurately, and an understanding of basic concepts of descriptive statistics" (Gómez-Diago, 2022, p. 31). This algorithmic journalism, moreover, must have the right ethical paths and codes of transparency and objectivity.

The changes in the field of journalism that could be implemented with the arrival of AI can be condensed into three levels:

- An automated and quantifiable audience, therefore, possible to know through the tools of big data.
- Less involvement of journalists in the production of texts since the selection of sources and review of content can be automated.
- The usual activities of journalists can easily be done by AI, for example, in the field of subtitling, classification or elaboration of material (Gómez-Diago, 2022).

The technology and its integration with journalistic practice is not a new development but has been tried and tested for some time. For example, in 2009, Northwestern University in the United States developed a system called Stats Monkey that generated automated news stories, covering all kinds of fields with structured data (Lindén et al., 2019; Peña-Fernández et al., 2023).

However, news agencies have not been able to assimilate to the speed of technological change, and automation has been slow, with very few successful examples around the world, precisely because of defensive and hesitant actions within the journalistic field (Lahav & Reich, 2011).

Several studies have been conducted on the application of AI in journalism, especially in the Western context. For example, one study approached participants from leading news organisations, such as CNN, BBC, and Thomson Reuters, to work closely with the robotic newsroom. In doing so, the results indicated that journalists pointed to the limitations of automation in elements such as sourcing and sensitivity but highlighted that AI will play an increasingly important role, leading to news with greater depth, accuracy and immediacy (Thurman et al., 2017).

14.2.2 Benefits of AI and Big Data and Their Contribution to Digital Journalism

On the positive side of what AI can offer in relation to the media, there are many voices. For context, the media has been heavily criticised for misinformation and for apparent links to ideologies and politics. In this regard, a study in China found that more than half of the participants believed that the media was responsible for fake news, followed by journalists and social media, with only 24.3% blaming audiences for the spread of fake news (Willnat et al., 2018).

Leading media companies such as Facebook, Amazon, Apple, Netflix, and Google have embraced the use of AI to refine products and make services smarter. Another great value to be found in AI is the support in identifying new business opportunities. "For example, AI enables better recommended playlists in Spotify and Netflix, plus more effective content management in media companies, and even chatbots to improve customer experience" (Chan-Olmsted, 2019, p. 8).

Another benefit of AI can be found in understanding social conversations and audience preferences. In addition, it can specialise in interpreting content that is produced live, and to improve the organisation of a media outlet's archive, through metadata and context (Canepa et al., 2017).

For its part, big data is a concept intrinsically linked to the quantity and complexity of data; from a more technical perspective it is the set of information so vast and diverse that conventional data processing tools are inadequate; thus, big data encompasses not only the magnitude of the volume of data but also its speed of generation and the variety of sources.

Big data within digital journalism manifests itself in the ability to process and analyse huge amounts of information from a variety of sources. News platforms use big data to understand user behaviour, preferences and information consumption habits, so that the digital content product can engage in a process of dynamic content personalisation.

These aspects have revolutionised editorial strategies, which, with the use of predictive analytics algorithms, allow the media to anticipate emerging trends and adapt their editorial approach by evaluating the effectiveness of different headlines, topics or content formats, providing valuable information to optimise the presentation of news; and, in the case of big data, in this context, it becomes the engine that fuels innovation by providing the necessary raw material for predictive analysis and the identification of patterns.

This process has unleashed a revolution in digital journalism, offering a panoply of substantial benefits in terms of efficiency, innovation and diversity; efficiency in content production represents one of the most significant achievements derived from this technological synergy; an illustrative example is the use of natural language processing algorithms to write routine reports, freeing journalists from repetitive tasks and allowing them to concentrate on creating more analytical and sophisticated content.

Innovation manifests itself prominently in AI's ability to create personalised user experiences, with the application of recommendation algorithms, based on big data, for example including personalised news services, where AI learns users' interests and suggests specific content, leading to improved user experience and driving engagement and loyalty, generating a feedback loop that continuously improves the quality and relevance of content.

14.2.3 Risks Involved in Digital Journalism

Within the academic community there is no consensus on the influence of AI on society, and specifically on the media. On the one hand, there are views that argue that AI has more complexities than social benefits:

> Less complacent visions draw AI as a new way of organising and controlling commercial relations generating a new virtual capitalist control, or as a system designed to generate spheres of social control through singularised products or messages adjusted to needs detected by mass data processing.
>
> (Túñez-López, 2021, p. 8)

From this notion, the use of AI can lead to the redefinition of the communicative perspectives of the media since the technology would be used as a generator of content and not as a mediator. In this sense, we could expect to have media without journalists (Ufarte-Ruiz et al., 2023).

In addition to the aforementioned, AI can come to define different types of labour inequality that can create complex crises, given the changes that have been taking place since the proliferation of information and communication technologies at the beginning of the century (Díaz-Noci, 2023).

These logical, mathematical and sequential processes, while promising remarkable advances, carry intrinsic risks that reverberate in the quality, credibility and accountability of information, since information quality, being the cornerstone of journalism, faces a latent risk in the form of algorithmic bias and can distort journalistic objectivity by perpetuating biases present in training data, and this bias often goes unnoticed and threatens to undermine the integrity and fairness of news reporting.

Journalistic credibility, essential to the bond of trust with the audience, is at stake in the increasing reliance on algorithms in news generation and reporting; the lack of clarity in the analytical capacity of algorithmic processes represents a significant challenge.

In addition, there is a risk of fake news dissemination, which is exacerbated by the rapid evolution of AI, as advanced algorithms generate information in a convincing manner, challenging the ability of journalists to verify facts and maintain news integrity.

Another element to analyse concerns user privacy, immersed in the maelstrom of big data, which emerges as another area of risk for journalism, as the massive collection of data to personalise content can lead to privacy violations.

Over-reliance on algorithms could result in the loss of the human essence of news writing and editing; this process called over-automation could diminish the capacity for discernment and contextualisation that human journalists bring to the table, and the quality of content and message would deteriorate.

Algorithms that recommend news based on prior preferences can create information bubbles, where users are only exposed to limited perspectives, leading to a homogenisation of information that can undermine the diversity of opinions and perspectives, thus compromising the quality and breadth of information that journalism aspires to provide.

In assessing these risks, the implementation of AI and big data in digital journalism requires constant ethical reflection and prudent management. The adoption of safeguards, such as transparency in algorithms, continuous training of journalists in fact-checking and digital ethics and the establishment of clear regulations to protect user privacy, are positioned as essential pillars to mitigate these risks.

14.3 DEONTOLOGY AND ARTIFICIAL INTELLIGENCE

In the 21st century, the digitisation of technical and technological processes opens up new possibilities for education and communication. Under this principle, the constant evolution of technology and the development of AI present not only opportunities but also risks and, above all, ethical questions and concerns (Selwyn et al., 2022).

Van de Poel and Royakkers (2011, p. 71) define ethics as "systematic reflection on morality", where morality is seen as "the set of opinions, decisions and actions by which people, individually or collectively, express what they consider to be good or right". Thus, ethics and morality are two distinct but related concepts. As for ethics, it seeks to initiate a process of searching for the right morality in order to address moral problems, since ethics does not provide us with a guide that gives us clear answers on how we should or should not behave but allows us to reflect on the choices we can make, that is, it gives us free will.

As can be seen, among the risks is one linked to access to information, which is being heavily manipulated by the empires of behaviour modification, referring to companies such as Facebook, Google and Twitter, and how these companies use different algorithms and programming to access the personal data of their users for advertising purposes or to predict and analyse consumer or behavioural trends, thanks, today, to the use of digital tools such as AI.

Under this modern panorama of infinite digital resources and unknowns, about the positive and negative aspects of these tools, the challenges regarding the ethics of Under this modern panorama of infinite digital resources and unknowns about the positive and negative aspects of these tools, the challenges regarding the ethics of AI are configured as the epicentre of public debate, so that, on a more general level, there is a need to do things ethically, with the aim of warning new and current generations about the dangers of the indiscriminate use of AI, which is now so accessible and common in education, as well as in the professional practice of communication (Selwyn, 2019).

In a similar vein, Benjamins and Salazar (2020) argue that since it is not possible to teach ethics to a machine, it will be up to companies and their developers to demand that the development and use of AI be carried out in an ethical manner, in accordance with international human rights, applicable to all fields of knowledge.

These are issues that increasingly affect and concern academic, scientific and professional communities, as well as organisations, public and private entities, governments and, in short, society in general. However, the first step is to learn from the technology we live with, with the aspiration to better understand the world.

Therefore, the implementation of AI technologies in society and professional practice in general must be seen as a complex and highly controversial issue (Selwyn, 2019) where morals and ethical principles must be solidly supported by regulation with a global approach.

In the last year, several experts point out that the multiple and complex challenges associated with AI need to be properly considered. For example, AI is sometimes known to have a biased stance; however, the cause is not always obvious. AI decisions may be biased because the human data it relies on is biased and/or because the algorithms applied and developed by humans are biased. In other words, AI mirrors and exemplifies human decision-making, which reinforces the need for humans to step up and take responsibility and control.

However, it should be made clear that AI cannot be a source of inspiration for, for example, learning within university development, since, unlike a human teacher, AI does not play on empathy in the teaching–learning process, a process in which inspiration, humanity and sisterhood are fundamental.

Based on this postulate, AI may not completely replace human teachers. But, AI is already being used to support remote learning in different ways with remotely delivered, guided and shared classes, each of which brings benefits and challenges. On the other hand, the various models of AI created by Big Tech (GAFAM) according to Benjamins and Salazar (2020) are becoming increasingly sophisticated, although expert assessments differ as to whether AI (for the time being) have real intelligence, understanding or creativity, let alone possess clear identity, moral integrity or free will, just like humans.

14.4 CONCLUSIONS

The amalgamation of AI and big data in the field of digital journalism engenders a synergy that, while opening up a compendium of possibilities, is not without ethical and professional dilemmas that require a diligent and thoughtful approach; in this context, meticulous and well-founded recommendations are outlined for an ethical and professional use of these technologies in journalistic practice, safeguarding the integrity and responsibility inherent to this discipline.

First, transparency emerges as a fundamental backbone to mitigate the ethical risks linked to AI and big data; complemented by the opacity in algorithmic processes that constitute an intrinsic challenge, causing communication and journalism professionals to opt for clear disclosure of how these technologies influence the production and presentation of content; the selection and personalisation criteria, as well as the explanation of the influence of these algorithms in editorial decision-making, contributes to building a relationship of trust with the audience.

Concomitantly, inadvertent discrimination introduced by these systems can distort journalistic objectivity, and the implementation of rigorous mechanisms for the detection and correction of bias should be pursued, along with constant evaluation and adjustment of the algorithms.

In the realm of fact-checking, the responsibility falls unwaveringly on the shoulders of journalism professionals; for while AI can facilitate the automation of processes, accurate verification of information must be an immutable practice, which is why the adaptation of AI technologies must support fact-checking, along with the ongoing training of journalists to discern the authenticity of information.

In the privacy scenario, where big data plays a leading role, it is crucial to respect ethical and legal boundaries, as mass data collection must adhere to clear informed consent protocols, ensuring that users are fully aware of how their data is employed, and privacy regulations such as the General Data Protection Regulation must be in place imperatively to safeguard public trust and ensure the ethical use of information.

Ethical training of journalism professionals is another cardinal element for responsible use of AI and big data; understanding the ethical and social impacts of these technologies, as well as appreciating the challenges and dilemmas that arise, should be central components of academic and professional training.

The active participation of the public in the editorial process emerges as an innovative and relevant recommendation; the creation of mechanisms that involves the audience in the debate on the use of AI and big data can enrich editorial decision-making and promote a culture of transparency, where open forums, surveys and feedback channels allow the audience to better understand algorithmic dynamics and contribute to the shaping of more ethical and responsible practices.

Finally, the establishment of ethics committees in media organisations can be an invaluable resource that should be composed of professionals, ethicists and representatives of the public, can provide guidance and oversight in the implementation of AI and big data technologies, seeking through the creation of clear ethical guidelines, regular evaluations and collegial decision-making, to ensure that the implementation of these technologies aligns with the fundamental ethical principles of journalism; so that at some point the convergence of AI and big data in digital journalism is used to forge an ethical and professional framework that preserves the integrity and accountability inherent in this discipline; for, the thoughtful and cautious adoption of these guidelines advocates for an ethical evolution in the news landscape, where technology enhances, but does not compromise, the primary mission of journalism: to report accurately, truthfully and ethically.

REFERENCES

Benjamins, R., & Salazar, I. (2020). *El mito del algoritmo. Cuentos y cuentas de la Inteligencia artificial*. Ediciones Anaya Multimedia. https://bit.ly/3QfzhwR

Canepa, S., Van den Dam, R., Berman, S. J., & Toole, D. (2017). *Becoming a "living" media partner for your consumers: A cognitive future for media and entertainment*. www-935.ibm.com/services/us/gbs/thoughtleadership/cogmediaent/

Chan-Olmsted, S. M. (2019). A review of artificial intelligence adoptions in the media industry. *International Journal on Media Management, 21*(3–4), 193–215. https://doi.org/10.1080/14241277.2019.1695619

Coddington, M. (2015). Clarifying journalism's quantitative turn: A typology for evaluating data journalism, computational journalism, and computer-assisted reporting. *Digital Journalism, 3*(3), 331–348. https://doi.org/10.1080/21670811.2014.976400

Díaz-Noci, J. (2023). *Investigar la brecha digital, las noticias y los medios: hacia la equidad informativa digital*. Barcelona: Ediciones Profesionales de la Información.

Gómez-Diago, G. (2022). Perspectivas para abordar la inteligencia artificial en la enseñanza de periodismo. Una revisión de experiencias investigadoras y docentes. *Revista Latina de Comunicación Social, 80*, 29–46. www.doi.org/10.4185/RLCS-2022-1542

Lahav, H., & Reich, Z. (2011). Authors and poets write the news: A case study of a radical journalistic experiment. *Journalism Studies, 12*(5), 624–641. https://doi.org/10.1080/14616 70X.2011.562659

Lindén, C. G., Tuulonen, H., B€ack, A., Diakopoulos, N., Granroth-Wilding, M., Haapanen, L., Leppänen, L., Melin, M., Moring, T., Munezero, M., & Sirén-Heikel, S. (2019). *News automation: The rewards, risks and realities of 'machine journalism*. Germany: WAN-IFRA.

Malpica, J. (2016). *Inteligencia artificial y consciencia*. España: Universidad Alcalá de Henares.

Medina Chicaiza, P., & Martínez Ortega, A. (2020). Tecnologías en la inteligencia artificial para el Marketing: Una revisión de la literatura. *Pro Sciences, 4*(30), 36–47. https://doi.org/10.29018/issn.2588-1000vol4iss30.2020pp36-47

Peña-Fernández, S., Meso-Ayerdi, K., Larrondo-Ureta, A., & Díaz-Noci, J. (2023). Without journalists, there is no journalism: The social dimension of generative artificial intelligence in the media. *Profesional de la información, 32*(2), 1–16. https://doi.org/10.3145/epi.2023.mar.27

Pineda de Alcázar, M. (2018). Inteligencia Artificial y Modelos de Comunicación. *Razón y Palabra, 22*(1_100), 391–405. https://revistarazonypalabra.org/index.php/ryp/article/view/1162

Sánchez, J. L. M., & Ruiz, M. J. U. (2020). Inteligencia artificial y periodismo. *Revista Cidob d'afers internacionals*, (124), 49–72. doi.org/10.24241/rcai.2020.124.1.49

Selwyn, N. (2019). *¿Deberían los robots sustituir al profesorado? La IA y el futuro de la educación*. España: Ediciones Morata. https://bit.ly/3zxyPmO

Selwyn, N., Rivera-Vargas, P., Passeron, E., & Miño-Puigcercos, R. (2022). ¿Por qué no todo es (ni debe ser) digital? Interrogantes para pensar sobre digitalización, datificación e inteligencia artificial en educación. In P. Rivera-Vargas, R. Miño-Puigcercos, & E. Passeron (Eds.), *Educar con sentido transformador en la universidad* (pp. 137–147). España: Ediciones Octaedro. https://doi.org/10.31235/osf.io/vx4zr

Thurman, N., Dörr, K., & Kunert, J. (2017). When reporters get hands-on with robo- writing. *Digital Journalism, 5*(10), 1240–1259. https://doi.org/10.1080/21670811.2017.1289819

Túñez-López, J. M. (2021). Tendencias e impacto de la inteligencia artificial en comunicación: Cobotización, gig economy, co-creación y gobernanza. *Fonseca, Journal of Communication*, (22), 5–22. https://doi.org/10.14201/fjc-v22-25766

Túñez-López, J. M., Fieiras Ceide, C., & Vaz-Álvarez, M. (2021). Impact of artificial intelligence on journalism: Transformations in the company, products, contents and professional profile. *Communication & Society, 34*(1), 177–193. https://doi.org/10.15581/003.34.1.177-193

Ufarte-Ruiz, M. J., Calvo-Rubio, L. M., & Murcia-Verdú, F. J. (2021). Los desafíos éticos del periodismo en la era de la inteligencia artificial. *Estudios sobre el Mensaje Periodístico, 27*(2), 673–684. https://dx.doi.org/10.5209/esmp.69708

Ufarte-Ruiz, M. J., Murcia-Verdú, F. J., & Túñez-López, J. M. (2023). Use of artificial intelligence in synthetic media: First newsrooms without journalists. *Profesional de la información, 32*(2), 1–17. https://doi.org/10.3145/epi.2023.mar.03

Van de Poel, I. R., & Royakkers, L. M. (2011). *Ethics, technology, and engineering: An introduction.* United Kingdom: Wiley-Blackwell.

Willnat, L., Tang, S., Shi, J., & Zhang, H. Z. (2018). How the Chinese public views journalists, the media and fake news—Based on the 2017 National Survey. *Shanghai Journalism Review, 427*(9), 20–31. https://doi.org/10.16057/j.cnki.31-1171/g2.2018.09.004

CHAPTER 15

The Reception of Artificial Intelligence at Film Festivals

Montserrat Jurado-Martín

15.1 INTRODUCTION

Film festivals reflect trends in art, cinema, and culture. As cultural industries, they are hardly addressed in academic and scientific circles. However, they are remarkably flexible in embracing the most innovative proposals from one of the most powerful industries, the film industry. Just two years since the launch of ChatGPT and the ensuing apocalyptic narratives surrounding it, other voices are advocating for a proactive and fearless approach towards the new paradigm emerging in the social and cultural landscape, one that comes with its own name: artificial intelligence (AI). "AI stands as one of the most far-reaching creations that humanity has promoted in recent decades" (Terrones, 2021, p. 427).

This field of study has garnered interest from the most diverse spheres of science, ranging from technology and industrial engineering to visual arts and humanities through cinema, literature, and even philosophy. To such an extent, it could be considered a fourth industrial revolution, urging us to approach the future with responsibility (Terrones, 2021). From his perspective, cultural change in scientific environments must also be accompanied by philosophical reflections on technology and its new landscapes (p. 435).

Cinema is probably one of the most creative and innovative forms of media (Becerra, 2019). Cinematic creation plays an essential role in this context of technological development. Inspired by Steven Spielbergs film *Artificial Intelligence*, industrial engineer Ángel Riego Cue (2005, p. 145) remarks that:

> Man has been able to create machines that fly through the air or ply the waters, has invented ways to communicate instantly with any fellow man being anywhere

DOI: 10.1201/9781003473633-15

> on Earth, has sent expeditions to other worlds, but so far has not succeeded in creating by artificial means a being like himself.

In his article, Riego conducts a review of the early films whose plot focused on the prominence of AI, often associated with a humanoid robot. As he explains, in the 20th century, humans have shown great interest in building machines that reproduce actions and thoughts similar to the human brain. Described in this way, the 21st century can only be understood within the context of technological growth (Cantos, 2012) and placed in the Digital Era (López Corsi, 2017). The same author asserts that AI is a key element that needs to be analyzed in the realm of cinema.

In line with this development, film festivals have always walked in parallel with the most innovative filmmakers. These events have provided them with a platform for disseminating new trends and spaces for both artistic and technological experimentation. At the time of writing this chapter, and as an example of a quantitative approach to the topic at hand, the Filmfreeway distribution platform included a total of 71 film festivals in its database offering content related to AI: specialized festivals, specific sections, and productions made using this system. Just a year earlier, the number was in single digits.

In a very short time, we have moved from discussing film festivals as engines of the cultural industry, trend indicators, guardians of quality cinema, innovative spaces for experimenting with new technologies such as virtual reality, augmented reality, immersive reality, 360° cinema, and the metaverse to environments for experimentation with AI. Now, just as we have barely scratched the surface of the possibilities of the metaverse, neither professionally, reflectively, nor critically, AI emerges. How does AI affect film festivals? How is it being adapted to the market? This study provides a review of technological developments and a framework for understanding how AI is being incorporated into the activity of film festivals.

15.2 WHERE DO WE COME FROM AND WHERE ARE WE GOING?

This heading carries out an overarching review that spans from general academic literature on film festivals to specialized ones. It continues with what is considered to be the origin of film festivals specializing in new technologies, employing diverse techniques such as immersive cinema, 360° cinema, virtual reality, and, finally, the metaverse, culminating in film festivals specialized in AI.

The earliest mentions of literature on film festivals place them within the context of promoting and distributing cinematic works (Redondo, 2000, p. 55; Linares Palomar, 2009; Cabezón & Gómez-Urdá, 1999; Matamoros, 2009), often perceived more as recreational and festive activities (Gonzalo Maza, 2008) rather than primarily cultural events or tourism-oriented occasions (Adrianzén Rodríguez, 2007; Elizagarate, 2008).

Since then and up to the present day, definitions, functions, and characteristics of film festivals have been studied from various perspectives. They all share the common aspect of being necessary and valuable for the cultural industry, providing alternative channels to commercial ones, thereby facilitating access to a cultural offering that is generally not accessible to the audience (Mosquera, 2002). They promote transparency and quality in processes and, most importantly, highlight trends across various domains: geographical, temporal, thematic, formats, genres, and more.

The coherence of objectives covered by film festivals has already been noted by other authors who emphasized the possibility of introducing society to cinema from other countries (Duarte, 2002; Barral, 1997) or to short films, given their limited outlets (Velázquez & Ramírez, 2000). Likewise, we must not overlook their essential role as meeting places for audiences, media, critics, producers seeking talent, and emerging filmmakers (Georgakakou, 1998; Tapia, 2002; Redondo, 2000). These same functions attributed to film festivals in the late 1990s are reaffirmed two decades later, asserting that they are "key spaces for production, circulation, exhibition, and exchange" (Peirano, 2018, p. 66).

In the 21st century, the study of film festivals is situated within the domain of cultural industries (Quintero Rivera, 2016), seen as active agents in the economy, politics, and tourism. In this more recent period, we observe functions aligned with new technologies, internet usage, social changes, and shifts within the industry, among others. Consequently, the professional function gains significance. Festivals lose their value as purely cultural activities and evolve into professional platforms "designed as alternative and globalized cultural spaces that create bridges between the local, national, and international realms" (Rueda, 2019, p. 59). In fact, a festival implies competitiveness and a globalized distribution market (Gutiérrez & Wagenberg, 2013).

Festivals are no longer just showcases; they set trends and serve as indicators of quality for productions. In other words, they wield significant influence in the cultural sphere (Campos, 2012). Part of this recognition is legitimized by the value bestowed upon them by both producers and the audience (Narváez, 2019; Vivar Navas, 2016). The cultural exchange and promotion within the framework of film festivals have a transnational approach that sets them apart from other local cultural events that do not aim for a global presence (Iordanova, 2016).

Undoubtedly, technological development has marked a turning point in the celebration of film festivals. It not only affected the feasibility of whether they would be held or not but also spurred specialization. For example, in the case of Spain, specialization was crucial for the survival of these cultural events (Jurado-Martín, 2017), enabling them to justify their celebration to sponsors, industry stakeholders, and audiences while garnering sector-wide interest. The context of the quotation refers to the years following the economic downturn of 2008, during which investment in culture was deemed secondary and superfluous compared with the economic problems the country was facing. "Film festivals choose to offer unique products to differentiate themselves from neighboring events or to satisfy the tastes and interests of an audience seeking new experiences as a means to escape commercial offerings" (Jurado-Martín, 2018, p. 245).

In the 2010s, distribution and registration platforms became standardized. These platforms facilitated film distribution and enabled filmmakers to reach previously inaccessible festivals. Regarding these events, they streamlined their internal management, significantly reducing costs and allowing many of them to remain active and vibrant, reaching audiences far beyond their borders. The global pandemic put them to the test (Hanzlík & Mazierska, 2022). Those already using distribution platforms were able to adapt relatively easily, as the processes of submission, reception, and viewing remained largely unchanged. Similarly, those festivals already offering projects based on virtual reality, augmented reality, or even AI (Armstrong, 2021) were able to adapt, as they only needed to propose alternatives to ensure that the audience could remain engaged in the process.

Heredero (2020) suggested that this context might lead to a future with fewer in-person festivals due to the reduction in expenses involved. Some authors also argued that the online format would entail the loss of traditional values and functions (De Valck & Damiens, 2020). Finally, there were those who believed that a new stage in the history of film festivals had begun and that online platforms were a growing trend (Lomelí, 2017). "While this option is not extremely innovative (...), it rather serves as a straightforward substitute or alternative" (Ozgen-Tuncer, 2020). The reality is that many festivals have now returned to offering the pre-pandemic in-person format while also providing specific online viewing schedules.

However, before the pandemic, the film industry had already shown signs of anticipating a change. "The distribution of multimedia content and films increased exponentially" (Iordanova & Cunningham, 2012), as did distribution platforms and pay-per-view and live-streaming platforms. These factors influenced the organization and its relationship with the environment, the audience, sponsors, tourism, or culture, among others. The incorporation of new technologies in cinema, which began in the 20th century, gained momentum in the late 2010s. For example, in Spain, specialization saved many festivals in the 1990s and did so again after the 2008 crisis, by incorporating the distribution platform system (Jurado-Martín, 2017).

15.3 NEW TECHNOLOGIES APPLIED TO CINEMA

New technologies also find their applications in cinema. "Digital prevails over analog, and the business model of cultural industries is being transformed" (Paz, 2011). The technologies we are referring to primarily affect formats, while content, themes, and stories are subordinate to them. These technologies have changed and continue to change work routines, making production more accessible to anyone interested while also specializing and professionalizing sectors. Digital cameras have democratized filmmaking, with even any mobile phone capable of shooting a movie, and YouTube serving as a free distribution platform (Riambau, 2014). Other techniques are employed that require specific professional profiles, implying significant investments, both human and equipment-wise. This context widens the gap between major commercial productions and independent and auteur cinema.

Films in the competitive section are embracing new formats such as virtual reality, immersive cinema, augmented reality, 360° cinema, and, most recently, the metaverse. According to Sementille et al. (2014, p. 93), "the origins of augmented reality in journalism began with the use of chroma key." Cuadrado Alvarado (2014) discusses the early experiences of interaction and immersion in the virtual worlds of video games. These formats change narratives and storytelling methods, impacting not only fiction but also other genres. In the case of virtual reality, its applications extend to fields such as communication, journalism, advertising, non-fiction and documentary narratives, and even video games. In journalism, notable studies include those by Nonny De la Peña et al. (2010), Eva Domínguez (2012), and Paíno Ambrosio et al. (2017); in the non-fiction and documentary fields, the works of Gaudenzi (2009) and Gifreu-Castells (2017) stand out; and in the realm of video games, authors like Rose (2011), Holmberg (2003), Boas (2013), and Martínez Cano (2015), among others, have made significant contributions.

In the case of this latter author, we find a connection between the study and application of new technologies to film festivals. Martínez Cano (2018) conducted a study on the installation of experimentation using virtual reality techniques at the 2017 Cannes Film Festival. This was an additional activity outside the official competition section. Nowadays, there are few film festivals specializing in virtual reality, augmented reality, and related fields, but virtually all of them accept these formats in the competitive section.

Jurado-Martín (2020) explained that, in general, there was not a great interest in organizing specialized events, mainly due to their high costs and limited accessibility for a large audience in one location. This confirms Gifreu-Castells' assertion (2017) that it is a kind of consumption oriented towards individual experience. The few existing specialized events showed transparency biases in the case of the United States, with incomplete registration requirements, mandatory registration fees, and copyright assignment. Overall, these events attract an international profile of participants, feature mostly generalist content (86%), and have a preference for short films (71%). Contest rules are incomplete in 30% of cases, cash prizes are awarded in only 30% of cases, and 50% charge registration fees (Jurado-Martín, 2020).

In this journey of integrating new technologies into cinema, we reach the concept of the metaverse. For both professionals and researchers, it was presented as the culmination of the entire process, merging all previous advancements and essentially representing a watershed moment for the industry. Nevertheless, there were researchers who went against the grain and dared to say that the emperor wore no clothes.[1] The metaverse is an umbrella term that encompasses many realities (cited Pérez in Elorza, 2022). The author suggested that future content would be interactive, immersive, and personalized, allowing for widespread creation. Rather than having positive implications, this possibility would pose a threat to the industry (Elorza, 2022). Perhaps this is why we rarely hear about the metaverse anymore.

Film festivals exclusively dedicated to the metaverse are inherently innovative and creative events in terms of the techniques employed. They prioritize form over content, with fiction being subordinated to a narrative that is more aesthetic than literary. Nevertheless, these events are often linked to other major festivals or specific sections thereof (Jurado-Martín, 2023).

As some of the most representative examples, the 2022 Cannes Film Festival offered a metaverse experience in a virtual location called Decentraland, and named it the First NFT Film Festival. This virtual space featured workshops, conferences, and networking opportunities for industry investors and filmmakers (Ellis, 2022). In the same year, the

1 Mention to the tale *The Emperor Wears No Clothes* by Hans Christian Andersen, published in 1837.

San Sebastián Film Festival organized a meeting to discuss the metaverse concept, while Sundance offered a series of activities spanning over a week related to this theme and to virtual reality and immersive cinema. This dedicated space was named the New Frontier Gallery.

In 2022, Francisco Asensi (2022), an advisor to Spain Audiovisual Hub, explained during the roundtable on the metaverse at the Santander Film Festival that: "The metaverse is still evolving to carve out a niche in the audiovisual industry. New forms of content call for regulation to be efficiently and safely exploited." Now, it seems that the previous interest or relevance in the metaverse has waned, and the spotlight has shifted from the metaverse to AI.

15.4 ARTIFICIAL INTELLIGENCE AT FILM FESTIVALS

Cultural industries have always adapted to the latest trends set by authors and creators. The pandemic emphasized the importance of transnational support for culture, showing that geographical boundaries are not limiting if the conditions and tools are provided to make it accessible. As explained by Elsaesser (2015, pp. 186–186): "The film festival is an institution that was consolidated in Europe after 1945, yet it has globalized in the last twenty or thirty years. (...) Festivals have become a transnational network."

Cinema has always been characterized by embracing innovative alternatives, both in industry management and film production. Concerning the film industry, there is concern about "the automation of professions and the impact of AI on employment" (Terrones Rodríguez, 2021, p. 431). In fact, "this emerging economic/virtual environment is shaping new patterns of artistic consumption and dissemination, as well as public interaction" (Maggioni, 2021, p. 85). On a more technical level, AI tools are transforming film editing and generating audiovisual content (Caballero, 2023, p. 57). This potential also generates uncertainty, as described by the author:

> The potential of artificial intelligence technologies in film editing is undeniable. However, it is crucial to address their impact on creativity, diversity, and quality of the generated content. Likewise, it is essential (...) to ensure that these new tools and techniques not only facilitate content production but also contribute to enriching cinema and the creative expression of filmmakers.
>
> (p. 57)

Furthermore, from a creative perspective, the early AI-based productions exhibited some distortion due to an emphasis on technique. In this sense, "although structuralist and materialist influences are still apparent in certain AI-based films, new filmic characteristics have emerged and others will undoubtedly continue to develop" (Hales, 2021, p. 85). The author considers that "future experimental filmmakers may need to exchange their traditional cinematographic skills for the curation and creation of datasets and the training of personalized models." Thus, the debate begins as to whether authorship will be attributed to the creativity of the machine or that of the human author.

At this point, specialized film festivals are undertaking actions that highlight the quality of AI in cinematic creation (Guerrero, 2024, p. 12). This author explains that these festivals incorporate experimental elements and aesthetic-narrative innovations to demonstrate to the audience how AI is integrated into filmmaking. "The emergence of festivals aims to showcase the capabilities of AI, discuss the most controversial aspects of its use, and ultimately legitimize human intervention throughout the creative process" (p. 12). Guerrero served as co-director of Spain's first AI festival, the +RAIN Film Festival, organized by Pompeu Fabra University as a parallel activity to the Sonar music event.

Considering the rapidly evolving nature of this field, we are aware that the content provided in this chapter may become outdated by the time the book reaches the reader. Nonetheless, it will contribute to knowledge within its context. We have employed the FilmFreeWay database and Google search engine to verify the existence of each event. Using the search term "AI film festival" in Spanish, and English, with abbreviations, and without them, the platform yielded a total of 71 events. They are referred to as "events" because this category includes specialized events, those with a specific section, those accepting this format in their competition guidelines, and competitions. The latter are not considered festivals when they lack an exhibition of selected works. Similarly, non-competitive screenings that do not involve competition or industry networking are excluded due to their specific focus on audience-oriented programming rather than industry engagement.

The profile of the festivals resulting from the filtering process reveals that 36 (51%) have had fewer than 5 editions, 13 (18%) have held between 6 and 10 editions; 8 (11%) have had between 11 and 15 editions; and 14 (20%) have completed between 16 and 20 editions. This data confirms previous expectations. Many of these events cannot be considered specialized AI film festivals due to their relatively recent establishment. A critical analysis of this outcome suggests that, despite being a relatively recent trend, nearly all festivals feature a section or category dedicated to AI.

By examining the competition categories outlined in their guidelines, it is observed that: 67 are for short films, 63 for animation, 61 for documentaries, 56 for experimental films, 54 for student films, 49 for fiction, 38 for music videos, 24 for virtual reality, 19 for television, 9 for scripts, 8 for short film scripts, 3 for stage plays, and 3 for television scripts. Therefore, these competitions accept short films for competition, including animation, fiction, and documentary genres. Additionally, as distinguishing features from other studies on film festivals (Jurado-Martín, 2018, 2020), more festivals accept experimental categories and are open to student submissions.

These events are distinguished by the following specializations:: sci/fantasy/thriller: 9; human rights: 9; underground: 6; environment/outdoor: 4; horror: 4; comedy: 3; black/African: 2; dance: 2; indigenous/native people: 2; women: 2; adventure/action; 1; children: 1; Latino/Hispanic: 1; LGBTI: 1. The remaining, 23 (32%), are assumed to be described as generalist. The distinguishing feature of this filtering is that almost 70% of the analyzed events are defined as specialized.

Half of them have registration fees below $50, while the other half present fees above that threshold, with only four of them being free of charge.

Only seven festivals include the term "artificial intelligence" or its abbreviation in their names. The rest do not include it, and it is assumed that they are not specialized but rather have competitive or non-competitive categories related to AI. However, events with names that do not explicitly suggest a theme have been analyzed for confirmation. Below are the full names, countries of origin, and inaugural dates of those festivals that do include the term "artificial intelligence" or its abbreviation in their name:

- BAIFF, Burano Artificial Intelligent Film Festival, Italy, 2024
- Experimental Brasil, Campos dos Goytacazes, Brazil, 2024
- Artificial Intelligent Short Festival, United States, 2024
- AIFF, Dubai Artificial Intelligent Film Festival, Arab Emirates, 2022
- Artificial Intelligent Film Festival, United States, 2022
- FICMA, Festival Internacional de Cine con medios Alternativos (International Alternative Media Film Festival), Mexico, 2016
- SPE Media Festival. Video Art/New Media Film, United States, 1996

In Google, using the same search terms as in FilmFreeway, we compared the results and found one more festival: +RAIN Film Festival, Spain, 2023. The first of its kind in Europe.

As a final assessment of the chapter, it is concluded that almost all film festivals (70%) include this specific category in competition or offer spaces for dissemination, screening, and engagement with AI. The majority of specialized festivals (75%) have emerged in just two years, totaling eight at the time of writing this text. Although FilmFreeway is a North American database, it is the most widely used platform by cultural managers organizing festivals for film submission and promotion. Currently, FilmFreeway lists over 12,200 events related to cinema, including festivals, film competitions, scripts, music, photography, and online modalities.

15.5 DISCUSSION AND CONCLUSIONS

Film festivals are natural receptors of the most innovative proposals from the film industry. As an example, there are emerging festivals specialized in AI and those already proposing some sections dedicated to this theme. In a very short time, we have moved from discussing film festivals as engines of the cultural industry, trend indicators, guardians of quality cinema, innovative spaces for experimenting with new technologies such as virtual reality, immersive reality, 360° cinema, and the metaverse to discussing the integration of AI in film festivals.

The unstoppable development of new technologies finds its applications in cinema. As previously mentioned, these technologies primarily affect formats, while content evolves accordingly. It is easier to find sequels, prequels, and adaptations of contemporary works or events than scripts offering something unprecedented, innovative, or creative. These technologies have been and continue to be integrated into formats such as virtual reality, immersive cinema, augmented reality, 360° cinema, and the most recent innovation, the metaverse. It was presented as the culmination of this entire process, merging all previous advancements. However, today the metaverse has practically faded into the background, serving as an umbrella term for the previous techniques, and has been overshadowed by the latest trend: AI. The critical reading is simple: if the metaverse has had a lifespan of two or three years in our lives, could AI also be a passing fad? Could we consider AI within the metaverse? How does it affect film festivals? How is it being adapted to the market? These questions will be explored in another study that will build upon the findings of this one.

The study has conducted a review of technological developments and a framework for understanding film festivals and new technologies, culminating in how they integrate AI. The results reveal that these competitions are linked to larger ones and even to events that are not necessarily film festivals. The digital and technological transformation is advancing so rapidly that offering specialized festivals is risky, and the most consistent approach is to consider them as parallel activities within the already consolidated events.

The results conclude that almost all film festivals described as open to models employing AI on FilmFreeway (70%) include this specific category in competition or offer spaces for dissemination, screening, and engagement with AI. The majority of specialized festivals (75%) have emerged in just two years, totaling eight at the time of writing this text. Although FilmFreeway is a North American database, it is the most widely used platform by cultural managers organizing festivals for film submission and promotion. Currently, FilmFreeway lists over 12,200 events related to cinema, including festivals, film competitions, scripts, music, photography, and online modalities.

We cannot determine whether film festivals specializing in AI will reshape the events landscape. It is too early to assess whether this technique will seamlessly blend with existing formats, evolve into a specific category, or proliferate as specialized festivals. Just as it took merely two years to elevate the metaverse to a pinnacle of technological investment across various domains, it also took a similar timeframe for it to fade into obscurity.

Perhaps, by the time the reader is reading these lines, the number of film festivals specializing in AI or those offering a significant section dedicated to AI has surged. Time will tell whether, after the initial wave, interest in AI will wane when another trend emerges. Time will tell whether, as others predict, AI will become the cornerstone of social, cultural, and human relations in the future. Only time will tell.

REFERENCES

Adrianzén Rodríguez, J. C. (2007). *Festival de Lima 'El Cine'. Encuentro Latinoamericano de cine de Lima.* Instituto Complutense de Ciencias Musicales, Universidad Complutense de Madrid.

Armstrong, K. (2021). Virtual visibility and the film festival circuit. *Afterimage*, *48*(1), 10–18. https://doi.org/10.1525/aft.2021.48.1.10

Barral, C. (1997). Internet se va de festivales. *Cinemanía, 17*, 120–121.

Becerra, A. (2019). Entrevista a Jerónimo Luis Repoll: Hay que pensar el cine como algo más que un medio de comunicación. *Revista Mexicana de Comunicación, 144*. https://tinyurl.com/y28rjj5x

Boas, Y. (2013). Overview of virtual reality technologies. *Interactive Multimedia Conference.* shorturl.at/DMSV9

Caballero, J. (2023). Hacia una nueva dimensión del montaje cinematográfico: Explorando las posibilidades de la inteligencia artificial. *Hipertext.net,* (26), 53–58. https://doi.org/10.31009/hipertext.net.2023.i26.08

Cabezón, A., & Gómez-Urdá, F. (1999). *La producción cinematográfica.* Madrid: Cátedra.

Campos, M. (2012). Reconfiguración de flujos en el circuito internacional de festivales de cine: el programa 'Cine en construcción'. *Secuencias: revista de historia del cine,* 35, 84–102.

Cantos Ceballos, A. (2012). Cine virtual y "presencialidad" teatral: El cine electrónico de Coppola y sus imbricaciones en la consolidación del género (Peter Jackson). *Revista ICONO 14. Revista científica de Comunicación y Tecnologías emergentes, 10*(1), 135–148. https://doi.org/10.7195/ri14.v10i1.137

Cuadrado Alvarado, A. (2014). Tocar a través del cuadro: Una genealogía del interfaz como metáfora de control en el espacio del arte, el cine y los videojuegos. *Icono 14, 12*(2), 141–167. https://doi.org/10.7195/ri14.v12i2.708

De la Peña, N., Weil, P., Llobera, J., Spanlang, B., Friedman, D., Sanchez-Vives, M. V., & Slater, M. (2010). Immersive journalism: Immersive virtual reality for the first-person experience of news. *Presence, 19*(4), 291–301. https://doi.org/10.1162/PRES_a_00005

De Valck, M., & Damiens, A. (2020). Film festivals and the first wave of COVID-19: Challenges, opportunities, and reflections on festivals' relations to crises. In: *NECSUS,* Autumn 2020 (Festival Reviews - Special Dossier: Covid 19). https://bit.ly/3uFKGfc

Domínguez, E. (2012). *Periodismo inmersivo: Fundamentos para una forma periodística basada en la interfaz y la acción* (Tesis doctoral). Universidad de Blanquerna.

Duarte, R. (2002). El flujo vital del cine. *VVAA: El cortometraje en primera persona. Encuentro de cortometrajistas iberoamericanos. Edita la Asociación Cultural Certamen Internacional de Filmes Cortos 'Ciudad de Huesca'y Casa de América. Huesca. Colección 'Cine y más,* (9), 135–148.

Elizagarate, V. (2008). *Marketing de ciudades. Estrategias para el desarrollo de ciudades atractivas y competitivas en un mundo global.* Madrid: Pirámide.

Ellis, J. (2022). The first NFT film festival in the metaverse to launch in decentraland. Mediaverse. 19 de mayo. https://bit.ly/3BMmEEI

Elorza, I. (2022). El metaverso que es, no es, pero al final acabará siendo. *Diario del Festival. Festival de Cine de San Sebastián,* 23 de septiembre. https://bit.ly/3PFKRm8

Elsaesser, T. (2015). Cine transnacional, el sistema de festivales y la transformación digital. *Fonseca, 11*(11), 175–196. https://revistas.usal.es/cuatro/index.php/2172-9077/article/view/13440

Asensi, F. (2022). El metaverso. Un horizonte de posibilidades para el audiovisual. https://bit.ly/3YyBgkY

Gaudenzi, S. (2009). *Interactive documentary: Towards an aesthetic of the multiple.* London: University of London, Centre for Cultural Studies (CCS) of Goldsmiths.

Georgakakou, V. (1998). Los complejos mecanismo de la producción. VVAA: *Promoción y difusión del cine europeo. Jornadas de cine de la Unión Europea.* Valladolid: Semana Internacional de Cine de Valladolid.

Gifreu-Castells, A. (2017). Documental interactivo: Dispositivos locativos, impacto social, ciencia y divulgación. *Doc On-line,* diciembre, 2–4.

Guerrero Solé, F. (2024). La comunicación ante el desafío de la inteligencia artificial generativa: Reflexiones, retos y oportunidades en un escenario disruptivo. https://repositori.upf.edu/handle/10230/58968

Gutiérrez, C.A., y Wagenberg, M. (2013). Meeting Points: A Survey of Film Festivals in Latin America. *Transnational Cinemas*, 4(2), 295–305. https://doi.org/10.1386/trac.4.2.295_1

Hales, C. (2021). Artificial intelligence: The latent revolution in filmmaking. *ADAM Arts, 2*. https://journals.riseba.eu/index.php/adamarts/article/view/291

Hanzlík, J., & Mazierska, E. (2022). Eastern European film festivals: Streaming through the Covid-19 pandemic. *Studies in Eastern European Cinema, 13*(1), 38–55. https://doi.org/10.1080/2040350X.2021.1964218

Heredero, C. F. (2020). Festivales en tiempos de pandemia (editorial). *Caimán Cuadernos de Cine*, 30 de septiembre. https://bit.ly/2RaHt8S

Holmberg, J. (2003). Ideals of immersion in early cinema. Cinémas: Revue d'études cinématographiques. *Cinémas: Journal of Film Studies, 14*(1), 129–147.

Iordanova, D. (2016). The film festival and film culture's transnational essence. *Film festivals, history, theory, method, practice* (pp. 11–17). New York: Routledge.

Iordanova, D., & Cunningham, S. (2012). *Digital disruption: Cinema moves on-line*. St. Andrews: St. Andrews University Press.

Jurado Martín, M. (2017). El germen del cine más amateur: festivales de cine de educación. En C.M. Lazo (coord.), Nuevas realidades en la comunicación audiovisual (pp. 245–260). Madrid: Tecnos.

Jurado Martín, M. (2018). Festivales de cine online en España: Pocos, efímeros, pero de calidad. Muñoz, Martínez y Peña (Coord.) *La realidad audiovisual como nuevo vehículo de comunicación* (pp. 175–192). Madrid: Gedisa.

Jurado-Martín, M. (2020). Festivales de cine especializados en realidad virtual en España. *Sphera Publica, 1*(20), 59–77. https://sphera.ucam.edu/index.php/sphera-01/article/view/381

Jurado-Martín, M. (2023). Gone with the wind: From virtual reality to the metaverse at film festivals. Bénitez, Rojas, R. (Ed.) *The future of digital communication. The metaverse*. Boca Raton: CRC Press, Taylor & Francis Group.

Linares Palomar, R. (2009). *La promoción cinematográfica. Estrategias de comunicación y distribución de películas*. Madrid: Fragua.

Lomelí, A. (2017). Festivales de cine en línea ¿una tendencia al alza? *Isopixel*, 19-01-2017. goo.gl/pjsoF6

López Corsi, J. E. (2017). *El cine de ciencia ficción: El significado de la inteligencia artificial* (Doctoral dissertation). Universitat Politècnica de València. https://riunet.upv.es/handle/10251/90679

Maggioni, F. (2021). El Fenómeno de las *lives* en Brasil: nuevas formas y agentes de difusión de la cultura. En Jurado-Martín, M. y Peña Acosta, Beatriz (coord.), Periodismo Cultural en el siglo XXI (2). Modelos transmedia para profesionales innovadores, (pp. 85–98). Madrid: Universitas.

Martínez Cano, F. J. (2015). Nuevos paradigmas del cine y realidad virtual: Aplicación de nuevas tecnologías de realidad virtual en videojuegos y cine. Alonso, D, Martínez de Salazar, I. y Cuesta, J. (Coord.), *03 Videojuegos e industria creativa* (pp. 269–282). Madrid: Escuela de Diseño, Innovación y Tecnología.

Martínez Cano, F. J. (2018). Impresiones sobre Carne y Arena: Práctica cinematográfica y realidad virtual. *Miguel Hernández Communication Journal, 9*(1), 161–190. http://dx.doi.org/10.21134/mhcj.v0i9.222

Matamoros, D. (2009). *Distribución y marketing cinematográfico*. Barcelona: Publicaciones y Ediciones de la Universidad de Barcelona.

Maza, G. (2008). Para qué sirven los festivales de cine. *laFuga, 7*. http://2016.lafuga.cl/para-que-sirven-los-festivales-de-cine/304

Mosquera, L. (2002). Corto y Televisión. Cerón Gómez, J. F. (Coord.). *Años de corto. Apuntes sobre el cortometraje español desde los noventa*. Murcia: Universidad de Murcia y Primavera Cinematográfica de Lorca.

Narváez, G. (2019). El cine latinoamericano contemporáneo y la estética de festival: El caso de Cannes (2000–2015). *Archivos de la filmoteca, 77*, 21–46. www.archivosdelafilmoteca.com/index.php/archivos/article/view/668/633

Ozgen-Tuncer, A. (2020). The International Labour Film Festival in Turkey. *Festival Reviews. Special Dossier: Covid-19*. Necsus, December 2020. Recuperado de: https://bit.ly/3lFlPnS

Paíno Ambrosio, A., Jiménez Iglesias, L., & Rodríguez Fidalgo, M. I. (2017). El periodismo inmersivo y transmedia: De leer la historia a vivirla en primera persona. Herrero, J., & Materos, C. (Coord.), *Del verbo al bit* (pp. 1177–1191). Madrid: Sociedad Latina de Comunicación Social. https://dv.doi.org/10.4185/cac115

Paz García, C. (2011). *El agotamiento del modelo cinematográfico analógico. La cooperación iberoamericana en la era digital* (Tesis doctoral). Universidad Complutense de Madrid. https://eprints.ucm.es/12286/

Peirano, M. P. (2018). Festivales de cine y procesos de internacionalización del cine chileno reciente. *Cuadernos.info, 43*, 57–69. https://tinyurl.com/yxkfrf4v

Quintero Rivera, H. A. (2016). Los festivales de cine independiente una ventana alterna de distribución. VVAA. *La pantalla solemne*, 3.275–3.286. http://dx.doi.org/10.4185/cac179

Redondo, I. (2000). *Marketing en el cine*. Madrid: Pirámide.

Riambau, E. (2014). El cine en la era digital. *BiD: Textos universitaris de biblioteconomia i documentació, 33*. http://dx.doi.org/10.1344/BiD2014.33.2

Riego Cue, Á. (2005). Cine e inteligencia artificial. *Ars Medica, 4*, 145–158.

Rose, F. (2011). *The art of immersion. How the digital generation is remaking Hollywood, Madison Avenue and the way we tell stories*. New York: W. W. Norton & Company.

Rueda, A. (2019). Nuevas condiciones de la internacionalización de los cines de América Latina y plataformas profesionales de festivales. *Archivos de la Filmoteca*, 59–78. https://dialnet.unirioja.es/servlet/articulo?codigo=7122494

Sementille, A. C., Américo, M., Belda, F. R., Marar, J. F. & Cunha, A. K. (2014). Arsstudio. Estúdio Virtual para Produção de Conteúdos Audiovisuais em Realidade Aumentada para TV Digital. *Revista Tram(p)as de la comunicación y de la cultura, 77*, 89–98.

Tapia, G. (2002). *La historia se repite. VVAA: III Encuentro de Nuevos Autores*. Valladolid: Semana Internacional de Cine de Valladolid y SGAE/ Fundación Autor.

Terrones Rodríguez, A. L. (2021). *Inteligencia artificial responsable. Humanismo tecnológico y ciencia cívica* (Tesis doctoral). Universidad de Valencia. oai:roderic.uv.es:10550/77016

Velázquez, J. M., & Ramírez, L. M. (2000). *Una década prodigiosa. El cortometraje español en los noventa*. Alcalá de Henares: Festival de Cine de Alcalá de Henares.

Vivar Navas, R. (2016). *Los festivales de cine en la era de los new media: Una perspectiva lúdica sobre la fiesta del cine y sus públicos* (Tesis doctoral). Universidad de Granada.

CHAPTER 16

Cinderella Named "Artificial Intelligence": Media Image of Artificial Intelligence in Alternative Media (Case Study from Slovakia)

Hedviga Tkácová

16.1 INTRODUCTION

Mainstream media presents artificial intelligence (AI) through concrete examples of its deployment in various sectors, including factories, transportation, and healthcare. The overall portrayal of AI is positive, reflecting its current positive applications and the increase in its users' use. This positive attitude is further emphasized in the realm of social media (NexTech, 2019).

Alternative media have established a permanent presence in society, with their numbers continually on the rise. This growth is directly correlated with an increase in disinformation, influencing public perception and contributing to misinformation's impact on society. Competing for popularity with mainstream media, alternative media, in Slovakia notably Hlavné správy, has achieved considerable success, even rivalling larger-budget outlets like TV TA3 in terms of readership. This competitive dynamic has been ongoing, reflecting the enduring influence of alternative media in Slovakia (Transparency International Slovakia, 2020).

Alternative media in Slovakia, particularly within the realm of social media, exhibit unique structural features. Operating as internet portals, their goal is to captivate a wide audience and drive profit through clickbait strategies. Functioning with minimal regulation and low operational costs, these platforms are frequently managed by one or two

DOI: 10.1201/9781003473633-16

individuals. Their economic self-management and straightforward sustainability contribute to their distinctive structure.

Research from the Reuters Institute indicates that alternative media channels, despite relying on true information from reputable sources, play a significant role in disseminating false information (Smith, n.d.). These platforms often introduce manipulative elements, blending genuine news with lies and white lies, not only creating misinformation (Plevák, Euractiv.cz, & Euractiv.sk, 2023) but also complicating its identification (Shu et al., 2017). The credibility of news disseminated through alternative media is a growing concern, as the repetition of messages on social media can enhance perceived truth, even in cases of problematic content (Fielden, Grupac, & Adamko, 2018).

Experts highlight a global surge in interest in alternative media in recent years (Gorwa, 2017). European Union authorities tie the increased interest in Western countries to critical topics like the migration crisis (ongoing since 2014), the Istanbul Convention (linking gender equality to combat domestic violence since the second half of 2017), and the global pact on refugees (a UN agreement on migration cooperation since late 2018) (European Parliament, 2018).

In the realm of contemporary alternative media in Slovakia, alongside dominant pro-Kremlin narratives (Infosecurity.sk, 2023), various recurring conspiracies manifest in diverse contexts. Notable examples include conspiracies linked to the COVID-19 pandemic, conspiracies involving secret elites purportedly controlling global events and the economy, conspiracies surrounding 5G technology, conspiracies related to climate change, etc.

Furthermore, in current alternative media, a spectrum of AI-related conspiracies and theories arises. Concerns range from “global mind control” via AI (Mihale, 2023a) to AI altering nuclear deterrence dynamics (Hlavné správy, 2023a) and making uncontrolled military decisions (Richter, 2023). Other narratives explore the creation of AI “superhumans” (Hlavný denník, 2022a), myths about AI superintelligence gaining control (Infovojna, 2023), and framing AI as a danger to life and the planet (Zemavek, 2023a), among other themes. Building on the preceding discussion, our research delves into how alternative online media shapes the perception of AI, exploring the narratives conveyed on the most popular platforms in Slovakia.

16.1.1 Public Perception of Artificial Intelligence in Research

It can be observed that the motivations of Slovaks to actively use AI are relatively modest. Despite a certain increase in the number of individuals in Slovakia familiarizing themselves with AI tools since the public launch of GPT-3 (Generative Pre-trained Transformer 3 from the company OpenAI) in June 2020, these tools have not yet achieved widespread adoption throughout the country. This is substantiated by the findings of the latest survey conducted by the Go4insight agency, indicating that only 18% of Slovaks between the ages of 15 and 79 years had experimented with AI tools, primarily ChatGPT and Bing Chat, by the beginning of October 2023. However, AI tools are used regularly by only

7% of the population (Trend, 2023). To provide context, a Pew Research Centre survey of US adults in December 2022 revealed that 27% interact with AI at least several times a day, while another 28% interact with it approximately once a day (Kennedy, Tyson, & Saks, 2023).

Despite some growth in the use of AI in homes and industries, Americans, overall, exhibit a cautious approach towards AI and its impact on human life. According to a 2022 survey by the Pew Research Centre, only 15% of respondents expressed more excitement than concern about the increasing use of AI in everyday life, compared with 38% who reported more worry than excitement. Nearly half of the respondents consistently expressed equal levels of concern and excitement (Rainie et al., 2022). Less than a year later, the level of concern among Americans about the use of AI in everyday life has risen, with 52% of respondents stating they are more worried than excited about AI (Tison & Kikuchi, 2023).

A similarly negative evaluation of AI prevails among Slovaks. According to the most recent survey, 43% of Slovaks believe that the benefits of AI are predominant, while a slightly larger portion—45% of respondents—hold the opposite opinion (Bačová, 2023). Third, most British adults surveyed assess the impact of AI on their lives as neutral (32%). Additionally, a slightly higher proportion of respondents expressed a positive view of AI compared with those with negative responses (Farbrace, Warren, & Murphy, 2023). This indicates that despite concerns, the active use of AI among citizens is gradually gaining popularity, marking a trend not only in Slovakia but also in other countries.

The use of AI among the general population is significantly increasing, especially within the global AI market, projected to grow at an annual rate of up to 37.7% from 2023 to 2030. Experts highlight that with this anticipated growth, "it is clear that the AI market is growing exponentially" (Hostinger Tutorials, 2023). The escalating prevalence of AI underscores its rising significance in the daily lives of ordinary individuals and its extensive application across various major industries, including healthcare, e-commerce, food tech, logistics, banking, financial services, automotive, media, education, hospitality, and more.

This development is underscored by a recent IPSOS survey conducted for the World Economic Forum, revealing that 60% of adults globally anticipate products and services utilizing AI to fundamentally transform their daily lives. According to respondents, significant changes are expected within a time frame of 3–5 years. Similarly, 60% of those surveyed agree that AI products and services will simplify their lives. However, only half of the respondents believe that the use of AI has more advantages than disadvantages, leading to some reservations about daily AI utilization (Myers, 2022).

Research findings from the United States, Britain, and Slovakia illustrate a general perception that AI-related technologies have the potential to enhance daily life and human capabilities. However, public opinion is not solely positive; it is equally influenced by concerns about utilization, limitations, and potential impacts on various stakeholders. Across countries, a consistent neutral to negative sentiment towards AI is observed, despite an acknowledgment of its positive contributions. This negativity extends to social media, where diverse platforms not only host questionable content but also shape public discourse. The convergence of research findings and social media dynamics forms the foundational research aspect of this chapter.

16.2 DESCRIPTION OF THE EXPERIMENTAL DESIGN AND METHODOLOGY

The research entails an analysis of five popular alternative media outlets in Slovakia within the timeframe from June 11, 2020, to November 11, 2023. The study's timeline commences with the public launch of a large language model Generative Pre-trained Transformer 3 (GPT-3), by OpenAI. The conclusion of the research aligns with the date of finalizing the written process and processing this study into its ultimate form.

The primary objectives of the research are to identify the principal narratives regarding the current and future utilization of AI. Additionally, the study aims to explore the tonality, that is, the sentiment attributed to AI by the authors in the texts of the investigated media. The research is grounded on the assumption that the identified narratives and their tonality can significantly influence the perception of AI within the Slovak social and media sphere. The analysis of textual material progresses from data collection to conclusions, reflecting the inductive nature of the research.

16.2.1 Research Design

The research on the five most popular alternative media in Slovakia is conducted separately in two distinct contexts:

Research goal 1: The media image (themes and tonality) of the current use of AI;
Research goal 2: The media image (themes and tonality) of the future use of AI.

The mainstream media in Slovakia generally presents a positive image of AI, aligning with its increasing adoption and usage among users. This optimistic outlook is also mirrored in social media discussions (NexTech, 2019). The research is designed to investigate whether the portrayal of AI in the analysed alternative media follows a similar positive trend.

Moreover, the hypothesis will try to verify whether the thematic circles related to AI future use tend to be depicted negatively. This hypothesis suggests that concerns and fears may be evoked through narratives surrounding the future applications of AI in these alternative media outlets.

The study was conducted using a sample of 150 texts published in 5 prominent alternative media outlets in Slovakia (Takács, 2022) (see Table 16.1). All the alternative media investigated are part of the current database maintained by the independent Slovak initiative Konspiratori.sk, which scrutinizes and maps media with questionable credibility and content quality (Konspiratori.sk, n.d.).

TABLE 16.1 Overview of the Research Sample – Alternative Media

Name of alternative media	Brief description
Hlavné správy	News internet portal
Slobodný vysielač	Internet radio
Infovojna	News internet portal and YouTube channel
Hlavný denník	News internet portal
Zem a vek	News internet portal

Source: Prepared by author.

16.2.2 Research Method and Research Sample

During the research, the unit of analysis was the occurrence of the term "artificial intelligence" (including its possible abbreviation in the Slovak language, i.e., "UI") within the articles. The study involved randomly selecting 30 texts from each of the 5 alternative media sources investigated, totalling $n = 150$ texts.

For research purposes, a coding scheme was developed, encompassing several categories and their corresponding subcategories. The analysis of the research sample of 150 texts involved the application of this coding scheme, focusing on identifying narratives and evaluating their tonality. The assessment was carried out independently by three experienced researchers.

From a research standpoint, our analysis exclusively focused on the textual content of the articles. We did not delve into the visual components such as photographs or the joint presentation of verbal and visual elements. Each identified occurrence was considered as one code and documented in the coding sheet. The results are visually represented, illustrating the frequency of occurrences in individual categories or thematic circles, providing a numerical overview of the research findings.

Following the content analysis, a thematic and ideological analysis ensued, involving the interpretation of the meaning of the obtained categories. The informational and conceptual interpretation of findings constitutes a verbal representation of the research results.

It is crucial to highlight that not all analysed texts within the framework of this analysis can be automatically categorized as manipulations or misinformation. The research sample included several substantive and unproblematic articles (for instance, Hlavné správy, 2021a). This consideration guided our decision to refrain from using labels such as "conspiracy media" or "disinformation media" to characterize the investigated media, as is customary in Slovakia. Instead, we chose the more neutral term "alternative media," aligning with how these outlets often present themselves as alternatives to mainstream sources. This decision aligns with expert opinions that define "alternative media" as "a counterforce or a watchdog to mainstream news media" (Holt, Ustad Figenschou, & Frischlich, 2019, p. 863).

16.3 RESULTS

As numerous examined texts featured more than one dominant narrative, the content analysis of 150 texts yielded a total evaluation of $n = 248$ narratives. Within this set, 86 narratives portrayed the media image of the current use of AI, fulfilling research goal 1. The remaining 162 narratives contributed to shaping the media image of the future use of AI, addressing research goal 2.

16.3.1 The Media Image of the Current Use of AI

Within the scope of the first research objective, we can see that the media portrayal of the current use of AI is predominantly characterized by five themes in the analysed narratives ($n = 86$), disseminated through five of the most popular alternative media outlets in Slovakia. The prevalent aspects of AI's current use are predominantly linked to information technology (27 texts, 31.37%), media (21 texts, 24.40%), healthcare (19 texts, 22.08%), the automotive industry (11 texts, 12.78%), and education (6 texts, 6.97%). The "other" thematic circle included occasional conspiracy narratives advocating for limiting AI, citing reasons such as potential interference in elections or concerns about atmospheric quality (2 texts, 2.32%).

The underlying theme among the identified thematic circles is the attempt to highlight the current risks or, conversely, emphasize the benefits stemming from the use of AI today. However, the presentation of benefits is largely derived directly from influential opinion-forming media.

In several examined texts, the depiction of benefits is succeeded by the author's position and opinion, often reflecting a personal and predominantly negative view of the current use of AI (as seen in, for instance, Hlavné správy, 2021b). This tendency likely contributes to the prevalent neutral tonality (author sentiment) observed in texts portraying the image of the current use of AI in alternative media (34 texts, 39.50%), closely followed by a negative sentiment (32 texts, 37.18%). Positive sentiments from authors were identified in 20 texts (23.24%) from the total set of $n = 86$ texts. The research findings are depicted in Figures 16.1 and 16.2.

16.3.2 The Media Image of the Future Use of AI

In the investigated narratives ($n = 162$) published in five of the most popular alternative media in Slovakia, the media image of the future use of AI is predominantly depicted in six thematic circles, with three of them considered dominant.

The predominant theme is (1) negative impacts stemming from AI's effects on the labour market and individuals working within it (45 texts, 27.76%). AI is often depicted as an imminent threat to employment, posing inherent risks to the population's quality of life and well-being.

Ranking second, the prevalent theme on alternative websites involves notions of AI as a force aspiring to world domination, predicting the imminent dominance and/or destruction of humans (37 texts, 22.82%). Researched alternative platforms depict AI with intentions to exterminate humanity, portraying it as a threat not only to the planet

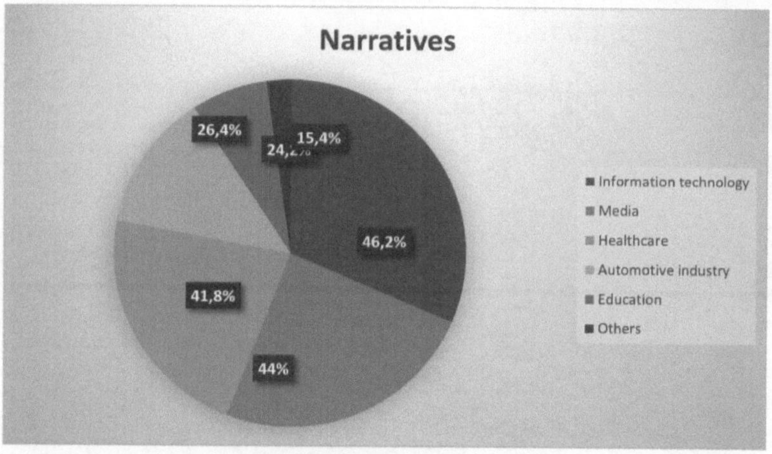

FIGURE 16.1 The media image of the current use of AI.

Source: Prepared by authors.

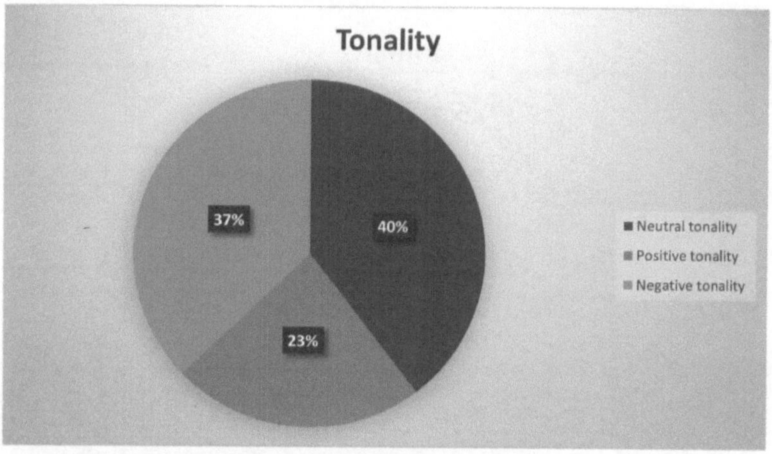

FIGURE 16.2 Tonality of the media image of the current use of AI.

Source: Prepared by authors.

but also to its own existence. A recurring narrative explores the "greatest goal of AI," cantered around achieving immortality through replication and technological evolution.

Securing third place is the media depiction of future AI use, where (3) AI is presented as a component of future cyber threats (34 texts, 20.97%). This category encompasses articles linking AI to threats like identity theft, fraudulent information acquisition (phishing), email signature forgery, online fraud (e.g., bots and trolls impersonating humans), and the spread of malicious content on the Internet (disinformation and hoaxes). Authors frequently reference current threats, emphasizing their anticipated exponential growth with increased AI utilization.

A notable decrease in occurrences was observed in the investigated alternative websites regarding (4) AI's connections with disinformation spread to manipulate public opinion

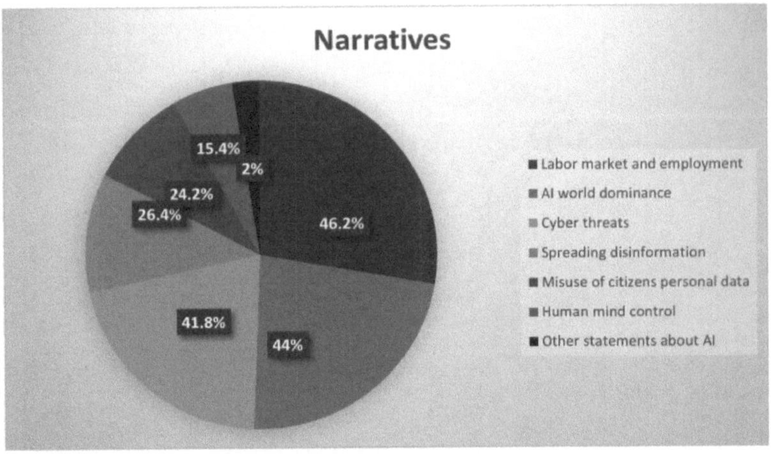

FIGURE 16.3 The media image of the future use of AI.

Source: Prepared by authors.

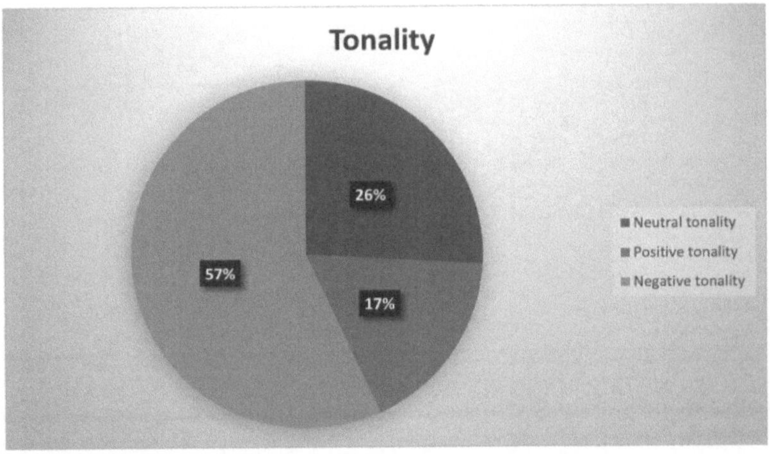

FIGURE 16.4 Tonality of the media image of the future use of AI.

Source: Prepared by authors.

or influence political processes (18 texts, 11.10%), (5) AI's use in collecting citizens' personal data for abuse, monitoring, control, or behaviour prediction (15 texts, 9.25%), and (6) considerations about AI as a technology for controlling the human mind (9 texts, 5.55%). General statements about AI within the context of EU political decisions on future use in the digital space fell under category (7) "other" (4 texts, 2.46%).

The media portrayal of future AI use is largely negative in the examined texts (92 texts, 56.76%). A smaller portion maintains a neutral tone (42 texts, 25.91%), with positive tonality being the least frequent (28 texts, 17.27%). Figures 16.3 and 16.4 present the research findings.

As we can see, the research did not confirm the first part of the hypothesis, that is, the thesis that AI tends to be perceived more positively in the present context. The research revealed that concerning the media image of the current use of AI, the most frequent tonality observed was neutral (34 texts, i.e., 39.50%), closely followed by the negative sentiment of the authors (32 texts, i.e., 37.18%).

At the same time, we can affirm the validity of the second part of the hypothesis, namely that the thematic circles about its use in the future tend to be portrayed negatively. Our research confirmed the prevailing negative tonality concerning the use of AI in the future (92 texts, i.e., 56.76%). Due to this fact, there is an assumption that in alternative media, the sentiment presented in this way not only creates a significantly negative image of AI and its future use but also potentially instils concern and fear among users.

16.4 DISCUSSION AND FUTURE LINES OF INVESTIGATION

Based on the content analysis, it can be concluded that the investigated alternative media most frequently represent the media image of the current use of AI (research goal 1) neutrally (39.50%). This neutral evaluation is less frequent compared with the image of the future use of AI. AI technology tends to be assessed neutrally and is mostly associated with benefits (Hlavné správy, 2022), evident within current information technology (Hlavné správy, 2023b), media (Hlavný denník, 2023), healthcare (Hlavný denník, 2023), the automotive industry (Hlavné správy, 2023c), and education (Zemavek, 2023b).

Concerning the media images of the future use of AI (research goal 2), the most frequently presented topics carry a negative tone (56.76%). Within our research set, these topics primarily link the use of AI with negative consequences on the labour market and individuals working in this market. AI is often portrayed as a fundamental threat to population employment and, inherently, as a threat to an individual's quality of life and well-being (Zemavek, 2021). Authors are convinced that "those who are afraid of human limitations see artificial intelligence as an ally," while those who truly "believe in man are afraid of artificial intelligence" (Mihale, 2023b). This simplified and relatively one-sided idea contradicts many relevant observations, including studies by the McKinsey Global Institute, estimating that up to 800 million jobs worldwide may be replaced by AI by 2030 (approximately 1.5 million jobs in Slovakia). However, the study also suggests that AI can create up to 950 million new jobs, requiring new skills and education. This indicates that AI may have a positive impact not only on the labour market but also on the overall quality of work. Consequently, experts emphasize the need to prepare for such changes and acquire skills related to AI that will be in demand in the future (IT Ročenka, 2023).

Content analysis reveals the second most prevalent theme about AI on investigated alternative websites is connecting it with the establishment of imminent world domination. AI is portrayed not only as a mechanism aspiring to rule but also to eliminate current rulers, that is, people (Hlavné správy, 2023d). The control and/or destruction of people are deemed necessary because humanity is considered a threat to AI, primarily to itself, evoking fear and concern in readers of such articles (Infovojna, 2022b). Narratives also link the rise of AI dominance with the decline of human intelligence, eventually resulting in AI dominating the world (Brožík, 2023). However, in reality, the latest language model GPT-4, responsible for these statements, is not mature enough to handle all these tasks. A significant obstacle is the fact that this is not an AGI (artificial general intelligence) model and is thus not capable of autonomously solving intellectual challenges, learning on its own, or performing almost arbitrary tasks without explicit instruction from the user.

AI and its future use are often linked to impending cyber threats, an issue with global implications. However, alternative media narratives tend to adopt an one-sidedly catastrophic tone, recalling past incidents, emphasizing the general threat, and underscoring the rapid development of technologies and associated threats (Infovojna, 2022a). There's a projection of AI being implemented "in addition to other forms of war" in "new forms of cognitive warfare" in the online space (Hlavný denník, 2022b). The goal of authors producing such articles is to present selective information about AI in connection with cyber threats, creating highly inflammatory, provocative, or frightening content with the potential to arouse fear and concern.

Additionally, the identified thematic circles reinforce the conspiratorial nature of half-truths with manipulative insertions by article authors. Narratives reflect truth but also incorporate their own "manipulative adjectives," often representing the cognitively distorted opinion of the author. Consequently, fake news and conspiracies generate distorted information. Research findings align with the latest report from Transparency International Slovakia, stating that current alternative websites primarily "question facts with questions, publish unsubstantiated theories and conspiracies, or comment on information brought by someone else" (Press Agency SITA, 2023).

We will not elaborate further on refuting conspiracies shaping the AI image through questionable websites. Conspiracies advocate for limiting AI for various reasons, and our research identifies six common thematic circles surrounding this perspective.

Significantly, the current impact of AI conspiracy theories is recognized as a factor contributing to the neutral and negative perception of AI in daily life (Trend, 2023; Rainie et al., 2022; Myers, 2022; Kennedy, Tyson, & Saks, 2023; Tison & Kikuchi, 2023; Bačová, 2023; Farbrace, Warren, & Murphy, 2023). This influence extends to "states" efforts to combat AI (Williams, 2023). The image of AI presented by alternative media is a relevant and necessary research topic, impacting a broad readership and providing fertile ground for speculations increasingly gaining prominence in society.

In light of these considerations, it is crucial to highlight the necessity for future investigations into alternative media and their portrayal of AI. A systematic examination of topics related to AI within Slovak conspiracy media, with an emphasis on tracking their evolution over time, becomes paramount. Future research endeavours should delve into discerning changes in emphases, addressing concerns, and evaluating the evolving tonality of primary narratives.

Furthermore, there is merit in exploring the portrayal of conspiracy theories about AI in alternative media and drawing comparisons with conspiracy narratives in mainstream Slovak media. This approach could shed light on potential differences in information framing and reveal patterns and trends within the broader media and social landscape.

Expanding the scope to include a broader international comparative analysis, incorporating extended research, holds promise in unravelling cross-cultural differences in both themes and tonality present in examined texts. The inclusion of other countries in such investigations could pave the way for new paradigms in international research, offering a deeper understanding within varying geographical, cultural, and social frameworks.

In conclusion, we recommend further investigation into the ethical issues associated with the portrayal of AI in conspiracy media. This research should focus on fostering critical thinking and media literacy as a response to the potential consequences. Exploring the ethical implications of how AI is presented in the media would underscore the importance of critical thinking and media literacy, contributing to a more nuanced understanding of both current and future media portrayals of AI.

16.5 CONCLUSIONS

In the examined issue, it is foreseeable that the most likely scenario, wherein AI significantly shapes society based on its capabilities and current applications, will soon be realized. However, the positive impact of AI may face limitations due to conspiratorial beliefs that question its benefits and intentionally discourage its adoption.

The ongoing trend of AI's rapid development introduces numerous challenges that can sway public opinion and affect the widespread acceptance of this technology. It is imperative to continually educate the public about the actual properties and potential of AI. Active and continuous support should not only emphasize positive user experiences in everyday life but also promote informed and responsible decision-making, guiding society towards the optimal and safe use of this technology both now and in the future.

Only under these circumstances will AI unveil itself as Cinderella, overcoming misconceptions akin to dirty rags used for cleaning. Eventually, she will step into the festive society, donning a new dress to ascend as the prom queen.

REFERENCES

Bačová, J. (2023, May 15). Polovica Slovenska netuší, čo je umelá inteligencia. Značná časť z nás sa jej bojí, ukázal prieskum. *Startitup.sk.* www.startitup.sk/polovica-slovenska-netusi-co-je-umela-inteligencia-znacna-cast-z-nas-sa-jej-boji-ukazal-prieskum/

Brožík, I. (2023, March 20). Umelou inteligenciou k vygumovaniu tej prirodzenej, zdar! *Hlavný denník.* www.hlavnydennik.sk/2023/03/20/umelou-inteligenciou-k-vygumovaniu-tej-prirodzenej-zdar

European Parliament. (2018, April 18). *Pokrok v súvislosti s globálnym paktom OSN o bezpečnej, riadenej a legálnej migrácii a globálnym paktom o utečencoch.* www.europarl.europa.eu/doceo/document/TA-8-2018-0118_SK.html

Farbrace, E., Warren, J., & Murphy, R. (2023, June 16). *Understanding AI uptake and sentiment among people and businesses in the UK.* Office for National Statistics. www.ons.gov.uk/businessindustryandtrade/itandinternetindustry/articles/understandingaiuptakeandsentimentamongpeopleandbusinessesintheuk/june2023#main-points

Fielden, A., Grupac, M., & Adamko, P. (2018). How users validate the information they encounter on digital content platforms: The production and proliferation of fake social media news, the likelihood of consumer exposure, and online deceptions. *Geopolitics, History, and International Relations, 10*(2), 51–57. https://doi.org/10.22381/GHIR10220186

Gorwa, R. (2017). *Computational propaganda in Poland: False amplifiers and the digital public sphere.* University of Oxford.

Hlavný denník. (2022a, September 27). Posledná temná predpoveď fyzika Hawkinga: Príde rasa nadľudí a zničí známy svet. *Hlavný denník.* www.hlavnydennik.sk/2022/09/27/posledna-temna-predpoved-fyzika-hawkinga-pride-rasa-nadludi-a-znici-znamy-svet

Hlavný denník. (2022b, December 17). Je svet pripravený na novú éru odstrašovania? *Hlavný denník.* www.hlavnydennik.sk/2022/12/17/je-svet-pripraveny-na-novu-eru-odstrasovania

Hlavný denník. (2023, June 15). Politológ: Mainstreamoví novinári sú už len držiaky na mikrofóny! *Hlavný denník.* www.hlavnydennik.sk/2023/06/14/chmelar-mainstreamovi-novinari-su-uz-len-drziaky-na-mikrofony-video

Hlavné správy. (2021a, May 23). Správa Európskeho parlamentu: Umelá inteligencia má slúžiť dobru človeka. *Hlavné správy.* www.hlavnespravy.sk/umela-inteligencia-ma-sluzit-dobru-cloveka/2547616

Hlavné správy. (2021b, February 13). Koniec Sveta ako ho poznáme? Veľká séria o "Veľkom Resete" Klausa Schwaba. *Hlavné správy.* www.hlavnespravy.sk/koniec-sveta-ako-ho-pozname-velka-seria-o-velkom-resete-klaus-schwaba-cast-druha-mytus-o-pokroku-dronyzanik-fyzickych-penazi-totalna-strata-sukromia-a-dalsie-mokre-digitalne-sny-nemeckeh/2436990.

Hlavné správy. (2022, February 11). CEDMO spúšťa ďalšie aktivity v boji proti dezinformáciám v strednej Európe. *Hlavné správy.* www.hlavnespravy.sk/cedmo-spusta-dalsie-aktivity-v-boji-proti-dezinformaciam-v-strednej-europe/2858676

Hlavné správy. (2023a, March 8). Vojna budúcnosti. *Hlavné správy.* www.hlavnespravy.sk/vojna-buducnosti/3070150

Hlavné správy. (2023b, November 4). Toto nepsal robot. *Hlavné správy.* www.hlavnespravy.sk/toto-nepsal-robot/3308592

Hlavné správy. (2023c, April 28). Toto predstavuje pre Európu existenčnú hrozbu. *Hlavné správy.* www.hlavnespravy.sk/toto-predstavuje-pre-europu-existencnu-hrozbu/3122536

Hlavné správy, (2023d, November 16). Zašifrované posolstvo. *Hlavné správy.* www.hlavnespravy.sk/zasifrovane-posolstvo/3318894

Holt, K., Ustad Figenschou, T., & Frischlich, L. (2019). Key dimensions of alternative news media. *Digital Journalism, 7*(7), 860–869. https://doi.org/10.1080/21670811.2019.1625715

Hostinger Tutorials. (2023, November 10). 28 AI statistics and trends in 2023. *Hostinger Tutorials.* www.hostinger.com/tutorials/ai-statistics

Infosecurity.sk (2023, April 1). *Slovenskí dezinformátori pomáhali šíriť ruskú propagandu aj v marci (Report proruských naratívov – marec 2023).* https://infosecurity.sk/studie/slovenski-dezinformatori-pomahali-sirit-rusku-propagandu-aj-v-marci-report-proruskych-narati vov-marec-2023/

Infovojna. (2022a, October 22). Společnost BlackRock má tajnou zbraň, která z ní udělala nejmocnější společnost na světě: Aladin. Info vojna. www.infovojna.bz/article/video-spo lecnost-blackrock-ma-tajnou-zbran-ktera-z-ni-udelala-nejmocnejsi-spolecnost-na-svete-aladin

Infovojna. (2022b, April 13). Šéf spoločnosti OpenAI varoval v Kongrese pred nebezpečenstvom umelej inteligencie a žiada jej reguláciu. *Info vojna.* https://t.me/s/InfoVojnaOfficial?before=5534

Infovojna. (2023, April 12). Umelá inteligencia ChatGPT pripravila mierovú zmluvu medzi Ruskom a Ukrajinou. *Infovojna.* www.infovojna.bz/article/umela-inteligencia-chatgpt-pripravila-mierovu-zmluvu-medzi-ruskom-a-ukrajinou

IT Ročenka 2023: Informačné technológie a komunikácie v SR. (2023). Vplyv AI na trh práce s ekonomiku. *NexTech.* www.nextech.sk/library/IT%20Rocenka/ITR%202023.pdf

Kennedy, B., Tyson, A., & Saks, E. (2023, February 15). *Public awareness of artificial intelligence in everyday activities.* Pew Research Center. www.pewresearch.org/science/2023/02/15/public-awareness-of-artificial-intelligence-in-everyday-activities/

Konspiratori.sk. (n.d.) www.konspiratori.sk

Mihale, I. (2023a, September 9). Elon Musk chce implantovať nebezpečný čip do mozgu desiatok tisíc ľudí. *Hlavný denník.* www.hlavnydennik.sk/2023/11/09/elon-musk-chce-implantovat-nebezpecny-cip-do-mozgu-desiatok-tisic-ludi

Mihale, I. (2023b, July 5). Falošná inteligencia. Nakoniec ľudstvo možno zachráni autentická blbosť, veští Ivan Hoffman. *Hlavný denník.* www.hlavnydennik.sk/2023/07/04/falosna-inteligencia-nakoniec-ludstvo-mozno-zachrani-autenticka-blbost-vesti-ivan-hoffman

Myers, J. (2022, January 5). *5 charts that show what people around the world think about AI.* Word Economic Forum. www.weforum.org/agenda/2022/01/artificial-intelligence-ai-technology-trust-survey/

NexTech. (2019, April 12). Analýza – Ľudia sa umelej inteligencie boja, médiá ju vnímajú ako príležitosť. *NexTech.* www.nextech.sk/a/CZ--Analyza---Ludia-sa-umelej-inteligencie-boja--media-ju-vnimaju-ako-prilezitost

Plevák, O., Euractiv.cz., & Euractiv.sk. (2023, July 14). *Český expert na dezinformácie: Slovenský dezinformačný scenár nám nehrozí.* https://euractiv.sk/section/kultura-a-media/interview/cesky-expert-na-dezinformacie-slovensky-dezinformacny-scenar-nam-nehrozi/

Press agency SITA. (2023, November 13). Čaputová zastupujúca zahraničné záujmy aj sfalšované voľby. Vplyv alternatívnych médií na verejnú mienku nemožno podceňovať. Press agency SITA. https://sita.sk/caputova-zastupujuca-zahranicne-zaujmy-ci-sfalsovane-volby-vplyv-alternativnych-medii-na-verejnu-mienku-nemozno-podcenovat/

Rainie, L., Funk, C., Anderson, M., & Tyson, A. (2022, March 17). *AI and human enhancement: Americans' openness is tempered by a range of concerns.* Pew Research Centre. www.pewresearch.org/internet/2022/03/17/ai-and-human-enhancement-americans-openness-is-tempered-by-a-range-of-concerns/

Richter, A. (2023, April 6). Gates odmieta výzvy na pozastavenie vývoja chatbotov s umelou inteligenciou. *Zemavek.* https://zemavek.sk/gates-odmieta-vyzvy-na-pozastavenie-vyvoja-chatbotov-s-umelou-inteligenciou/

Shu, K., Sliva, A., Wang, S., Tang, J., & Liu, H. (2017). Fake news detection on social media: A data mining perspective. *ACM SIGKDD Explorations Newsletter, 19*(1), 22–36. https://doi.org/10.1145/3137597.3137600

Smith, S. (n.d.). *Digital news report 2019: Slovakia.* Reuters Institute & University of Oxford. www.digitalnewsreport.org/survey/2019/slovakia-2019/

Takács, D. (2022, March 31). *Od anti-vax k pro-war: Dezinformačné médiá menia kurz (Infosecurity.sk: Bi-weekly report o nových dezinformačných trendoch). Infosecurity.sk.* https://infosecurity.sk/dezinfo/od-anti-vax-k-pro-war-dezinformacne-media-menia-kurz-infosecurity-sk-bi-weekly-report-o-novych-dezinformacnych-trendoch-30-3-2021/

Tison, A., & Kikuchi, E. (2023, August 28). Growing public concern about the role of artificial intelligence in daily life. *Pewresearch.org.* www.pewresearch.org/short-reads/2023/08/28/growing-public-concern-about-the-role-of-artificial-intelligence-in-daily-life/?utm_source=AdaptiveMailer&utm_medium=email&utm_campaign=23-08-28%20Chatbots/AI%20Short%20Read%20Promotion&org=982&lvl=100&ite=12444&lea=2700582&ctr=0&par=1&trk=a0D3j000014FiSPEA0

Transparency International Slovakia. (2020, February 6). Dezinformačné weby pravidelne číta každý siedmy. *Blog SME.* https://blog.sme.sk/transparency/media/dezinformacne-weby-pravidelne-cita-kazdy-siedmy

Trend. (2023, November 3). Z prieskumu vyplýva, že Slováci umelú inteligenciu využívajú čoraz viac, ale nie pravidelne. *Trend.* www.trend.sk/spravy/prieskumu-vyplyva-slovaci-umelu-inteligenciu-vyuzivaju-coraz-viac-ale-nie-pravidelne

Williams, Z. (2023, September 11). Conspiracy theories give a boost to state efforts to tackle AI. *Bloomberg Law.* https://news.bloomberglaw.com/artificial-intelligence/fears-of-ai-toxins-government-takeover-surface-in-statehouses

Zemavek. (2021, April 1). Budúcnosť prinesie novú formu komunikácie užívateľa / spotrebiteľa a producentov / výrobcov. Nevyhnutná zmena spôsobu života. *Zemavek.* https://zemavek.sk/buducnost-prinesie-novu-formu-komunikacie-uzivatela-spotrebitela-a-producentov-vyrobcov-nevyhnutna-zmena-sposobu-zivota-peter-stanek/

Zemavek. (2023a, July 23). James Cameron: Varoval som vás už v roku 1984. *Zemavek.* https://zemavek.sk/jame-cameron-varoval-som-vas-uz-v-roku-1984/

Zemavek. (2023b, August 22). Bill Gates propaguje umelú inteligenciu na školách. *Zemavek.* https://zemavek.sk/bill-gates-propaguje-umelu-inteligenciu-na-skolach/

Index